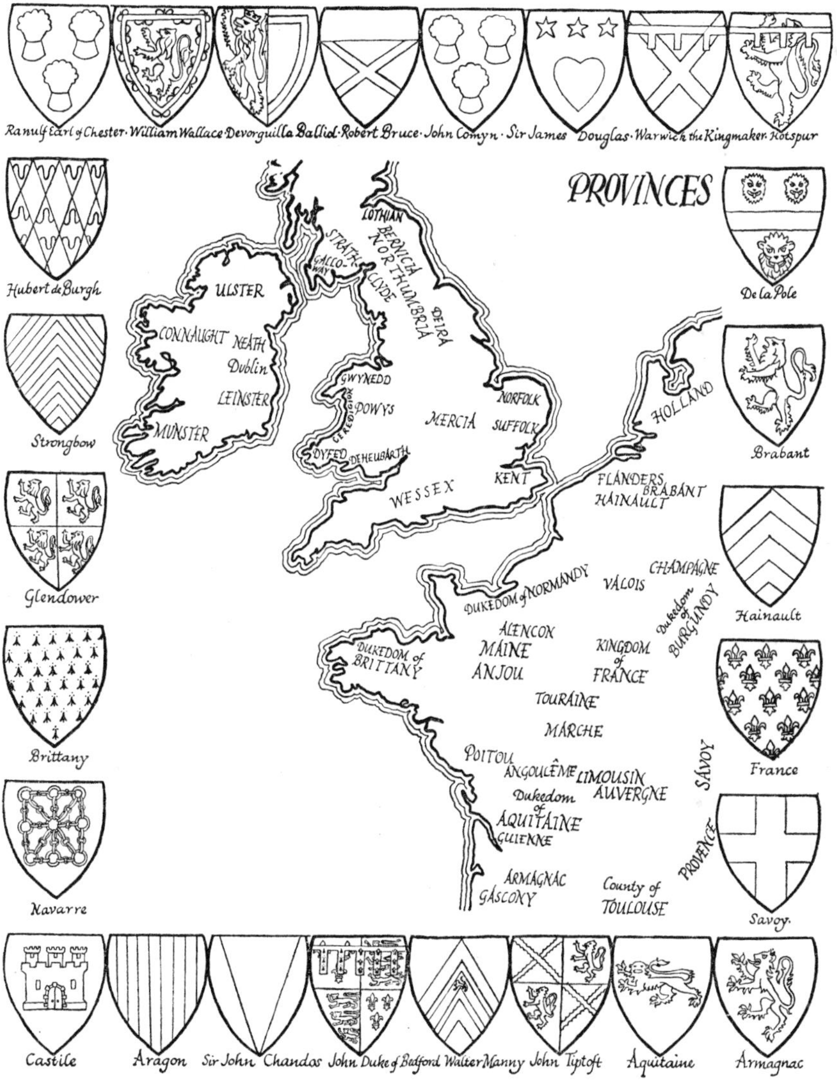
Ranulf Earl of Chester · William Wallace · Devorguilla Balliol · Robert Bruce · John Comyn · Sir James Douglas · Warwick the Kingmaker · Hotspur
PROVINCES
Hubert de Burgh
De la Pole
Strongbow
Brabant
Glendower
Hainault
Brittany
France
Navarre
Savoy
LOTHIAN
BERNICIA
NORTHUMBRIA
STRATHCLYDE
GALLOWAY
DEIRA
ULSTER
CONNAUGHT
MEATH
Dublin
LEINSTER
MUNSTER
GWYNEDD
POWYS
CEREDIGION
DYFED
DEHEUBARTH
MERCIA
NORFOLK
SUFFOLK
WESSEX
KENT
HOLLAND
FLANDERS
BRABANT
HAINAULT
DUKEDOM of NORMANDY
VALOIS
CHAMPAGNE
Dukedom of BURGUNDY
DUKEDOM of BRITTANY
ALENCON
MAINE
ANJOU
KINGDOM of FRANCE
TOURAINE
MARCHE
POITOU
ANGOULÊME
LIMOUSIN
AUVERGNE
SAVOY
Dukedom of AQUITAINE
GUIENNE
PROVENCE
ARMAGNAC
GASCONY
County of TOULOUSE
Castile · Aragon · Sir John Chandos · John Duke of Bedford · Walter Manny · John Tiptoft · Aquitaine · Armagnac

WHO'S WHO IN HISTORY

VOLUME ONE: BRITISH ISLES
55 B.C. to 1485

WHO'S WHO IN HISTORY

Vol. I. British Isles
55 B.C. to 1485

by

W. O. HASSALL

General Editor: C. R. N. Routh

BASIL BLACKWELL
OXFORD
1960

PRINTED IN GREAT BRITAIN BY
BILLING AND SONS LIMITED, GUILDFORD AND LONDON

GENERAL INTRODUCTION

DISRAELI once wrote in *Contarini Fleming*, 'Read no history, nothing but biography, for that is life without theory'—a sound piece of advice for the general public in the twentieth century, when theory is all too apt to swamp experience and when there is, perhaps, a greater demand for genuine history for the general public than ever before. Not a bad piece of advice, within limits, for the student of history in the public, grammar and secondary modern schools today; not without a wholesome reminder for students at the universities.

The *Dictionary of National Biography* is one of the great literary and historical achievements of British historians. Sir Thomas Browne was apt to enshrine a profound truth in the language of the seventeenth century—'diuturnity is a dream and folly of expectation'. Not even the *D.N.B.* can escape that devastating truth, and in fact the *D.N.B.* needs to be completely revised. *Who's Who in History* does not pretend to provide that revision and the authors of the four volumes wish to acknowledge their great debt to the *D.N.B.* Any criticisms are made only in the hope that they may further historical knowledge and scholarship and help to bring up to date the still invaluable articles of the *D.N.B.*

Three general objectives have been kept in view in the writing of the biographies—that they should be as accurate as possible, as up to date as possible and as full as space allows. Where space is limited there is bound to be a conflict between the length of the biographies and the number of the biographies. We have tried on the one hand to avoid scrappy biographies and on the other not to omit any name which everybody would expect to find in a biographical dictionary.

The difficulties begin when the hard core of 'inevitables' has been satisfied: clearly, not everybody will agree with the final selection of the 'rest'. In making this selection, we have been guided to some extent by the decision to try to make each volume a portrait of the age with which it deals and the four volumes something like a general outline history of Britain. Each generation alters its historical perspective; the hard core remains the same, but the personalities in the second rank change from time to time. We have ruthlessly cut down the enormous number of ecclesiastics who swell the volumes of the *D.N.B.*, while we have tried to lay more stress on those classes of people who are now recognized to have been immensely important in their own day—*e.g.* the merchants and travellers of the sixteenth century.

The decision to make each volume a portrait of its own age compelled another decision, to abandon the traditional alphabetical sequence and to adopt a chronological sequence which has sometimes in the later volumes had to be modified by a grouping of subjects, so that the general portrait of the age will also provide a portrait of each section of that age. To overcome the obvious defects in that method, the index of each volume has been prepared with the utmost care, and alphabetical indexes at the ends of the volumes should greatly help readers to find what they are looking for easily and quickly.

The ground-plan for the four volumes is as follows:

Volume 1, Roman and Medieval down to 1485, by W. O. Hassall.

Volume 2, Tudor down to 1603, by C. R. N. Routh.

Volume 3, Stuart and early Georgian, by P. Hill.

Volume 4, late Georgian and Victorian, by B. Rees and E. W. Gladstone.

There is bound to be a spill-over from one age to the next. We have as a general rule included each biography in the volume which covers the years of a man's greatest importance—for example, Sir Walter Raleigh appears in the Tudor volume, although he was executed in the Stuart period, while Robert Cecil, Earl of Salisbury, appears in the Stuart volume although he was born in the Tudor period. Such names appear in the index of both volumes.

Biographies are to a great extent verbal portraits which come more easily to life with the help of a painted portrait. These volumes are liberally illustrated: great care has been taken to select only authenticated portraits and to make sure that the present location of each one is accurately stated.

In each volume there are one or two genealogical trees, a glossary of technical terms, and very short general bibliographical notes of the standard text books which may prove useful to the general reader. At the end of most biographies one or two suggestions for further reading are added, which may be helpful to the student.

C. R. N. R.

INTRODUCTION

This book illustrates our history by assembling brief sketches of the chief actors in the drama. It indicates the background, actions, passions, purposes and, when possible, the physical appearance of individuals. It is intended to entertain and instruct the amateur, whether still studying history at school, or an educated adult interested in the lives and works of our predecessors. It adds little to the sum total of organized historical knowledge, but it marshals many significant facts into an interesting and convenient new pattern. It is no mere rearrangement and summary of some of the important lives scattered through the *Dictionary of National Biography* where those with ready access to a large public library can profitably study some of the 30,378 lives scattered alphabetically in its sixty-three volumes. *Who's Who in History* is enabled by virtue of being the *Dictionary's* younger brother to include some modern re-assessments and newly learned facts which lurk in more recent monographs and learned periodicals. It even contains some new lives.

Who's Who in History does not assume as correct any special attitude to history. The fact that it is concerned with individuals is not meant to suggest that the course of events is necessarily often altered much in the long run by great men; for however great a man is, his thoughts are limited by his birth and surroundings and his actions cannot go further than the practical possibilities of time and place allow. Opinions of historians have sometimes differed widely in assessing the characters and actions of some prominent people, just as well-informed people in our own generation are not always agreed about the rightness or wisdom of living generals or statesmen. In such cases this book sometimes prefers to indicate what have been the conflicting opinions of rival schools of thought, rather than to anticipate the Day of Judgment by giving a pithy verdict on matters of debate, such as whether Richard III was a dastardly villain or a maligned hero. This does not mean that it attempts to blur the contrast between black and white by condoning crime or debunking whatsoever is of good repute. If informed opinions clash both sides should be heard; for the attitudes of different parties and sects show that informed opinion can differ widely about a well-known public figure even during his lifetime.

It has seemed better to devote some of the available space to the presentation of portraits of people in the second rank of fame, rather than to lengthen the portraits of kings and archbishops to the exclusion of representatives of other spheres of activity. The lives of the kings give some sketch of the main actions of their reigns, but under the heading 'Henry III' many important facts contained in the lives of men like Simon de Montfort will not be repeated. For a continuous account of military, constitutional or political history the lives must accordingly be supplemented by good text-books such as the Oxford *Histories*. References to these are not repeatedly inserted in the biographical notes at the end of articles, although such text-books are in fact often of the utmost value, even from a narrowly biographical point of view, for further study and as a source.

Such text-books are, however, sometimes here supplemented by personal details which may have seemed trivial to the constitutional or economic historians in their specialist fields but which observant eyes thought worth recording. Such details sometimes give readers rare glimpses of historical characters as individuals and real human beings.

The arrangement of the lives is chronological not alphabetical, but there is of course an alphabetical index at the end of the book. This chronological arrangement brings together friends, enemies and relations. A king is thus accompanied by some of his chief subjects, and lives of the actors in any great drama are never widely separated and are not thrown into such incongruous company as they are by the conventional alphabetical arrangement. Thus it is easy to find all the great lives of one period, including some whose names are less familiar but whose lives are significant. The dates of one life overlap those of the next in a long succession, so that there is no artificial break between reigns, or between the Saxon, Norman and Early English periods, in the long procession of historical characters.

Dates are given, when known, for births and deaths, and in the case of kings the period of the life, not of the reign, is thus given, unless otherwise stated. In arranging the lives dates of death, not of birth, have had to be followed, if only because the dates of birth of medieval people are often unknown.

Pedigrees of royal families are included to indicate the chief relations of every English king. These pedigrees link up one with another and would thus for instance enable the curious to trace the descent of Henry VII right back to his mythical ancestor, the heathen god Woden. When characters are included in these pedigrees, cross-references are given to enable a reader to find the names of other members of the family circle of each and to study particular individuals against their family backgrounds. A very large number of us today are descended from Edward III and a pedigree of both his paternal and maternal ancestors shows how very cosmopolitan Edward III's ancestry was. It is useful to follow up clues provided by the pedigrees and to read the lives of those who died in the decades immediately preceding or following any particular life, as this shows a figure in the perspective of his period and of his family.

It is not possible in this book to discuss at length the wider implications of particular historical crises, though sidelights are given from the angle of different people on different sides. Where eye-witness accounts of such events survive, cross-references have been inserted, by request, to the relevant pages of *They Saw it Happen, 55 B.C.–A.D. 1485*, to which this volume is a companion. The title is abbreviated as '*T.S.I.H.*, i.'

Readers unfamiliar with medieval history will find themselves introduced to people whose world was very different in certain respects from ours. It was a world which assumed such fundamental facts as the concentration of much political and administrative influence and authority as a matter of course in the hands of the clergy, whether Saxon saints or Norman or English bishops; and this is reflected in the fact that, apart from royal persons, Godwin is the only layman with a biography included in the five centuries between the death of St. Cuthbert in 687 and the Norman Conquest. By the fifteenth century the proportion of laymen to ecclesiastics had much increased. The authority of the Catholic Church was accepted for most of the time in most of Britain and indeed by the subjects of all medieval biographies in the book except supporters of the early Celtic Church, Wyclif and Oldcastle.

Prominent features of political life were the rivalry between the law courts of kings and Church, the great power of English kings in France as Dukes of Normandy and Aquitaine, and the absence of an overwhelmingly strong central government. The uneasy relationships between the rulers of England and Scotland and between the English and the Welsh helped to increase the importance of the powerful Anglo-Norman barons of the Welsh and Scottish borders. Such facts mattered much, and though it is not the function of this book to discuss them they are illustrated by many of the lives. In speaking of a world so different from ours the use of words with technical meanings cannot be wholly avoided, and such words are defined in a glossary on pages xix-xxii for the benefit of those who abandoned this fascinating period at school after the age of 12–13 owing to a belief that the age of the nineteenth century, Mr. Gladstone and the Factory Acts is more vivid than that of the Hundred Years' War, Wat Tyler and the Peasants' Revolt.

A word of explanation is necessary for the number of thirteenth- and fourteenth-century Oxford men mentioned and the absence of Cambridge men. This is not local bias. Oxford happened to be of international importance in those centuries, and Cambridge rose rapidly in status in the fifteenth century thanks to pious royal generosity.

Gratitude is due to Mrs. Arrowsmith and to the girls of Holton Park Grammar School, to my wife and to my son Tom, for reading the draft and eliminating obscurities and repetitions; to Jackson Son and Co. for allowing me to reprint some of

Jordan of Fantosme's lines on William the Lyon; to the Athlone Press for allowing the drawings of pre-reformation English cathedrals on the end-paper to be based on models photographed in Sir Bannister Fletcher's *History of English Architecture*; to Mr. J. D. A. Thompson of the Ashmolean Museum for selecting casts of coins for plates 1 and 3; to all owners of originals and of copyrights of photographs named in the list of plates; to the Public Record Office for finding original documents with royal autographs; and to Mr. G. W. Lyttleton for writing articles on Chaucer, Langland, Gower, Lydgate and Malory. Last but especially thanks are due to the artist, Cory Hassall. She made facsimiles for reproduction with line-blocks of many figures on seals and effigies and from many medieval illustrated manuscripts, and these form a valuable supplement to the half-tone plates listed below which are chosen to represent the chief kinds of media used in medieval times.

One end-paper shows the positions of the Anglo-Saxon kingdoms and the chief counties and dukedoms of France. The arms in the margin are some of those associated with the areas on the map. The 'charges' on these shields would have been distinguished by differing 'tinctures' or contrasting metals and colours. It is possible to indicate these by conventional methods of shading, with horizontal lines for azure (or blue) and vertical lines for gules (or red), but this has not been done here as it would have made the charges less distinct. This absence of tincture makes the arms of Ranulf of Chester appear to be identical with those of John Comyn, whereas in fact the golden sheaves of corn or 'garbs' are on a blue ground for the former and on a red ground for the latter. In the same way the arms of Aragon and Provence are only distinguished by their tinctures.

On the other end-paper, showing ecclesiastical England and Wales, the arms of a number of bishoprics are accompanied by the arms of Archbishops of Canterbury and those of three great Bishops of Winchester. Heraldry arose in the thirteenth century to distinguish individuals who would otherwise be indistinguishable owing to their armour. In a medieval 'Who's

Who' heraldry is of the utmost importance and its understanding was as necessary to the knights and squires of the Hundred Years' War as aircraft recognition was to the anti-aircraft gunners of 1940. It will be noticed that this end-paper shows Old St. Paul's, not Sir Christopher Wren's familiar seventeenth-century structure, and the ancient and not the modern arms of York. The diocese of Coventry and Lichfield is represented by the medieval cathedral of Lichfield because the church at Coventry only became a cathedral in the late nineteenth century. The ancient church which is now Oxford Cathedral is not indicated as it only became a cathedral at the Reformation. Until then it, with Northampton and Buckingham, lay in the diocese of Lincoln and this is indicated on the end-paper by the position in which the word 'Lincoln' is written, well to the south of Lincoln Cathedral.

The coloured dust jacket is a fine symbol of English medieval history. It represents the Battle of Hastings, but the artist has not attempted to show the armour of the eleventh century. He was a Frenchman working in the fifteenth century and he shows the armour of his own period. The knights are those of the concluding phase of the Hundred Years' War when the heirs of the Norman knights who had conquered England at Hastings were finally expelled from Normandy as English intruders. This colourful mêlée thus spans the centuries and bridges the Channel, and a picture which purports to illustrate one famous event when Norman conquered Saxon in fact gives an accurate picture of warfare at the end of the Gothic period.

Nine important people were born before 1485 but are not included in this book as they lived on into the period covered by Volume 2, where their lives will be found. These are Margaret, Countess of Richmond, the mother of Henry VII, Elizabeth of York, his wife, Henry of Richmond, later Henry VII, William Caxton, Wynkyn de Worde, Richard Fox, later Bishop of Winchester, Warham, later Archbishop of Canterbury, Tunstall, later Bishop of Durham, and Morton, later Archbishop of Canterbury.

LIST OF PLATES

1. Coins of twenty rulers, from casts at the Ashmolean Museum, Oxford: Cunobelinus, Claudius, Carausius and Magnus Maximus (obverse and reverse: Claudius has a triumphal arch after conquering Britain); Offa, Alfred, Athelstan, Ethelred, Cnut, Edward the Confessor, Harold, William I, William II, Stephen and Matilda, Henry III, Alexander III of Scotland, Edward I, John Baliol, Edward III and Henry IV. Original sizes.

2. Claudius. Photo from Ipswich Museum from portrait head found in the River Alde at Rendham, in private possession.

3. Trajan, with earliest representation of Britannia. Enlarged from cast of coin, Ashmolean Museum, Oxford.

4. Six 'portraits' from the Bayeux tapestry: Edward the Confessor; Harold and Stigand; Odo, William I and Robert of Normandy (Curthose). Photo: Victoria and Albert Museum. *Cf.* drawings from seal of Edward the Confessor and from effigy of Robert.

5. William I of England and William the Lyon of Scotland. Seals in the typical, formal, romanesque style of both the beginning and of the end of the Norman period. The artist conveys the idea of majesty and does not make an individual portrait. British Museum.

6. King David of Scotland (bearded) and his son Malcolm 'the Maiden' (1141–65) (beardless). This clearly shows differentiation at an early date between two faces. Illuminated initial reproduced from a charter by permission of His Grace the Duke of Roxburghe.

7. Eleanor of Aquitaine and her husband Henry II, Berengaria of Navarre and her husband Richard I. From funeral effigies engraved by C. A. Stothard. That of Berengaria is from L'Espan Abbey and the rest from Fontevraud. The effigies at Fontevraud were restored (after damage during the French revolution) since these engravings were made. Stothard visited revolutionary France in order to record them. He was later accidentally killed when making similar drawings in a church elsewhere.

8. Three scenes drawn by Matthew Paris to illustrate his *History*. Battle of Bouvines, Siege of Lincoln, and Henry III as seen by

Matthew Paris. Henry is carrying the blood of Christ in procession. The article on Matthew Paris refers to line-blocks in the text taken from his original drawings.

9. Henry III on horseback and enthroned. Simon de Montfort riding with his hound and blowing his horn (centre). One seal of Henry supplements another. Such equestrian seals are a common type for great laymen. Seals, British Museum.

10. Monk and Friar, from illuminated manuscripts. Matthew Paris, self-portrait, Corpus Christi College MS., Cambridge. Roger Bacon, fifteenth century, MS. Bodley 211.

11. Arms of Bigod (1), Edmund Earl of Cornwall (2), Ferrers (3), FitzAlan (4), FitzWalter (5), Grey of Rotherfield (6), Hastings (7), Latimer (8), Earl Marshal (9), St. John (10), Segrave (11), and Vere (12). Glass, Dorchester Abbey (Oxon.), *c.* 1300. Arms of individuals who happened to be benefactors of the Abbey typify great families of whom only a few individual representatives can find places in the book. Photo, I. H. Taylor.

12. John de Warenne, Aymer de Valence, Roger Bigod, and Humphrey de Bohun (with the famous Bohun swan). Seals from the 'Barons' letter to the Pope', 1301, to which are attached numerous baronial seals. Casts, Society of Antiquaries, London.

13. Robert Bruce and Edward I. Seals, British Museum.

14. Courtly scenes from an illuminated manuscript Chronicle of the Counts of Flanders (fifteenth century). Edward III as prince does homage to Charles IV of France, 1325. His mother, Queen Isabel, on her way to catch up with her doomed husband, Edward II, welcomed at Oxford. The pointed headdress is typical of fifteenth-century Flanders, not fourteenth-century England. Holkham MS. 659, by permission of the Rt. Hon. the Earl of Leicester, who has allowed the publication of all the pictures in this manuscript on coloured film-strip.

15. Soldiers of the Hundred Years' War, from the same manuscript. The Battle of Crécy, showing an early cannon ball, and the unsuccessful negotiations before the Battle of Poitiers. From Holkham MS. 659. The fifteenth-century artist puts the soldiers of the fourteenth century into the armour of his own day.

16. Edward III, enthroned and on horseback. Sixth seal, 1340–72, British Museum. Compare the style of Nos. 5 and 9 with this typical fourteenth-century work with its 'decorated' style of architectural framework.

GLOSSARY

AUGUSTINIAN CANONS (Austin canons, Canons regular or Black canons). Members of a religious order following the so-called Rule of St. Augustine (of Hippo, 354–430), based on a letter of advice which he wrote for nuns. They began to appear in the second half of the eleventh century and reflected a feeling that clergy attached to large churches should lead a common life. They took vows like monks, but served parish churches which belonged to them.

BARON. A lord holding land directly from the king in return for military service. Under a weak king like Stephen (d. 1154) barons tended to make war and peace with one another like independent sovereigns (p. 80). The greater barons had family ties with the royal family as well as with each other. See pp. 44–5, 58–9, 78, 149, 152, 160 and 166 and plates 11 and 12.

BENEDICTINES (Black monks). Their monasteries were independent communities in which the monks swore to remain, obeying the abbot in accordance with the rule of St. Benedict of Nursia (480–543). In 1066 Benedictine monasteries were the only centres of art and education in England and during the following fifty years the number of Benedictine monks and monasteries, situated in every rich valley, was greater than before or since. See pp. 37–9. Famous Benedictines included in this book are St. Augustine, St. Birinus, Benedict Biscop, St. Aldhelm, Bede, St. Aethelwold, St. Dunstan, Ealdred, Lanfranc, St. Anselm, William of Malmesbury, Alexander Nequam, Matthew Paris and Thomas de la Mare (d. 1396).

BRETWALDA. A title given to some outstanding early Saxon kings before England had become a single united kingdom. It means 'ruler of the Britons'. See pp. 15 and 16.

CANONIZATION. Members of the Early Church used to accord the honour of a place in public worship to local martyrs without great formality or reference to a central authority. The first time that the Pope 'canonized' or declared anyone to be a saint and eligible for a place in public worship was in 993. In 1170 the Pope first denied that bishops might do this on their own authority. At first canonization involved less formality and cautious delay than came to be customary with the lapse of centuries. St. Thomas Becket (d. 1170) and St. Francis of Assisi (d. 1226) were canonized within two years of their deaths. Seventeenth-century papal decrees have distinguished between full canonization and a lower form of recognition called beatification. The common procedure for beatification now takes the form of a lawsuit in which evidence of worthiness is carefully considered and not only sanctity but also miracles must be proved in face of the criticism of an official nicknamed 'the Devil's advocate'. Before the solemn ceremony of canonization can take place in St. Peter's further miracles must follow beatification. The Patriarch of Constantinople and the Holy Synod of the Russian Church also canonize saints.

CANON LAW. The word canon is derived from a Greek word for cane or reed which is used in the sense of a straight rod or rule. Canon law is the collection of the official rules of the Church. These applied to many matters such as wills and marriage which are now subject to the laws of the state.

CARTHUSIANS. This was a strict order of monks founded in about 1084 by St. Bruno. The name is derived from Chartreux, a wild place near Grenoble (France). The lives of Carthusians were so ordered as to have much in common with those of hermits, for they lived in separate cells and did not sleep and eat together in common dormitories and refectories like other monks. See p. 103.

CISTERCIANS (or White monks). This order was founded at Cîteaux (1098). See pp. 75–7. They first came to England in 1128 at Waverley (Surrey) and forty houses were founded between 1132 and 1152 beginning with Rievaulx and Fountains (Yorkshire). They had a strongly centralized organization, unlike the Benedictines. In England their head was the Abbot of Rievaulx. They flourished especially in the North and their monasteries were founded in wild, uncultivated areas. They were great sheep-farmers and their architecture is marked by simplicity. Their lives were industrious and their rules strict. See p. 107.

CLUNIACS. Benedictine monks dependent on the great abbey of Cluny (Burgundy). Their first English foundation was at Lewes (1077). They had more elaborate observances than other Benedictines. See pp. 61, 91, 94.

DOMINICANS (Black, or Preaching Friars). Followers of St. Dominic (d. 1221), a champion of the Church against heresy, whose mission was to travel around propagating the faith. Their churches were built especially wide so as to enable large congregations to hear them. Their friaries were only built in towns, often on pieces of land which had been hitherto left undeveloped.

EXCOMMUNICATION. Expulsion from all part in Christian life. Its dreadful consequence was exclusion from the society of the faithful and from the sacraments which were necessary for the avoidance of Hell. Geoffrey de Mandeville (d. 1144) lay unburied for twenty years because he had been excommunicated, but every English baron attended the court of King John at Christmas 1209 in spite of his excommunication. See pp. 112 and 119.

FEUDAL. In accord with the medieval social system in which land was held in return for service to a superior. See p. 74.

FIEF. Land held in return for military service due to a lord. See pp. 58-9.

FRANCISCANS (Friars Minor or Grey Friars). Followers of St. Francis of Assisi (d. 1226). They took vows of poverty and dwelt in their popular preaching on the sufferings of Christ. Though they originally differed from the Dominicans in having a more emotional and a less intellectual approach to religion they produced great scholars before the end of the thirteenth century. See pp. 122 and 127. Great Franciscans in this book are Roger Bacon (p. 144), Pecham (p. 143) and Ockham (p. 169).

FRIARS. First appearing in the thirteenth century, the Dominican, Franciscan and other Friars were missionaries vowed to remain unmarried. They abandoned the monks' ideal of fixed residence devoted to prayer in isolation from the world, but accepted the authority of a strong organization subject to the Pope. In the fourteenth century they aroused the opposition of the Lollards. See pp. 119 and 127.

HERETIC. One who chose a belief contrary to the teachings of the universal church, the propagation of which would cause the eternal damnation of souls in the next world and the destruction of the unity of the Church in this world. If they could not be convinced of their error it seemed better to burn them. See pp. 184-6, 216 and 239.

INTERDICT. Suspension by authority of church services in a district. This was very serious when life centred round the Church and Hell was a reality in the minds of all. Becket threatened to put England under an interdict (1208–13) because King John would not recognize Stephen Langton as Archbishop. See pp. 111, 117 and 239.

JUSTICIAR. A powerful official responsible only to the king and wielding royal power as the king's representative.

LEGATE. An official representative of the Pope. See p. 116.

LOLLARD. An early protestant, a heretic who followed Wyclif (d. 1384). See pp. 184–6, 216.

MONKS. Men devoted to a life of religion, lived in common under vows of poverty, obedience and chastity. See also Benedictine, Cistercian and Cluniac. The friars regarded them with jealousy.

Motte. An earth mound raised for defence in Norman times. There are good examples at Oxford and Thetford. See p. 54.

Papacy. The office and authority of the Pope as successor of St. Peter and vicar of Christ, demanding a loyalty from all Christians which was greater than loyalty towards earthly kings.

Perpendicular. The style of architecture used in fifteenth-century England.

Prelate. Any high official of the church such as a Bishop or Archdeacon.

Relief. A fine paid to a feudal superior by an heir before entering his inheritance.

Sanctuary. A holy place where fugitives other than witches or heretics were free from arrest. It is first mentioned in the laws of Ethelbert in 600. See p. 124.

See. The official seat of a bishop for administration. See end-paper where the vast area administered by the Bishop whose seat was at Lincoln is indicated.

Seneschal. A steward.

Simony. The sin of buying an official position in the Church. The word is derived from the name of Simon Magus, a magician who offered the apostles a fee for instruction in the gift of the Holy Spirit by the laying on of hands.

Templars. In 1118 nine knights swore to defend the Christian kingdom of Jerusalem and were given part of the palace, near the Temple. From this they derived their title of Knights Templars. They adopted strict rules modelled on those of the Cistercians in 1128, adding a cross to the white habit which they had copied from the Cistercians. For all their Christian devotion and severity of life they soon acquired many lands and great privileges as an Order and this aroused jealousy of their wealth and power. This at last led to their ruthless suppression (1307–12). See p. 114.

Tester. An ornamental headpiece of architectural design made to accompany a monumental effigy. See p. 205.

Translation. The ceremonial removal of the relics of a saint to some suitable shrine, or the transfer of a bishop from one see to another. See p. 123.

Coins from the Ashmolean Museum, Oxford.

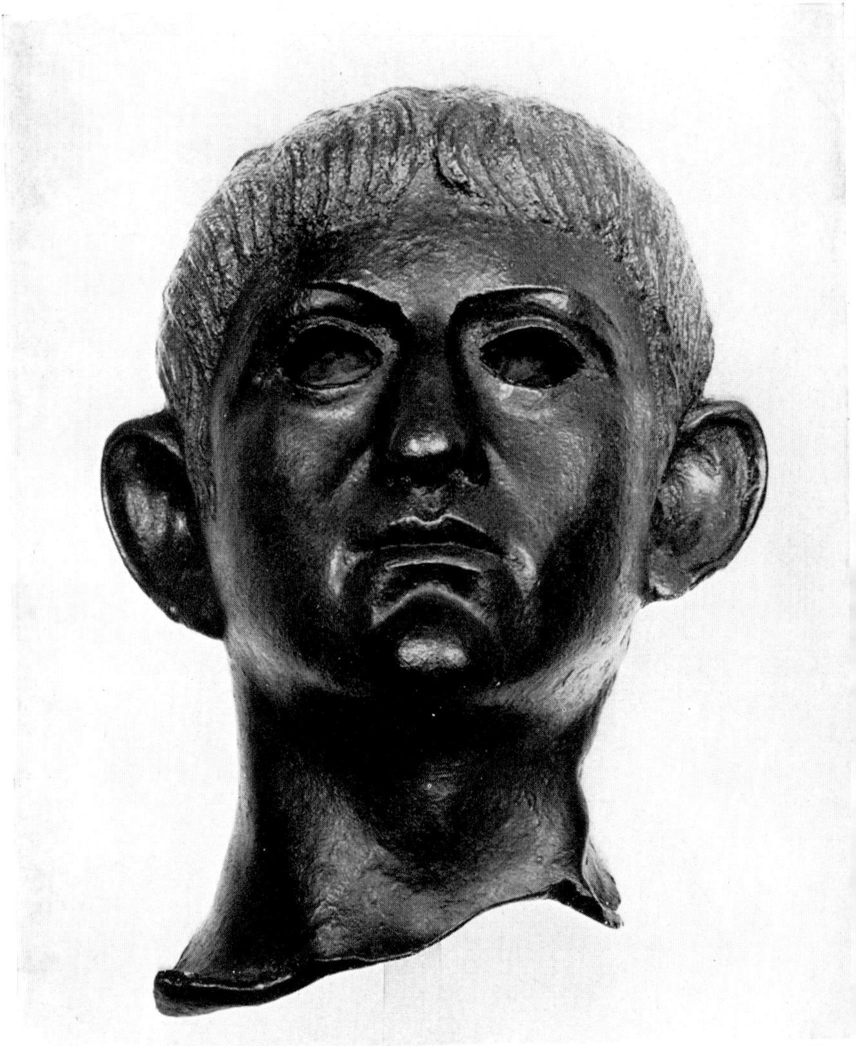

Plate

Claudius

CUNOBELINUS (d. *c.* 42) (Cymbeline in Shakespeare), son of Tasciovanus, was king of the Catuvellauni in Hertfordshire, the chief tribe in south-east Britain (*c.* A.D. 15 to *c.* 42). His forerunner, Cassivellaunus, submitted to Cæsar, swearing not to molest the adjoining Trinovantes of Essex, a tribe, like his own, of recently arrived Belgic invaders; but Cunobelinus conquered them and moved his capital from near St. Albans (Verulamium) to Colchester (Camulodunum, the fortress of Camulos, lord of battles). Here his moderately anti-Roman kingdom reached its greatest power and prosperity while Roman fashions displaced Celtic, and southern luxury imports came in exchange for cattle and the wheat portrayed on Cunobelinus's coins. Cunobelinus's son, Amminius (pro-Roman unlike his brothers Togodumnus and Caractacus), fled to the Emperor Gaius at Mainz. Gaius wanted to invade and built a lighthouse at Boulogne (A.D. 40). By A.D. 43 Cunobelinus was dead, Claudius invaded Britain, Togodumnus fell and Caractacus retreated westward to fight on for nine years. Eventually he was defeated in Wales and fled to the Queen of the Brigantes in the North. She sent him in chains to the Romans, and he was led through Rome in triumph. Claudius personally entered Camulodunum. See plate 1 (coin).

C. M. Matthews, 'The True Cymbeline', *History Today*, vol. VII, 1957, pp. 755–9.

I. A. Richmond, Roman Britain, *The Pelican History of England*, reprinted 1958, pp. 12, 15. See plate 1 (coin).

CLAUDIUS (**Tiberius Claudius Drusus Nero**) (10 B.C.–A.D. 54) was born in Gaul at Lyons, and was the brother of the Emperor Tiberius. His family despised him because he was sickly and feeble. He had not been allowed to take an active part in affairs, and his tastes were literary, but at the age of fifty the army made him emperor as successor to the murdered Caius Cæsar, nicknamed Caligula. In Rome he allowed his wives and his favourite freed slaves to lead him into acts of cruelty. He wrote historical works (now lost), and he conquered the southern part of Britain (43). Hitherto various factors had prevented the successors of Julius Cæsar from making a Roman province in Britain. Claudius had troops to spare; because Caligula had made an unsuccessful attempt at invasion it would have looked like weakness to abandon the scheme. Augustus had said that Britain was too poor and too friendly to justify an expedition; but time had made it richer and anti-Roman feeling was growing there. Claudius put Aulus Plautius in command. Cæsar's plan of a night voyage from Boulogne was adopted. As in 55 B.C. the prospect of the sea-crossing made some unwilling to go. This time Dover was avoided and the Romans disembarked in the land-locked harbour of Richborough. There they built landward defences of which 700 yards still remain. Plautius forced the passage of the Medway and advanced to the Thames. Claudius followed with his guards and elephants. According to the inscription on his triumphal arch he suffered no losses and received the submission of eleven kings at the enemy capital, Colchester. There he laid out a new town (A.D. 49–50) as centre of a Roman province with Plautius as governor. It had a great and costly new temple with Claudius himself for God. This and the confiscations of land were most unpopular. Claudius also built a new city at Verulamium (St. Albans) and made it an independent municipality. He made Cogidubnus, a pro-Roman chief at Chichester, a subject-king and 'provincial governor of Britain'. Claudius also made a subject-king out of Prasutagus, chief of the Iceni, a tribe in what later became East Anglia. The Iceni regarded the enemies of Claudius at Colchester as their own enemies. Claudius did not remain personally in Britain for long, but he is important as the first of a line of Roman Emperors who were to rule Britain for about as long a period as separates medieval from modern times. His fourth wife poisoned him with a 'mushroom'.

R. Graves, *I, Claudius*, 1934, and *Claudius the God*, 1934.

BOADICEA (d. A.D. 60–1), more accurately Boudicca, was Queen of the Iceni. The Iceni inhabited what is now East

Anglia and preferred Rome to the Belgic tribes ruled by Cunobelinus, though they resisted disarmament. Her husband, Prasutagus, a rich king subject to Rome, tried to protect his daughters' interests by making the Emperor co-heir with them; but Decianus Catus, the imperial agent, confiscated royal and other property, the palace was sacked, Boadicea flogged, her daughters raped and the nobility enslaved. Frightened investors, like the moralist Seneca, withdrew capital lent to those who copied expensive Roman habits. Boadicea rebelled and the conquered Trinovantes joined the Iceni to massacre the panic-stricken Romans at Colchester, London and St. Albans, which were all indefensible. Ashes, bones and a bronze head of Claudius, cast into the river from his hated temple at Colchester, still record British vengeance, though Decianus Catus escaped to Gaul. Suetonius ferociously crushed the rebels and famine helped the Roman revenge. Boadicea poisoned herself. Mercifully Classicianus opposed Suetonius and violence abated. Tacitus, anxious to glorify the rule of his father-in-law Agricola by contrast, belittled Classicianus, but the two halves of his tombstone (found separately in 1852 and 1935) commemorate an official who brought peace and alleviated the results of Roman injustice. The British queen who burnt London is represented by a statue near the Houses of Parliament and inspired romantic verses by William Cowper:

> 'Rome, for empire far renowned,
>   Tramples on a thousand states;
> Soon her pride shall kiss the ground,
>   Hark! The Gaul is at her gates'.

R. G. Collingwood and J. N. L. Myres, *Roman Britain and the English Settlements*, reprinted 1949, pp. 99–104.
T.S.I.H., i, 7 (Tacitus translated).

CNAEUS JULIUS AGRICOLA (A.D. 37–93) was born on 13th June, 37, at Fréjus (Provence). His father was executed by Caligula but nonetheless he obtained a careful education. A pithy *Life* by his admiring son-in-law, Tacitus, is the sole surviving biography illustrative of Roman Britain; though there exist the autobiographical memoirs of Julius Cæsar and St. Patrick, before and after the period of occupation. Agricola served Suetonius Paulinus (A.D. 60) against Boadicea's rebels and returned under Cerialis and fought the Brigantes. He was a quaestor (63), governor of Aquitaine (74–6), consul (77) and finally governor of Britain for seven years. He completed Frontinus's conquest of Wales (78) by massacring the Ordovices (78) and Cerealis's conquest of Brigantia by building forts (79). He advanced to the Forth and the Clyde (81) and into central Scotland (83), winning a decisive battle at Mons Graupius and building a fifty-acre camp at Inchtuthill. Next year he felt that his victory was wasted, for Domitian recalled him and he lived in retirement until 93. He had actively encouraged the spread of Roman ways. Archæological students of Roman Scotland are supplementing Tacitus from the evidence of 'brochs' (towers) and hillforts. If two fifteenth-century manuscripts had not preserved the text of Tacitus, Agricola would hardly be remembered but for his inscriptions from the forum at St. Albans and on a leaden pipe of A.D. 79 from Chester.

Sir G. Macdonald, *The Roman Wall in Scotland*, 1934.
A. R. Burn, *Agricola and Roman Britain* (Teach yourself History Series), ed. A. L. Rowse, 1953.
T.S.I.H., i, 9 (Tacitus translated).

HADRIAN (76–138) succeeded his cousin and friend, Trajan, as Emperor (117). He was of Spanish origin, and had seen service on almost every part of the Roman frontier and at Trajan's death was in command in Syria. His policy was to preserve peace and his rule was probably one of the happiest periods in history, though there was an important war against the Jews (131–6). He spent much of his time travelling in person throughout his provinces, remedying whatever seemed amiss and reorganizing the frontiers. He loved Athens and was a patron of learning and the arts and encouraged the construction of fine public buildings. His biography states that in Britain he 'set many things right'; and his architectural activity at the baths and forum of Wroxeter are recorded there in an inscription which used to stand above the gate of the forum. At Verulamium too an effort was made to improve the town. The most impressive monument of Hadrian's rule is preserved in Hadrian's wall. It was a boundary between the Roman south and the barbarian north and enabled traffic to be controlled and customs levied. Two million cubic yards of material, largely rock, had to be removed to dig the ditch of the wall and a similar quantity had to be moved for the wall itself. Hadrian surveyed (120–130) the frontiers personally, bare-headed and in all weathers, and a friend wrote some doggerel lines saying how he would not like to be the Emperor on his British walking-tour: *Ego nolo Cæsar esse, Ambulare per Britannos.* In both Britain and Germany he adjusted the frontier line so that in its detailed siting it was less comfortable but more efficient. Hadrian's visit to Britain was made in 121 or 122. The wall from the Tyne to the Solway is still one of the most impressive works of man in Britain.

J. Collingwood Bruce, *Handbook of the Roman Wall*, latest revised edition.

M. AURELIUS MAUSAEUS CARAUSIUS (d. 293) was a Menapian from a Low-Country tribe. He was appointed by Maximian, colleague of the Emperor Diocletian, to command a strengthened Romano-British navy to suppress Channel pirates (285). His interceptions brought vast booty and he foiled Maximian's plan to arrest and execute him by crossing to Britain and becoming an independent emperor (286–7). A naval invasion was routed and Carausius was recognized as emperor astride the Channel; but Constantius Chlorus, Diocletian's new commander in Gaul, took Boulogne (293), and Carausius was murdered by his paymaster and short-lived successor, Allectus (d. 296).

Handsome coins, minted at London, portray Carausius, aged about forty, with 'a massive head, short straight nose, bearded jowl, and bull-neck' (plate 1).

P. Webb, *The Reign and Coinage of Carausius*, 1908.
A. G. Carson, 'The British Empire of Carausius', *History Today*, vol. 4 (1954).

MAGNUS MAXIMUS (flourished 383–8) was a Spaniard who served in Britain under the Emperor Valentinian's general, Count Theodosius. Valentinian's successor was his son Gratian. Gratian was a Christian and made death the penalty for neglect or even ignorance of the divine laws; but his love of hunting and shooting led him to admire the skill of his Scythian soldiers so much that he shocked Roman opinion by personally appearing in public in Scythian fur garments. Meanwhile Magnus Maximus was defeating the Picts and the Scots, and his ability and courage inspired a respect which the Emperor Gratian did not. In 383 Maximus proclaimed himself Emperor, with general approval in Britain. He was said to have married the daughter of a grandee in Caernarvonshire and the Welsh of later times said a chapel there was his. The rise of Maximus was fatal for the defence of Britain, for he crossed to Gaul with his best troops. Apparently many civilians also emigrated when he went and to this time belongs the story of St. Ursula and 11,000 noble virgins from Britain. They were intended brides of the emigrants, lost their way, and were murdered by Huns, savage raiders from central Asia, at Cologne. Maximus said that he accepted the title of Emperor because it was forced upon him, and he was welcomed by the army in Gaul, near Paris. Gratian's remaining troops murdered their master near Lyons and Maximus became ruler of north-western Europe. He was too busy defending the Rhine to help Britain, and Hadrian's wall was overrun as it had been in the reign of Valentinian. No coins later than Gratian are found along it. Theodosius the Younger, who shared the Roman Empire with Gratian, thought it best to make an alliance with Maximus, and the Roman Empire was divided peacefully between them and Valentinian II. Maximus was the first ruler to shed the blood of heretics, which he did in spite of opposition from his wife's hero, St. Martin of Tours. The first heretic killed for his opinions was the noble and learned Bishop of Avila (Spain), Priscillian (385). Maximus used the wealth of his provinces to pay an army of German barbarians with whom he hoped to conquer Italy, but Theodosius defeated him in a two months' campaign (June-August, 388) with the aid of Huns and other barbarian mercenaries from Asia. Maximus was captured at Aquileia, and was led before Theodosius still wearing his imperial robe, diadem and purple slippers. The soldiers then cut off his head. Welsh princes claimed descent from Maximus. See plate 1 (coin).

E. Gibbon, *Decline and Fall of the Roman Empire*, ed. J. B. Bury, 1896.

Most popular books are not based on sufficient knowledge of the evidence, but Kipling gives an inspired glimpse of this exciting period in 'A centurion of the Thirtieth' and 'On the Great Wall' in *Puck of Pook's Hill*, 1908.

ST. NINIAN (d. ? 432) was the first missionary of North Britain. He was a Romano-Briton who went on a pilgrimage to Rome and was there educated. On his return he visited Tours and was there much impressed by the monastic arrangements of St. Martin. Ninian converted the Picts of Galloway. He built a Great Monastery dedicated to St. Martin. Bede says this 'stately church (wherein he and many other saints rest in the body) is still in existence among the English nation. The place belongs to the province of the Bernicians, and is generally called the White House, because he there built in 397 a church of stone, which was not usual among the Britons'. Ninian's work is commemorated in the name of St. Ninian's Well, and in St. Martin's church within the walls of the Roman fort, at Brampton in Cumberland.

A. P. Forbes, *Lives of St. Ninian and St. Kentigern*, 1874.

ST. GERMANUS (d. 448) was the son of noble parents and studied at Rome. His rather pagan hunting habits shocked the Bishop of Auxerre (Gaul), for he used to hang the heads of his kills in the middle of Auxerre. Later, like other aristocratic Gallo-Romans in the dark days of the collapse of the Roman empire, Germanus was persuaded to become bishop. When he became in his turn Bishop of Auxerre, Germanus became so austere that he abstained from luxuries, even oil and salt. He treated his wife as a sister and slept on boards covered with ashes. His miracles became so powerful that once when some people complained that their cocks would not crow, he blessed the chicken food and thereafter they crowed so much that they became a public nuisance.

At that time the universal church was vexed at the growth of a heresy called after its founder 'Pelagian'. Pelagius, a stout old Romano-Briton of independent mind, refused to believe that unbaptized babies were so wicked that they necessarily lost Heaven and he even thought that the clergy might marry. He had been condemned for heresy (418), but his followers in Britain grew in influence. St. Germanus came to Britain with St. Lupus, Bishop of Troyes, to prevent the spread of this heresy among Romano-British Christians. In describing this visit the *Life of St. Germanus* gives a precious glimpse of Britain in a dark period about which historical information is scarce. Germanus came and routed his richly dressed opponents and their numerous disciples near Verulamium (St. Albans, 429), with 'a torrent of eloquence and the thunders of the Apostles'. Then he converted conservative and backward Britons who were still heathen. Germanus even led the Britons to military triumph over heathen Saxon invaders at what was called the Alleluia Victory (430), because he drew up the Britons and bade them shout 'Alleluia'. The cry re-echoed from the sides of a valley and the noise caused the foe to flee, doubtless fearing an ambush of overwhelming strength. The valley where this happened has been identified with Maes-y-Gamon near Mold in Flintshire. He died at Ravenna (Italy). His body was brought to Auxerre for burial and all the bridges were mended on the route thither. There are many legends in Wales about Germanus.

There is a bibliography of Germanus in J. F. Kenney, *The Sources for the Early History of Ireland*, 1920, i, 163.

ST. PATRICK (389–461) was the chief apostle of Ireland. In his autobiographical *Confession* he writes: 'I, Patrick the sinner, am the most illiterate and the least of all the faithful, and contemptible in the eyes of very many. My father was Calpurnius, a deacon, one of the sons of Potitus, a priest, who belonged to the village of Bannavem Taberniæ. Now he had a small villa hard by, where I was taken captive. I was then about sixteen years of age . . . and I went into captivity to Ireland with many thousands of others'. Patrick's father was a wealthy *decurion*, a local Roman magistrate, and his home could not have been at Dumbarton as the *Dictionary of National Biography* states, for such an official could only have lived south of the Roman wall. It may have been near Bristol. Patrick, whose name was then Sucat (warlike), was sold to Miliuc, chief in Antrim, whom he served as a stockman in the wilds for six years before obeying a dream to find a ship and go home. Two hundred miles away he found a ship (for exporting wolf-dogs) and sailed to the Loire, then a trading centre. After wandering through devastated areas he studied in Gaul, before returning to his parents in Britain. In spite of their opposition he determined to preach in Ireland. He sailed round the coast after a discouraging reception at Wicklow to Strangford Lough where a chief gave him the use of a barn. There he began the conversion of Ulster, enforcing strict discipline on his followers and impressing the Irish by paying his way and, if an admiring biographer is right, even using his ample wealth to pay Irish believers. He could not stop all pagan practices such as well-worship. Eventually he established his headquarters at Armagh. He apparently died in 461 (not 493 as generally stated).

An autobiography records the thoughts of Patrick, alone of all who lived in this dark period. It is an open letter, called *The Confession*, written to answer foes who cast in his teeth a moral lapse committed at the age of fifteen. Patrick also wrote an *Epistle to Coroticus*. This protests against ill-treatment of his Scottish converts 'with the sign of the Cross still fragrant on their foreheads' by the pagan soldiers of a supposedly Christian king. The most famous of many legends about Patrick is that he expelled snakes from Ireland. His acceptance as a saint comes from popular tradition as he was never formally canonized at Rome. After Patrick had converted Ireland, it became a centre of Christian influence throughout Europe.

J. B. Bury, *Life of St. Patrick*, 1905.
Mrs. Helena Concannon, *St. Patrick*, 1931.

ARTHUR (*c*. 496), the most romantic figure of our past, was a champion of Roman Britain against heathen Saxon invaders. He commanded a body of well-armed cavalry, such as were used in the last days of their Empire by the Romans. He won an important victory at Mount Badon (496) (see p. 11). This battle was probably fought somewhat to the south-west of the Upper Thames, but attempts have been made to identify it with various sites from Bouden Hill in Linlithgow to Badbury (Dorset). Arthur may have been the son of Uther Pendragon, brother of Ambrosius Aurelianus, and he was a general whose commission was not confined to any one of the small kingdoms into which Britain was divided. He was not a king, but there is no reason to doubt his existence, though the eleven other victories attributed to him by Nennius may be fictitious. As a symbol of chivalrous and Christian resistance Arthur became a popular figure of Romance, reflecting in turn the knightly ideals of the reign of Stephen in the '*History*' of Geoffrey of Monmouth, and the courtly aristocratic spirit of the fourteenth-century tournament in *Le Morte d'Arthur*, written, by Sir Thomas Malory in 1469–70, and printed by Caxton (1485), and of Alfred Tennyson's *Idylls of the King*. Nennius (?8th century) is the first to mention Arthur: 'The warlike Arthur with all the kings and armies of Britain fought the Saxons. Many were nobler, but he was twelve times chosen general, and triumphed twelve times'. Nennius names twelve victories. Of them, Mount Badon occurs in Gildas (d. ?580). Doubters think that Arthur was a god, not a real man. Certainly Queen Guenevere, Mordred, Sir Lancelot and Sir Guy are characters of legend not history.

Sir E. K. Chambers, *Arthur of Britain*, 1927.
J. Lindsay, *Arthur and his Times*, 1958.

ST. GILDAS (496–?580), considered the wisest of the Britons by Alcuin (see p. 28), was the gloomy author of *The querulous book about the destruction of Britain*. He regards the triumph of of the heathen Saxons as a punishment for sin. Gildas was born in the year of the battle of Mount Badon. This has been variously assigned to 493, 516 and 520 and it seemed that the date could never be known with certainty; but Professor

Hawkes has carried forward the historical detective work of C. E. Stevens and J. N. L. Myres to prove that it actually occurred in 496. Gildas hesitated to write for some ten years and then wrote his book forty-three years after the battle (539), apparently in the Breton monastery of St. Gildas at Ruys near Vannes. His work only survives in two manuscripts, both at Cambridge. He tells how Gurthigern (Vortigern), the British king, made the fatal mistake of inviting the Saxons to come and repel the invasions of the northern nations (the Picts), in or about 443. He complains of lack of information, saying his sources were full of gaps and were not clear.

D. B. Harden ed., *Dark-Age Britain, Studies presented to E. T. Leeds*, 1956.
T.S.I.H., i, 11 (Gildas translated).

ST. DAVID (**Dewi Sant**) (*c.* 520–88) was son of Sant, a Brythonic sub-king of Ceredigion (see map on the end-paper), and Non, daughter of a local Goedelic notable, and was cousin of many other Welsh saints. He studied for ten years at Ty Gwyn (not Whiteland) near St. David's. He founded Ty Ddewi (St. David's) and other monastic centres and went to strengthen Christianity in Ireland for Ainmire, its High King. He is patron saint of dozens of south Welsh, Devon, Cornish and Breton churches, the only officially recognized Welsh saint, and the most famous Welsh bishop. David is first mentioned in a tenth-century manuscript of the *Annals of Wales*. The basic *Life* by Rhygyfarch, Bishop of St. David's (1088–96), errs in saying that he lived 147 years. It says nothing of his being archbishop or about leeks; and the original reason why leeks are worn on his day is unknown. In one legend David is made head of the Welsh church because he could shout louder than the other bishops. Geoffrey of Monmouth's twelfth-century *History of Britain* fancifully makes Arthur David's nephew.

E. Rhys, *Life of St. David*, 1927.

ST. COLUMBA (**COLUMCILLE**) (521–97), born near Gartan Lough (Donegal), was a pupil of St. Finnian (d. 550), and grandson of a convert of St. Patrick. He crossed to Scotland (563) to convert its heathen inhabitants and founded a religious community on Iona (St. Colm's Isle or Hy). He wrote on monastic discipline and penance, enjoining early rising for lie-a-beds, blows for the boisterous and abstinence for the greedy. He encouraged private confession. His biographer, Adamnan, calls him a contrary man, tender and irritable, rude and courteous, grateful and revengeful. Columba was tall with bright eyes and the front of his head was shaved. He wore a cassock and hood of undyed homespun wool. His bed and pillow were stone. He is not the same as **St. Columban** (543–615), another Irishman, whose name is the same in Latin, Columbanus. Columban is a symbol of the light and learning which came back to the Continent from remote Ireland, for he went to France (585) and Lombardy (612), taught heathen tribes, settled in the Tyrol and died at Bobbio (Piedmont). Both Columba and Columban loved animals and on the last evening of Columba's life an old horse rubbed its head against him and he blessed it. Birds would settle on Columban's shoulder and nestle in his hood. Barbarian invasions severed Rome from Britain and Ireland, and differences in custom grew up between Celtic and other Christians. Their tonsure and the date of keeping Easter differed. Columban wrote to Pope Gregory the Great about the date of Easter but had no answer. The dispute ended in 663 (see p. 21).

Miss Lucy Menzies, *St. Columba of Iona* (The Iona Community), 1950.

ST. AUGUSTINE (d. between 604 and 609), first Archbishop of Canterbury, was Prior of St. Andrew's in Rome when Pope Gregory the Great chose him to lead a mission to England. The 'barbarous, fierce, and unbelieving nations, whose very language was unfamiliar' terrified him, but he landed in Thanet (597) with forty monks. They chanted the litany in procession, carrying a silver cross and a picture of the Crucifixion, and Ethelbert, King of Kent, received them kindly, though he was somewhat suspicious of magic. Ethelbert's capital was Canterbury, and there Augustine used a church 'built in honour of St. Martin while yet the Romans inhabited Britain'. Bishop Liudhard, chaplain of Ethelbert's Christian queen, Bertha, had used it. In it Augustine baptized Ethelbert on the eve of Whitsun. He was allowed to have the king's palace as his own, and was consecrated at Arles Bishop of the English. At Christmas he baptized ten thousand converts. He used to refer even trifling points to Pope Gregory, who warned him not to let his miracles cause conceit. He dedicated to St. Pancras a former heathen temple and rebuilt Christ Church, Canterbury, another former Romano-British church. He held a conference at Aust on the Severn with the Welsh Christians, hoping to unite with them, but failed because they regarded as a symptom of pride his failure to rise from his seat to meet them. He consecrated Justus (d. 627) and Mellitus (d. 624) as Bishops of Rochester and London, and Lawrence (d. 619) to succeed himself at Canterbury. Gregory intended London and York to be twin headquarters of the English church, but the fact that little Canterbury has an archbishop today and London only a bishop is the historical consequence of the fact that Ethelbert was the strongest king in England in 597. St. Augustine is to be distinguished from his namesake, the Bishop of Hippo (N. Africa), a much greater man and one of the greatest writers of the Church (d. 430).

H. H. Howorth, *Augustine the Missionary*, 1913.

ETHELBERT (d. 616) was great-grandson of Hengist, the Saxon conqueror of Kent, and reigned fifty-six years. Before becoming king (560) he married a Frankish princess, Bertha, who was a Christian. Thus Augustine came (597) to a court ripe for conversion. A coin found in St. Martin's church (Canterbury), crudely minted after a Frankish model, bears the name of her chaplain, Liudhard. This marriage was not the only link between south-eastern England and the more civilized people across the Channel, for Frankish and Kentish ways of ploughing and measuring land were alike and Kentish charters followed Roman forms, and the laws of Ethelbert were made 'according to the Roman fashion' soon after. Ethelbert's influence, after the death of his enemy Ceawlin, King of

KINGS OF DEIRA, BERNICIA AND NORTHUMBRIA

YFFE, 12th in descent from Woden

AELFRIC

OSRIC d. 634

OSWIN d. 651

AELLE, 1st K. of Deira

EDWIN K. of Northumbria d. 633 = ETHELBURGA dau. of Ethelbert K. of Kent

EANFLED = OSWY K. of Bernicia and then of all Northumbria d. 670

EGFRITH K. of Northumbria d. 685

EOPPA, descendant of Woden 1st K. of Bernicia

IDA d. 549

ACHA = ETHELFRITH K. of Northumbria d. 617

OSWALD d. 642

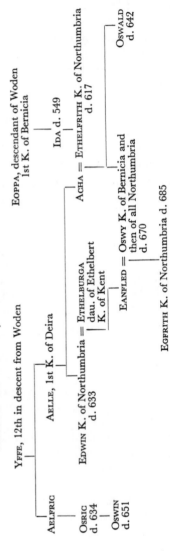

Wessex (593), became great enough to ensure Augustine's safety at a conference in the distant and unconverted west of England. He was supreme over all the English south of the Humber, a position which led to his being reckoned *Bretwalda.* Before he died the leadership passed to Raedwald, King of the East Angles, who led a reaction against Christianity.

Margaret Deanesley, 'Canterbury and Paris in the reign of Aethelberht', *History*, N.S. xxvi, 1941, pp. 99–104.

Ethelbert's laws, recorded in a single manuscript, the *Textus Roffensis*, are translated by Dorothy Whitelock in *English Historical Documents, c. 500–1042*, 1955.

EDWIN (?585–633) had to flee from the King of Bernicia (Northumbria) at the age of three on the death of his father, Aelle, King of Deira (Yorkshire) (588). Then Rædwald, King of East Anglia, defeated Ethelfrith, King of Bernicia, and made Edwin king of both Deira and Bernicia, uniting them to form the important kingdom of Northumbria. Edwin conquered a British enclave in the West Riding (Elmet) and won victories over Welsh and Scots, though it is untrue to say that Edinburgh commemorates his name. His Kentish queen, Ethelburga, and her chaplain Paulinus (see p. 16), converted him and even Coifi, his chief priest, to Christianity. Coifi personally desecrated the pagan temple and many were baptized. Edwin began to build a stone church for Paulinus in York, his capital. Bede says that the calm of Edwin's dominions was proverbial and that a mother with a babe might cross the land from sea to sea unharmed; and that he placed stakes with copper drinking-vessels hanging from them at wayside springs and that nobody abused these, either through fear or love of him. Even in peace-time a standard-bearer preceded him as he rode round his realms and in the streets his dignity was marked by an impressive banner, probably like one recently excavated at Sutton Hoo, borne before him. Jealousy of Edwin united Cadwallon, a British king, with Penda, King of Mercia (see p. 18); and they slew him, then aged forty-eight, at 'Heathfield' (Hatfield Chase, Doncaster) (633). Edwin's work was a continuation of English expansion begun by Ethelfrith who had beaten the Welsh at Chester (616); and after Edwin's death it was Ethelfrith's sons, and grandson, Oswald (634–42), Oswy (642–70) and Egfrith (671–85), who ruled Northumbria in the days of its greatness (see pedigree, p. 14). Edwin was the fifth of the outstandingly powerful English kings called Bretwalda.

R. H. Hodgkin, *History of the Anglo-Saxons*, first printed 1935.
T.S.I.H., i, 14 (story of Coifi).

ST. OSWALD (d. 642), son of Ethelfrith King of Bernicia, fled from his victorious kinsman, Edwin (617), to Iona with his brother, Oswy. Edwin represented a rival branch of the family and owed much to Roman Christianity; but Oswald in his seventeen years' exile caught the spirit of Celtic Christianity there. Triumphant Britons, who hated both the royal houses of the North, slew Oswald's elder brother in the 'hateful' year (633–4) when Edwin fell. Oswald returned with twelve thegns, and, erecting a wooden cross by Hadrian's Wall and invoking St. Columba, slew King Cadwallon, Edwin's British enemy, at Heavenfield (634). Oswald summoned Aidan from Iona to convert his new subjects to Celtic Christianity (635), giving him Lindisfarne near the stronghold of Bamborough. The heathen Penda of Mercia slew Oswald at Maserfield (642) as he had slain Edwin less than a decade before. The mutilated body wrought miracles and the head was in due course carried in St. Cuthbert's coffin to Durham (1104).

J. L. G. Meissne, *The Celtic Church in England*, 1929.

ST. PAULINUS (d. 644) was a tall dark Roman with an aquiline nose and a stoop, sent by Pope Gregory (601) to take to Augustine the mantle or 'pall' which distinguishes its wearer as archbishop. He was to help organize the English church in two provinces, with an archbishopric for the northern one at York. Each province was to consist of twelve sees ruled by bishops. He went as bishop when the Kentish princess Ethelburga married Edwin of Northumbria (625). Like Augustine he profited by toleration at court and, skilfully taking advantage of various crises, he converted Edwin.

Plate 3

Coin of Trajan with earliest representation of Britannia
(Ashmolean Museum)

Edward the Confessor

Harold and Stigand

Plate 4

Odo, William I and Robert of Normandy

Bayeux Tapestry

Paulinus established himself at York, with its proud Roman traditions, and there Edwin helped him build round a temporary wooden church a stone one dedicated to the Roman saint, Peter. Edwin's conversion was the occasion of a famous speech, comparing life to a sparrow speeding through the hall during a winter feast from darkness into darkness. Paulinus made many mass baptisms after preaching in the open air, especially by the Swale above Catterick Bridge (N. Riding), for in all Bernicia there was then not yet one church, altar or even preaching cross. After Edwin's defeat at Hatfield (633) Paulinus fled with Ethelburga and became Bishop of Rochester, where he died on 10th October, 644. He was buried there but some of his bones and teeth were kept as relics at York. Paulinus had fled, taking his church ornaments with him, before his own archbishop's pall arrived, and no archbishop received a pall for York until Egbert (d. 766). His deacon, James, went on working in Northumbria until the time of Bede (d. 735). St. Paul's church at Lincoln is really dedicated to Paulinus.

R. H. Hodgkin, *History of the Anglo-Saxons*, 1935.
T.S.I.H., i, 14 (the sparrow story).

ST. BIRINUS (d. 650), a Benedictine monk, landed in Wessex (634) with a commission from Pope Honorius to evangelize the unconverted English. He baptized Cynegils, King of Wessex, with Oswald, King of Northumbria's support as sponsor (635), and became Bishop of Dorchester on Thames, a little town with Roman associations at an important Thames crossing near Benson (Oxon) (636). He baptized Cynegils' sons Cwichelm (636) and Cuthred (639), though Cynegils' successor Coenwalch remained heathen until he was converted during a temporary exile in East Anglia. Birinus was buried at Dorchester (Oxon), whence the body was taken to Winchester, capital of Wessex (676). There Cnut gave it a new shrine (1035). In 1150 it was returned to Dorchester. Stained glass at Dorchester shows Birinus, Cynegils, Oswald and Honorius.

J. S. Field, *St. Berin, the Apostle of Wessex*, 1902.

ST. AIDAN (d. 651) was a brave and gentle Scot who left Iona (635) to help King Oswald. An earlier mission had failed to reconvert the Northumbrians, through, Aidan believed, impatience with ignorant audiences. Oswald gave Aidan Lindisfarne, a rocky island suitable as a site for a monastery like Iona, though near Bamborough, the capital. There Irish Christians trained young Englishmen. Aidan was the first bishop and he introduced the rule of St. Columba. Similar monasteries appeared and Aidan travelled round preaching, retiring at times for solitude to Farne Island and visiting Oswald at Bamborough. At his prayer the wind changed and saved Bamborough from fire after Penda had slain Oswald (642) and was attacking it; and once Aidan stilled a tempest with consecrated oil. Bede says that Aidan 'never out of awe hesitated to rebuke rich sinners. He never gave money to men of influence, but only food, if he was entertaining them'. Aidan was bishop of both Bernicia and Deira, the separate kingdoms of Oswy and Oswin. Oswy murdered Oswin and twelve days later Aidan died of a sudden illness, heartbroken, beside his church of Bamborough (31st August, 651). Aidan was buried at Lindisfarne, but Colman took some of his relics to Ireland (663) (see p. 20). See picture, p. 22.

A. C. Fryer, *Aidan, the Apostle of the North*, 1884.

PENDA (?577–655) became King of Mercia when aged fifty and was first to make it powerful and independent of Northumbria. He was descended from Woden (see pedigree, p. 30). He despised bad Christians and championed heathenism though sometimes in alliance with Cadwallon (d. 634) of Gwynedd. He slew two Christian kings of Northumbria, Edwin at Heathfield (Hatfield Chase, 12th October, 633) and Oswald at Maserfield (perhaps Oswestry, 5th August, 642), and three kings of East Anglia. He divided Northumbria into its separate component parts, Bernicia and Deira, as it had been originally and he expelled Cenwalh, King of Wessex (645). His son Peada became a Christian. Oswy of Northumbria slew Penda near the river Winwæd (15th November, 655) and Mercia temporarily lost its ascendancy. See p. 30.

ST. CEDDA (CEDD) (d. 664) was educated with his brother Ceadda by Aidan at Lindisfarne. King Oswy recalled him from converting the Middle Angles at Peada's request (653) to convert the East Saxon subjects of Sigeberht. Finan consecrated him Bishop of the East Saxons (654). He built monasteries and churches and accepted the Roman date of Easter at Whitby (663). Sigeberht's murder (660) seemed to fulfil a prophecy uttered by Cedd who had rebuked him for feasting with a thegn who was living in sin. Cedd died of yellow plague at his newly founded monastery of Lastingham, Yorks., on 26th October, 664. Thirty of his followers died of it soon after. It was so devastating that the East Saxons thought they had offended the old gods, and abandoned Christianity.

Bede, *Ecclesiastical History*.

OSWY or OSWIU (*c.* 612–70) succeeded his brother Oswald as King of Bernicia (642) and became ruler of all Northumbria after the murder of Oswald (642) (see pedigree, p. 14). He made it possible for the Roman Christianity of Paulinus, and Edwin at York and the Celtic Christianity of Aidan, and Oswald at Iona to flourish until their differences required and received settlement at Whitby (663); for missions to penetrate Mercia and Essex (653); and for the unifying organization of Theodore, Archbishop of Canterbury, to grapple with the local ambition of Bishop Wilfrid. Oswy slew Penda at Winwæd (655) and temporarily re-established Northumbrian power, but during most of his reign Mercia was predominant under Penda and his son Wulfhere (658–75). Oswy was the seventh of the English kings whose exceptional authority earned the name Bretwalda. He died on 15th February, 670, aged fifty-eight and was buried at Whitby, where his daughter, Aelflæd, succeeded Hild as abbess.

ST. CEADDA (CHAD) (d. 672), disciple of Aidan and converter of the Mercians, is the patron saint of over forty churches. He was trained in Co. Louth (Eire) and succeeded his brother Cedd as Abbot of Lastingham, Yorks., but King Oswy made him Bishop of Northumbria in place of Wilfrid who was lingering in Gaul (664–9). Theodore (see p. 23) condemned Ceadda's consecration and he modestly retired to Lastingham. Theodore then made him Bishop of the Mercians, insisting that when travelling far he should ride instead of always walking and even personally lifting him on to a horse. Whenever the wind blew loudly Ceadda used to pray for all mankind. He built a cathedral at Lichfield and there his Gospel Book is still preserved, a monument of seventh-century illustration. He died of pestilence on 2nd March, 672, seven days after hearing angelic singing. He is sometimes confused with his brother, Cedda.

ST. COLMAN (676), Bishop of Lindisfarne, was defeated by St. Wilfrid at the Synod of Whitby (663, see p. 24), and had to admit that St. Peter was greater than St. Columba and that the Celtic church must bow to Rome. He did not accept the Synod's decision but preferred to withdraw from Northumbria. Apparently he would have feared the anger of his countrymen if he had done otherwise. He founded a monastery at Inishbofin (Ireland), and there died.

ST. ETHELDREDA (AETHELTHRYTH or AUDREY) (?630–79) was one of the four sainted daughters of King Anna of East Anglia (see pedigree, p. 30) and a virgin though twice married. After twelve years' marriage, her second husband, Egfrid, son and successor of King Oswy of Northumbria, let her retire to her aunt Ebba's 'double monastery' (for monks and nuns) at Coldingham (Berwickshire). A year later she went to the Isle of Ely, which had been given her by her first husband, the prince of the fen-men, and founded another double monastery. Her strict life included abstinence from baths, except thrice yearly before great festivals. She died of plague. When a doctor lanced a tumour under her jaw, she said that this reminded her of her former necklaces. This is why cheap necklaces were sold at fairs on the anniversary of her death, 23rd June. From them is derived the word 'tawdry' (St. Audrey). Her body was removed from her wooden coffin to a marble sarcophagus brought from the

Roman ruins of Grantchester (Cambs.), and Ely cathedral has grown around her tomb.

Bede, *Ecclesiastical History*.

ST. HILD (HILDA) (614–80), great-niece of King Edwin and sister-in-law of Anna, King of the East Angles, was baptized by Paulinus (627) and became a nun at the age of thirty-three. Aidan recalled her from East Anglia to Northumbria, where she became Abbess of Hartlepool and later of her own foundation of Streoneshealh or Whitby. These houses contained both nuns and monks. Of the Whitby monks five, including Wilfrid and John of Beverley, became bishops. The most famous monk there was the poet Cædmon, of whose divine gift of song Bede tells. At her nunnery of Whitby a Synod took place in what Bede calls 664 but in what we should call 663. It was a meeting to decide whether the date of Easter should be according to the custom of the Roman or of the Celtic church. The Celtic Christians of Iona and the converts of Augustine's Roman mission had both worked well; but it was hard for them, now they were in contact, to work together and it was absurd to see Edwin and his queen keeping Easter on different dates so that one fasted with the Bernicians while the other feasted with the Deirans. Hild died, loved and respected, aged about seventy-six, after a six years' succession of feverish attacks, on 17th November, 680.

Lina Eckenstein, *Woman under Monasticism, Chapters on Saint-lore and Convent Life between A.D. 500 and A.D. 1500*, 1896.
T.S.I.H., i, 16 (Synod of Whitby).

ST. CUTHBERT (d. 687) was the most celebrated Northumbrian saint when the Northumbrian kingdom flourished. He was a Bernician boy who rejected boyish sports and became pious after an angel had cured a tumour on his knee. As a shepherd on Lammermuir he saw Aidan's soul carried heavenward (d. 651, see p. 22). He became a monk at Melrose under Eata, a disciple of Aidan, and there the prior, Boisil, greatly influenced him. Expelled from Ripon for his loyalty to the old Celtic church usages (661), he moved to Lindisfarne where he adopted Roman ones (664). He went preaching in remote villages which others were afraid to visit, because of their poverty and ignorance. He built a lonely hut on Farne Island with no window save in the roof (676) and he always wore a

Cuthbert sees Aidan carried to Heaven
(University College, Oxford, MS.)

robe of undyed wool. He refused to be Bishop of Hexham, but succeeded Eata as Bishop of Lindisfarne (684). He was learned but humble, tall, kind and happy, but of austere life and left by a plague with a fatal internal tumour. In 686 he withdrew to Farne where he died (20th March, 687). After many removals to avoid the Danes his incorruptible body finally rested at Durham with the head of King Oswald (d. 642). Many believed that Alfred's last words were 'Honour God and St. Cuthbert' and those who flocked to his shrine made Durham cathedral outstandingly noble and its bishops outstandingly powerful. A monk of Lindisfarne and the Venerable Bede both wrote his *Life*.

B. Colgrave, *Two Lives of St. Cuthbert*, 1940.

BENEDICT BISCOP (*c.* 628–89), a thegn of King Oswy of Northumbria, went to Rome (653), travelling many miles with Wilfrid. He returned there four times, buying books, relics and pictures, and was fired with loyalty to Roman as opposed to Celtic usages. He became a monk at Lérins and conducted Theodore for Pope Vitalian to Canterbury (667). There he stayed as abbot at the abbey of SS. Peter and Paul for two years. King Egfrith gave him land on which he built monasteries at Wearmouth with stone and even glass windows (674), and Jarrow, the home of Bede. He died on 12th January, 690, after three years of paralysis, and his pupil, Bede, wrote his life. Aethelwold moved his bones to Thorney.

R. L. P. Milburn, *Saints and their Emblems in English Churches*, 1957.

ST. THEODORE OF TARSUS (*c.* 602–690) was a learned Cilician who came to Rome aged sixty-six (667) and was sent by Pope Vitalian to be Archbishop of Canterbury after a delay of four months to let his shaven hair grow enough to receive the Roman tonsure. The abbot Hadrian (from North Africa) had refused the appointment and recommended Theodore instead, agreeing to go with him to watch his orthodoxy. They inspected England together and Hadrian became Abbot of SS. Peter and Paul's at Canterbury. Theodore filled vacant bishoprics and held reforming synods (673, 680, 684) and established unified ecclesiastical authority over the realms of England. Wilfrid long opposed his subdivision of Northumbria into four new dioceses but Ethelred, King of Mercia, co-operated (679) in the subdivision of Mercia into five sees. Theodore compiled a *Penitential*, long a confessor's text-book, now preserved in an eighth-century manuscript at Corpus Christi College, Cambridge. He was the first archbishop whom all the English church obeyed. He introduced the study of Greek—which was to disappear again owing to the havoc wrought by the Danes—

and after him England produced English bishops. Little regarded in the Middle Ages, Theodore's name was included in the calendar of the 1928 Prayer Book. He was an administrative genius, best appreciated in an age of bureaucracy more respectful of organizers than of mystics or military heroes.

G. F. Browne, *Theodore and Wilfrith*, 1897.

ST. WILFRID (634–709), the handsome and well-mannered son of a thegn at Ripon (where he became abbot), was educated at King Oswy's court, Lindisfarne and Canterbury. He died at Oundle aged seventy-five and was buried at Ripon. At Whitby (663) he successfully asserted Roman instead of Celtic practices in accord with ideas learnt from Benedict Biscop at Rome. He became Bishop of Northumbria, but his friend Oswy replaced him by Ceadda because he had gone to Gaul and lingered there (666–9). When reinstated he built Ripon and Hexham churches, where his stone crypts can be seen, and fitted glass windows in York Minster. He resisted the reforms of Archbishop Theodore who aimed at subdividing such large dioceses (678). He encouraged Etheldreda to become a nun (672) to the annoyance of her husband, King Egfrid, who imprisoned him (680–1). In the first of two temporary exiles, he converted Sussex and built a monastery at Selsey. On Egfrid's death he made peace with Theodore and returned (686–7) until 691. He walked to Rome at the age of nearly seventy and settled renewed differences with Theodore. In old age he devoted himself to his churches and indeed forty-three ancient churches are dedicated to him. He is confused with Wilfrid, Archbishop of York (718–37), in the article in the *Dictionary of National Biography*.

Eddius Stephanus, *Life of Bishop Wilfrid*, ed. and trans. by B. Colgrave, 1921. Eddius, brought from Kent to Northumbria as a singing master by Wilfrid, was his devoted supporter.

ST. ALDHELM (EADHELM) (?640–709) was a pupil of Theodore and Hadrian at Canterbury, teacher, singer, harpist, poet, Abbot of Malmesbury (975). He disliked arithmetic and was the first Englishman to write Latin verse, a poem about virginity. He built churches at Malmesbury, Bruton, Wareham, Frome and Bradford. The famous Saxon church at Bradford-on-Avon may be two and a half centuries later than his, and his stone church at Malmesbury, the finest in England, was rebuilt by the Normans. When visiting Pope Sergius I (*c.* 700) his chasuble, embroidered with peacocks and long afterwards preserved, was miraculously supported on a sunbeam in the Lateran church. His relative, King Ine of Wessex, made him become Bishop of Sherborne, where he built a handsome church, now destroyed. His contemporary, Bede, admired his 'notable book against the error of the Britons in not celebrating Easter at the proper time'. Perusal of it converted many of the British subjects of the West Saxons. He died in Doulting church near Shepton Mallet (709) and 'Bishop's Stones' (crosses) were built where his body rested on its way to Malmesbury.

W. B. Wildman, *Life of St. Ealdhelm*, 1905.
Aldhelm, in E. S. Duckett, *Anglo-Saxon Saints and Scholars*, 1947.

ST. GUTHLAC (663–714) was a princely Mercian warrior who became a saint. A good translation of a *Life*, written in turgid Latin by an East Anglian monk, has recently recalled his former fame as a hermit who dwelt for fifteen years on a haunted burial-mound on an island in the fens where Crowland Abbey was to rise.

B. Colgrave, ed. and trans., *Felix's Life of St. Guthlac*, 1956.
T.S.I.H., i, 18.

ST. JOHN OF BEVERLEY (d. 721), a pupil of Archbishop Theodore and monk of Whitby, was ordained by Bede. He often used to seek solitude in a wood near Hexham where he became bishop (687) before becoming Bishop of York (705). He founded a monastery at Beverley whither he retired and died on 7th May, 721. He was one of the most popular saints of northern England. Beneath his banner the Battle of the Standard went against the Scots (1138). Henry V attributed his victory at Agincourt, which took place on his anniversary, to John's intercession.

Rev. J. Raine, *The Priory of Hexham*, vol. 1 (Surtees Soc. 44), 1864.

ST. FRIDESWIDE (?680–735) was the first abbess of a monastery at Oxford which she founded (*c.* 730) as a princess who fled to a life of contemplation in a pigsty at Binsey near Oxford to escape a royal marriage. The earliest biographies of her are twelfth century. She became patron saint of the City and University of Oxford. Her wealthy shrine was plundered (1538) and her bones mingled with those of Peter Martyr's wife (1557) so that religious partisans might hesitate to scatter relics which they hated for fear of desecrating those which they respected. From the late twelfth century her monastery was occupied by regular canons. Wolsey suppressed it (1525) and its church is now the chapel of Christ Church and the cathedral of the post-reformation diocese of Oxford.

F. M. Stenton, 'St. Frideswide and her Times', *Oxoniensia*, vol. 1 (1936), p. 112.

THE VENERABLE BEDE (673–735) was the leading Northumbrian in an age when Northumbria led western Europe intellectually. Once chiefly thought of as a theologian, he is now appreciated as one of the greatest historians. He is the chief source for early English history up to 731. He sifts evidence and gives sources whether written or oral. A study of his works has enabled an idea to be formed of the composition of his large working library. He could read Greek, and Archbishop Laud's Greek manuscript of the Acts in the Bodleian (Oxford) is a text which Bede actually used. His life was spent as a priest in Jarrow monastery, observing its discipline and loving to learn, teach and write. He was admitted as a local seven-year-old boy for education by Abbots Benedict Biscop and Ceolfrid. Ceolfrid was once left by plague as Bede's sole companion. Bede was admitted deacon at nineteen and priest at thirty. His next twenty-nine years were passed annotating the Bible out of the Fathers for the use of himself and his brethren. Out of nearly 150 of his works 40 are known. These include his English Church History, Lives of the Abbots and of

St. Cuthbert and an Epistle to Egbert, Archbishop of York. Bede popularized the practice of dating events from the Incarnation. He had just time to finish a translation of St. John's Gospel before he died on Ascension Day, 25th May, 735, though his feast is 27th May. His relics were stolen from Jarrow and lie at Durham (1020) under an inscription:

Haec sunt in fossa
Bedæ venerabilis ossa.

Bede, his Life, Times and Writings, ed. A. H. Thompson, 1935.

ST. BONIFACE (or WYNFRITH) (*c.* 674–754) was born at Crediton (Devon) and was educated at Exeter and Nursling (Hants.). Ordained priest when thirty, he went to civilize the lands from whence the Saxons came. Failure to convert the Frisians, whose King, Radbod, was hostile, did not prevent him from refusing the abbacy of Nursling and returning to Frisia, with Pope Gregory II's authority, to labour for three years with Willibrord, Bishop of Utrecht. With further papal support and letters from Charles Martel, King of the Franks, he evangelized Hesse and Thuringia, destroyed an emblem of paganism by felling Thor's oak at Geismar, built a chapel with its timber, and founded Fritzlar monastery. Gregory III made him archbishop (732) and Pope Zacharias legate. He subdivided Bavaria, Thuringia and Hesse into bishoprics and held councils to regularize church practices, but resigned his archbishopric (753) and returned to Frisia. On June 4th, 754, 'the Apostle of Germany', with his friends, was massacred in camp near Dokkum, raising the Gospels in vain as a shield. Their books were cast into the reed-beds but were recovered later unstained. His correspondence survives. His life shows how England had become a centre of civilization instead of the barbaric outpost which Augustine had known.

C. H. Talbot, ed. and transl., *The Anglo-Saxon Missionaries in Germany, being the lives of SS. Willibrord, Boniface, Sturm, Leoba, and Lebuin, together with the Hodoeporicon of St. Willibald and a selection from the correspondence of St. Boniface*, 1954.
G. W. Greenaway, *St. Boniface, 3 biographical studies*, 1955.

OFFA (d. 796), King of the Mercians, called 'of blessed memory' by Alcuin. After forty-one years' reign Ethelbald of Mercia was murdered by his own household in 757. Offa at once expelled his successor. His victories gave him such influence that he could revoke without permission a grant made by 'his thegn' the King of Kent, and could make Lichfield an archbishopric (788) and could behead the King of East Anglia (794). In 779 he captured from Cynewulf, King of Wessex, Bensington, a royal estate strategically situated at the point where the important Icknield Way crosses the Thames and where the Thames at the Goring gap divides the Chilterns from the Berkshire Downs. His daughters married kings, he traded and corresponded as an equal with Charlemagne and he made his coinage conform to that of the Franks; but there is no chronicle of Mercia or biography to recount his acts and his Laws have perished. Asser wrote within a century of Offa's time that he 'bade make a great rampart between Britain and Mercia' from sea to sea. The northern end of Offa's Dyke is lost but apparently reached the sea at Prestatyn. It was built in separate sections to a single plan, included strong natural positions, sought open views towards Wales, controlled routes, and is indeed comparable with Hadrian's Wall. It has made Offa's name live, long after Mercia ceased to be chief among England's seven realms. See plate 1.

Sir Cyril Fox, *Offa's Dyke*, British Academy, 1955.

ALCUIN (**ALBINUS, FLACCUS or EALWHINE**) (735–804) was born at York and studied in its cloister school under Archbishop Egbert (732–66), its founder, and Ethelbert, with whom he travelled abroad as part of his education. When Ethelbert became archbishop (767) Alcuin undertook teaching and became the master (778). He loved Virgil and managed the library, which he describes in a poem, and which was unsurpassed in western Europe. On returning from a visit to Rome (781) he met Charlemagne, the Frankish king, at Parma, and agreed to organize great educational reforms. Except for two years (790–2), Alcuin remained abroad. He educated the royal family, including Charlemagne, for eight years, but settled at Tours (796) and as abbot made its school the Frankish equivalent to York. He died there aged sixty-nine (804). Alcuin links the scholarship of Bede's Northumbria with the revival of learning under Charlemagne. He was Europe's greatest scholar and through him York influenced all western literature. His philosophical works and versified annals matter less than his three hundred letters which reflect for us the history of his times.

E. S. Duckett, *Alcuin, Friend of Charlemagne: His World and His Work*, 1951.

EGBERT (**EGGBERHT**) (d. 839), King of the West-Saxons, was son of an under-king of Kent, and was exiled in youth by King Beorhtric of Wessex as the representative of a rival branch of his family. He first fled to Mercia but King Offa allied himself with Beorhtric, his son-in-law, and refused him asylum, so he went to Charlemagne's court for some years. He returned and became king (802), inspired by Frankish military and imperial ideas. He defeated 'West Welsh' rebels at Camelford (Devon) (825), and Mercians in a 'river of blood' at Ellandune (near Swindon), and conquered his ancestral kingdom of Kent. East Anglia successfully defied its Mercian masters and sought his peace and protection. Mercia submitted (826) and Egbert invaded Northumbria (829) and temporarily united all the English for the first time under one overlord, though separate kingdoms kept their own rulers, like Wiglaf in Mercia and Egbert's son Ethelwulf in Kent. Ethelwulf succeeded him after a reign of thirty-seven years and seven months. They made a perpetual alliance with the Archbishop of Canterbury (838) and Ethelwulf gave a tenth of his land to the church. See pp. 30–1 (genealogy).

ST. SWITHUN (806?–862) was a famous Bishop of Winchester and friend of Egbert and Ethelwulf. His biography tells more of his miracles occurring after his death than of his earthly life, a testimony to his hold on popular esteem. Hundreds of miracles followed the removal of his body by St. Aethelwold into the cathedral (the Danes had burnt it the

GENEALOGY OF THE SAXON KINGS OF ENGLAND

The English monarchy is the oldest European institution with the exception of the papacy. The history of the house of Wessex became the history of the English monarchy. King Egbert (802–39) was the founder of the dynasty. His mythical descent from Woden ran: Woden – Baeldaeg – Brand – Beorn – Frithugar – Freawine – Wig – Gewis – Esla – Elesa – Cerdic – Cynric (?534–60) – Ceawlin (560–92) – Cuthwine (d. 584) – Cuthwulf or Cutha – Coelwald – Cenred (d. 690) – Ingild – Eoppa – Eafa – Ealhmund, under-king in Kent, 784–86 – Egbert. From Woden's seven sons the kings of the seven Anglo-Saxon kingdoms all claimed descent. Ethelbert of Kent was seventh in descent from Wehta through Wehta's great-grandson, Hengist. Anna of East Anglia was tenth in descent from Casere. Penda of Mercia was twelfth in descent from Weolthelgeat. Aella of Deira was twelfth in descent from Weagdeag. Ida of Bernicia was twelfth, and Cerdic was ninth, in descent from Baeldaeg. For the Biblical and Roman ancestry claimed by the Welsh princes see pp. 36–37. The Tudor kings claimed descent from both.

Egbert 802–39

Osburgh (1) = Ethelwulf k. 839–58 = Judith (2) d. Charles the Bald k. of France

Athelstan, k. of East Anglia, 829– Sub-k. of Kent, 839–

Ethelbald = Judith his stepmother k. 858–60

Ethelbert k. 860–6

Ethelred I k. 866–71

Ethelswith = Burhred k. of Mercia

Alfred k. 871–901 = Ealhswith d. of Ethelred Mucel, ealdorman of Gaini

Aethelflaed Lady of Mercia d. 918 = Ethelred ealdorman of the Mercians

Edward the Elder k. 901–24

Ethelgifu Abbess of Shaftesbury

Aelfthryth = Baldwin II of Flanders

Ethelweard

Athelstan k. 924–40

Edmund I k. 940–6

Edred 946–55

Edgyth = Emperor Otto the Great

Edgifu = K. Charles the Simple of France

Edwig = Elfgifu daughter of Aethelgifu k. 955–59

Ethelflaed (1) = Edgar = Elfthryth (2) k. 957–75

Edward 'the Martyr' k. 975–8

Cnut (2) = Emma = Ethelred II 'the Redeless' (1) k. 1017–35 k. 978–1016

Edmund Ironside k. 1016

Athelstan d. 1015

Edwig killed 1017

Ealdgyth = Edric Streona

Alfred murdered 1036

Ealdgyth daughter of Godwin sister of Harold 1066 = Edward the Confessor k. 1042–66

Goda = Drogo Count of Mantes

Edward the Exile d. 1057

Ralph the Timid Earl of Hereford d. 1057

Duncan I killed by Macbeth 1040

Edgar Atheling d. 1106

St. Margaret d. 1093 = Malcolm III, King of Scots Canmore k. 1054–93 (see pedigree p. 85)

Matilda = Henry I (See pedigree p. 55)

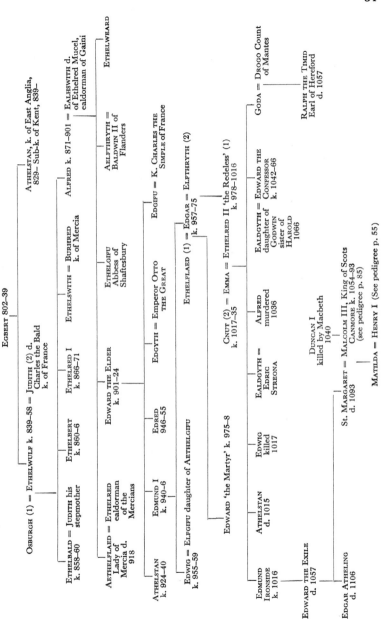

year before his death and he was buried outside it), and the monks grumbled at having to keep returning thanks in church for them. There is no support for the story that it rained for forty days after the removal. When he was employing men to make a stone bridge over the Itchen they upset a market woman's basket of eggs, but he miraculously mended them.

ST. EDMUND (841–70) was born at Nürnberg but was adopted by the King of the East-Angles whom he succeeded (Christmas, 855). In 866 he bought off the Danes but later he fought them and met defeat. He refused the Bishop of Elmham's advice to accept their terms and was tied naked to a tree (which stood until 1849) at Hoxne. He was scourged and riddled with arrows and finally beheaded by Inguar (20th Nov., 870). A wolf guarded his head in a thicket and drew the attention of those who sought it. The memory of his justice and gentleness fostered such tales, and his body was moved to Bedericsworth where Bury St. Edmunds grew up round the shrine of Edmund, the last king of his people.

Lord F. Hervey, *The History of King Edmund* (Corpus Christi College, Oxford MS 197), 1929.

ALFRED (849–901), King of the West-Saxons, was first called *Great* in the seventeenth century. He was the youngest child of King Ethelwulf (d. 858), born to Queen Osburgh at Wantage when the Danes were first settling in England (see pedigree, p. 31). He died before his fiftieth birthday. His father sent him when aged four (853) to be blessed by his godfather, Pope Leo IV, in Rome. Thither he returned (855) with his father, and on the way home they visited Charles the Bald, King of France. After Ethelwulf died (858) his three sons, Ethelbald, Ethelbert and Ethelred reigned successively. Alfred was sixteen when Ethelred succeeded (865) and he supported him loyally. An influx of Danes into East Anglia (866) fanned into Northumbria and Mercia (867). Alfred, aged twenty, married a Mercian and repelled the Vikings for three years. In 870 they first invaded Wessex. Alfred beat them at Ashdown (871). That year Alfred became king, aged

William I (Seal, British Museum)

Plate 5

William the Lyon (Seal, British Museum)

King David and his son Malcolm (Roxburghe Charter)

Plate 6

twenty-two, and he fought the Danes for fifteen more years (871–86). Nine battles occurred in 871; Wessex was exhausted and Alfred bought 'peace' with Danegeld (871–5). In 874 Guthrum invaded East Anglia and by 877 overran Mercia, Northumbria, and East Anglia. Alfred withdrew to the Isle of Athelney (Somerset) and planned and recruited for seven weeks. The story of how he carelessly burnt the cakes in a peasant's cottage there is a late insertion into Asser's *Biography*; but a jewel in the Ashmolean Museum, Oxford, which Alfred had made, was actually found there. In May, 878, he mustered his men at Egbert's stone near Penselwood (Somerset) and defeated Guthrum at *Ethandune* (Edington, Wilts.). The Vikings surrendered at Chippenham 'terrified by hunger, cold and fear' after fourteen days' siege. Alfred nobly refrained from massacre, gave his enemies food and peace, and stood godfather at Guthrum's baptism. By the Treaty of Wedmore Alfred sought conditions whereby Danes and English could co-exist, with Watling Street as frontier. He then turned to reconstruction (886–92).

Alfred foresaw further attacks; therefore defence was urgent. He built ships to prevent Danish landings and organized a professional mounted striking force. He divided the militia or *fyrd* into two halves, one to fight until relieved by the other. The Danes had established fortified bases provisioned from their surroundings and Alfred turned these into English strongholds which later grew into towns. These dispositions thwarted the Danes (892–6). After defence came education. Alfred imported foreign teachers, scholars and craftsmen and compelled freemen to learn letters. He himself learnt Latin so as to translate the most instructive Latin works, though he was over twelve when he learnt to read English, and was already nearly forty. In 892 he began his vast translations of Gregory's *Pastoral Care*, Bede's *Ecclesiastical History*, Orosius' *World History* and the writings of Augustine. He inserted original notes including descriptions of Northern lands. His preface to the *Pastoral Care* records his educational theories. His reign saw the commencement of the *Anglo-Saxon Chronicle*, a history, written from the standpoint of the Wessex royal house, which continued for two centuries and is unique to England. Alfred compiled a legal code expanded from those of Ethelbert of Kent, Ine of Wessex and Offa of Mercia. It defended the weak, limited blood-feuds and emphasized the duty of each to his lord. By applying it to Kent and English Mercia this code tended towards national unity. He was personally active in its administration for lack of competent subordinates. Alfred encouraged the arts and brought in foreign craftsmen to help rebuild houses and churches and design gold and silver ornaments and stone-work. British, Irish, continental and oriental influences are apparent.

Alfred may be called the first, and is certainly the noblest, of English kings, patient, modest, gentle and unselfish, strong and enduring in war, yet merciful in peace. He is the most memorable man in history. See plate 1 (coin).

B. A. Lees, *Alfred the Great, the Truth Teller*, New York, 1915.
T.S.I.H., i, 19.

ASSER (d. ?909), monk of St. David's and Bishop of Sherborne, came out of the extreme west at Alfred's request and was surprised to find himself asked to stay at the court (884). He hesitated while seeking advice and eventually divided his time between St. David's and Wessex. Alfred became his hero and Asser wrote Alfred's life up to 893. He is the source of the story that Alfred's mother showed an illuminated poetry book to her sons and encouraged Alfred to study by promising it to the one who could first read it.

E. Conybeare, *Alfred in the Chroniclers*, 1900.

EDWARD THE ELDER (870–924), King of the Anglo-Saxons, continued the Danish wars of his father Alfred and by one of the greatest military achievements of the dark ages gained the overlordship of Danes as well as English, even in Northumbria; but the fame of his father and of his son, Athelstan, eclipsed his own. His sister Aethelflæd (Ethelfleda), the Lady of Mercia (d. 918), helped to conquer Danish Mercia, fortifying centres like Chester (907), Tamworth, Warwick and Hertford.

Edward inherited Wessex, Kent and Sussex and conquered Mercia, Essex and East Anglia, exacting homage from Scotland, Wales and Strathclyde as well as Northumbria.

W. S. Angus, 'The Chronology of the Reign of Edward the Elder', *English Historical Review*, vol. 53, 1938. See p. 31.

ATHELSTAN (895–940), son of the martial Edward the Elder, was reared by his aunt, Aethelflæd (d. 918), the Lady of Mercia. (See pedigree, p. 31.) Crowned King of Wessex at Kingston (Surrey) (925), he crushed minor kings. When his brother-in-law the King of York died (927) he was the first southern king to take control of Northumbria, summoning its nobles to his assemblies and endowing churches like York, Ripon and Beverley. Even Constantine the Scot acknowledged him lord (927), Welsh princes attended his court (931–5), and five of his sisters married continental princes. He defeated a Norse invasion abetted by Constantine at Brunanburh (937), a victory celebrated in the Anglo-Saxon Chronicle in song:

> 'There also the aged Constantine, the hoary-headed warrior, came north to his own land by flight. He had no cause to exult in that crossing of swords. He was shorn of his kinsmen and deprived of his friends at that meeting-place, bereaved in the battle, and he left his young son on the field of slaughter, brought low by wounds in the battle. The grey-haired warrior, the old and wily one, had no cause to vaunt of that sword-clash; no more had Olaf . . .'

Athelstan's laws combated theft, oppression and fraud and mitigated severity to young offenders. He was a celebrated benefactor of monasteries and collector of books and relics and the *Annals of Ulster* proclaimed him 'pillar of dignity of the western world', though his empire collapsed when he died childless. William of Malmesbury says he was fair-haired, slender and of middle height. He was buried at Malmesbury. See plate 1 (coin).

A. Campbell, *The Battle of Brunanburh*, 1938.

T.S.I.H., i, 24 (Athelstan's laws about trial by ordeal).

HYWEL DDA or HOWEL THE GOOD (d. 950) wrote down Welsh law in a more systematic code than the Saxon kings made in England. He is the greatest Welsh king and traced his pedigree back to Anne, cousin of the Blessed Virgin. He is the only Welsh ruler to have coins minted. He inherited Ceredigion (see map, on the end paper), from his father Cadell ap Rhodri (909). He married Elen, daughter of Llywarch ap Hyfaidh, last of the old princes of Dyfed, and went to Rome on pilgrimage in the year of her death (928). Her pedigree is traced through King Arthur to Constantine the Great (323) whose mother Helena the Welsh regarded as British. By this marriage he was able to form the united south-west Welsh kingdom of Deheubarth. He submitted to Edward the Elder (918) and was one of the five kings who made peace with Athelstan (926). His name appears on many charters granted by English kings (931–46). He maintained peace with England even during the united action against Athelstan which ended in the Battle of Brunanburh (937); for he was a statesman, an admirer of Alfred and a friend of Athelstan, not a pugnacious nationalist. His name 'the Good', rare for any king and applied to no other Welsh ruler, marks out his virtues in contrast to Hywel the Bad, a north Welsh prince slain by Saxon treachery (984). His code was not what we call laws, being intended to describe existing customs, not to change them. According to the oldest manuscript of the 'North Welsh Code' the bad state of Welsh law led him to summon six men from each district to Y Ty Gwyn av Tav (the White House on the Tav), an otherwise unimportant place in Dyfed. These six included two clerks to prevent any ordinances contrary to scripture. 'Then he published the law, backed by his authority. Their curse and that of God and the Welsh was called down on any who broke it, unless altered by the agreement of the country and the lord'. Some of his legal maxims were: 'A contract breaks a custom'; 'It is wrong for you to own what is mine'; and 'Every injury that a person unwittingly commits, let him wittingly redress'. Much of the code discusses minute details, not general principles.

Prof. J. E. Lloyd, *Aberystwyth Studies*, vol. 10 (Hywel Dda millenary volume), 1928. For long Welsh princely pedigrees see *Cymmrodor*, vol. 9 (1888), pp. 169–71.

EDGAR THE 'PEACEABLE' (944–75), King of the English, was son of Edmund the Elder, a hero of his half-brother Athelstan's victory of Brunanburh. Edgar's elder brother, Edwig, died on 1st October, 959, after four years' reign. Edgar was not crowned until 973, at Bath. It is the earliest Coronation to be minutely described. Then six (or eight) kings accepted his lordship at Chester. Edgar kept the allegiance of the Danelaw by avoiding interference and he even ravaged Thanet for ill-treating some York merchants. His laws encouraged trade, protected the currency and were moderate, except for an extreme severity for withholding church dues. Later generations much respected them. Critics disliked his 'heathen manners' and 'foreign vices', but his support for monastic reform made monastic writers believe him divinely rewarded. Risings against monasteries followed his death, loyalty to his sons, little Edward the Martyr and Ethelred, was divided, and Viking raids restarted. In 975 the northern version of the Anglo-Saxon Chronicle sings his praise, 'In this year died Edgar, ruler of the Angles, friend of the West Saxons and protector of the Mercians. It was widely known throughout many nations across the gannet's bath (the sea), that kings honoured Edmund's son far and wide, and paid homage to this king as was his due by birth. Nor was their fleet so proud nor host so strong that it got itself prey in England as long as the noble king held the throne'. He was strong and handsome, but small and cruel. See p. 31.

W. H. Stevenson, 'The Great Commendation of King Edgar', *English Historical Review*, vol. 13, 1898 (The subject kings at Chester).

ST. AETHELWOLD (908?–84). His mother, a Winchester woman, had a prophetic dream before his birth about a lofty standard and a golden eagle, and when standing at mass in a crowded church, she felt the boy's soul enter her. After teaching him awhile the bishop sent him to Abbot Dunstan at Glastonbury (whom he had ordained at the same time) for further instruction. He became a monk and would have travelled abroad, but King Edred's mother interfered and made Edred give him Abingdon, then a deserted little monastery (954). Edred gave money and helped measure new foundations. Aethelwold himself broke all his ribs when a huge post fell, but things prospered and in 956 he obtained the first important endowment, an estate at Cuddesdon (Oxon.). After Edgar's accession Aethelwold sent a monk to study Benedictine customs at Fleury and with his support introduced them at Abingdon and he expelled worldly secular clerks from Winchester, Chertsey, Milton (Dorset) and Ely. The married clerics in the Old Minster were replaced by Abingdon monks. Athelstan made Aethelwold Bishop of Winchester (963). Aelfric, his pupil and biographer, says he visited the monasteries which he helped Dunstan to found, correcting the foolish with rods; at Winchester his opponents even tried to poison him. He never ate meat except during a three months illness and towards the end. He was often ill in bowels and legs. He liked explaining books in English to youths, some of whom became important. To him is attributed the translation of the Rule of St. Benedict. In the new monasteries flourished a school of illumination called the Winchester School. A supreme example is the 'Benedictional of St. Aethelwold'. When old he would read Latin at night, and once he fell asleep so that the candle fell on his book; but it was not damaged. He died on 1st August in the 22nd year of his episcopate, in the reign of King Ethelred. It was the work of such men which made Cnut (d. 1035) respect the church.

D. J. V. Fisher, 'The Early Biographers of St. Ethelwold', *English Historical Review*, vol. 67 (1952), pp. 381–91.

ST. DUNSTAN (924–88) was of noble Somerset birth, nervous and good at crafts. He was educated at Glastonbury, and studied writing, harping and painting as well as theology. He was once accused before Athelstan of being a wizard. He resisted the temptation to marry and became a monk. He thought marriage wicked in priests. On Athelstan's death

(940) King Edmund made him a courtier but he excited jealousy and was exiled when the court was at Cheddar, until Edmund repented when in peril on a cliff. Dunstan became Abbot of Glastonbury (*c.* 945). An early *Life* says that Edmund's brother and successor, Edred, liked Dunstan and deposited his charters and treasures with him at Glastonbury, but Edred's will shows that equal confidence was placed elsewhere and Dunstan's admiring biographer exaggerated his political influence, though mainly interested in his sanctity. Later monastic writers marked their respect by introducing more

St. Dunstan (self-portrait)

miracles, but no account survives written by those who opposed his church reforms and Benedictine monastic usages.

Edmund's young son Edwig (955) preferred his bride's company to his proper seat at a state banquet, but Dunstan dragged him back to the feast and was exiled; yet he enjoyed the favour of Eadwig's brother and rival Edgar who made him Bishop of Worcester (957), Bishop of London (959) and Archbishop of Canterbury (961). Dunstan crowned Edgar's son, Edward the Martyr (975), and directed his ecclesiastical policy until Edward's murder (978). He regarded the sorrows of Ethelred's reign as expiation for that murder.

Modern writers have struck a balance between regarding him first as a meddlesome villain and then as a hero like Alfred and Athelstan. He is now no longer seen as a 'chief minister' responsible for Edgar's secular acts as well as church reform; but he remains one of the greatest Archbishops of Canterbury, sharing with St. Aethelwold the unpopularity and the glory of the tenth-century Benedictine revival.

Eleanor Shipley Duckett, *Dunstan of Canterbury*, 1955.
T.S.I.H., i, 23.

ST. ALPHEGE (AELFEAH) (954–1012) was a monk at Deerhurst (where a window commemorates him), Abbot of Bath, Bishop of Winchester (984), Archbishop of Canterbury (1006) and a supporter of St. Dunstan's fight for an unmarried priesthood. The Danes, enraged by a massacre in 1002, took Canterbury (1011) and imprisoned Alphege on shipboard at Greenwich for seven months. He had condemned heathenism and the sale of slaves and had annoyed the pagans by confirming King Olaf Tryggwesson of Norway. He would not allow ransom to be raised from his tenants and the Anglo-Saxon Chronicle tells how, on 19th April, 1012, when drunk with wine of the South, his captors pelted him with bones and ox-heads, and one Dane killed him with a blow by the back of an axe. Florence of Worcester says that this man acted from pity, having been confirmed the previous day. Alphege was buried at St. Paul's and was a favourite saint of London. Cnut moved his body to Canterbury (1023). Lanfranc disputed his right to a martyr's crown, but Anselm disagreed (see p. 60).

ETHELRED II (986–1016), when aged ten, succeeded his brother, Edward the Martyr (see pedigree, p. 31). Ethelred's stepmother was apparently guilty of the murder of Edward at Corfe (14th March, 978), and it remained unavenged. The name 'Ethelred' means Noble Counsel, but thirty-three years' misrule justifies the punning nickname 'Redeless' (ill-counselled). The nickname first occurs in the thirteenth century, and is more correct and pointed than 'Unready', for Ethelred ever followed bad advice, especially that of Edric Streona, whom he rivalled in treacherous frightfulness. Danish raids were renewed (978–91) and inefficiency let them culminate in invasion (991–1012). Conquest (1013–6) by a 'Great Army' exasperated a writer of the Anglo-Saxon Chronicle who tartly observes that troops were always in the wrong place and that leadership was feeble and vacillating. Perhaps even Alfred would have been unable to control Northumbria, but Ethelred could not even control his own son, and even his charters are worded in an apologetic tone. The Chronicler records the details of pointless annual atrocities. Unaided, local heroes struggled in vain. The Song of the Battle of Maldon describes how a noble thegn, Brihtnoth, and the men of Essex (991) fought and fell. London too stood steady (994, 1013 and 1019); but though Ethelred occasionally resisted the Danes instead of ravaging friendly territory, he bought off the victors with 'Danegeld', trying to appease them with blackmail money (991, 995, 1001 and 1012). Ethelred's fear of treachery made him violent and he ordered (1002) a general massacre of Danes on a single day. The Danes were said to be plotting to murder him and his nobles when assembled in the Witan. Ethelred fixed the massacre for St. Brice's day. At Oxford the Danes fled to the minster of St. Frideswide's where the Saxons burnt them and it. Later writers added details, first including Danish women and then English women who associated with Danes. A basis for this mention of women may be the fact that Gunhild, sister of the Danish leader and wife of an English traitor, was murdered. In dying she apparently made the correct but easy prophecy that her death would bring England sorrow. A later account describes throat cutting, disembowelling, and the banging of babies' heads against door posts, and even dogs being urged to bite off women's breasts. Still later, bears were said to be used, with even less probability, for this. Lastly John of Wallingford (d. 1214) gives more convincing details. He says that the Danes were too popular with the English women, because they were so well groomed, combing their hair daily and bathing weekly. He says that the massacre was arranged for a Saturday as that was their bath-night. He does not mention St. Brice, but in 1002 November 12th fell on a Saturday. He leaves out dogs and bears and is content with cutting off the breasts of some women and 'planting' others in the ground.

Danish poetry tells how Sweyn swore on the 'bragging cup' to punish Ethelred. In 1013 Wessex, and even London, followed the Danelaw in accepting Sweyn's authority: and Ethelred fled to Rouen to the Norman relations of his wife, Emma. Sweyn died of apoplexy when threatening Bury St. Edmunds Abbey (3rd February, 1014), and the Witan recalled the ailing Ethelred for 'no lord would be dearer to them than their natural Lord, if only he governed better'. Sweyn's son, Cnut, had to flee, but a year of Ethelred taught Wessex to prefer Cnut again (1015), though Ethelred's son, Edmund 'Ironside', resisted elsewhere (1015–6). Ethelred died in London on 23rd April, 1016, when Cnut was preparing to besiege it, and was buried in St. Paul's. His widow married Cnut.

A translation of the Song of the Battle of Maldon is in Dorothy Whitelock, *English Historical Documents 1042–1189*, 1953.

M. Ashdown, *English and Norse Documents Relating to the Reign of Ethelred*, 1930. See plate 1 (coin) and p. 31.

EDMUND IRONSIDE (d. 1016) fought the Danes during the reign of his father, Ethelred II, and thereafter his seven months' reign was a heroic struggle against Cnut. The traitorous Edric Streona perhaps murdered Edmund (30th November, 1016) shortly after peace was made. See p. 31.

M. L. R. Beaven, 'King Edmund I and the Danes of York', *English Historical Review*, vol. 33, 1918.

AELFRIC (*c.* 950–1020) was a pupil and biographer of St. Aethelwold. His friend Alphege sent him to Cerne where he taught and became abbot before becoming the first Abbot of Eynsham (1005) where he died. His many writings, including Forty-five *Catholic Homilies* and *Lives of the Saints*, helped the growth of literature. He supported the religious revival inspired by the Benedictine monasteries. His views on the Mass are now regarded as orthodox by Catholics, but Elizabethan Anglicans believed that he supported their attitude. His canons, pastoral letters, paraphrase of the Pentateuch and Latin Grammar are less familiar than his fascinating *Colloquies*, dialogues to teach Latin; which give intimate details of Saxon daily life.

S. H. Gem, *An Anglo-Saxon Abbot: Aelfric of Eynsham*, 1912.

T.S.I.H., i, 25 (Aelfric's *Colloquies*).

CNUT OR CANUTE (?994–1035) was the foster son of Thurkil the Tall (d. about 1024), leader of a Viking army in English pay, and later his champion and chief adviser. He ruled an empire surrounding the North Sea and lies at Winchester. In youth he accompanied his father, Sweyn, against Ethelred (1013) and was proclaimed King of England by his army when his father fell (3 Feb., 1014). He was temporarily expelled, mutilating some hostages at Sandwich on his way back to Denmark, but returned (1015) to ravage Wessex. After the deaths of Ethelred (23 April, 1016) and Edmund Ironside (Nov., 1016) he was acknowledged king and married Ethelred's widow, Emma. Having become King of all England (1017) he became King of Denmark (1019) and Norway (1028). He left England and Denmark to his son Harthacnut (d. 1042) and Norway to another son, Sweyn.

Cnut's laws (1020–30) reflect his enthusiastic admiration for the Church. They forbid every heathen practice, worship of idols, sun, moon, fire, flood, wells, stones or trees, together with witchcraft and divination. Norse poems praise him and his early life as a ruthless Viking warrior: 'Never younger than you did prince set out in war . . . you made war in green Lindsey . . . you made corslets red in Norwich . . . you won no less renown on Thames' bank'. Yet he vowed to rule justly, and though he was a conqueror who had to reward his followers with land and maintain soldiers and a fleet at the cost of his defeated subjects, he promoted some of the leaders of the English Church, of which he was a devoted disciple, patronized Bury St. Edmunds and Winchester abbeys and made Godwin Earl of Wessex. He was proud to be honoured at Rome by Pope and Emperor and was the first Viking to be accepted in the circle of Christian kings. If the story of Cnut and the waves is untrue, it truly reflects the repute of one who, for all his foreign thegns, was troubled less by his English subjects than his own folk. His power saved England from invasion despite raids from Wales (1039) and Scotland (1040) and he spared English landowners. See p. 44 and plate 1 (coin).

L. M. Larson, *Canute the Great and the Rise of Danish Imperialism*, 1912.
T.S.I.H., i, 34 (story of the waves as first told).

EMMA (?987–1052) was the daughter of Richard the Fearless, Duke (943–96) of the Normans, sister of Richard the

Good (Duke, 996–1026) and aunt of Dukes Richard (III) and Robert the Devil. (See pedigree, p. 31.) She was born in the middle of a long period of surprisingly tranquil progress, which

Emma and Cnut (Hyde Abbey Register)

was only seriously marred by a peasants' revolt (997). The children and other relatives of Emma's mother, Gunnor, became heads of great baronial families destined to win fame in both England and Normandy in the next century. Such were the counts of Eu, Brionne, Mortain and Bellême, the

FitzOsberns, Montgomerys, Beaumonts, Giffards, Tancarvilles, Warennes, Mowbrays and Mortimers. Emma herself, Henry of Huntingdon calls the gem of the Normans. Ethelred, well-advised for once, hoped to strengthen his hand against the Danes by reaching an agreement with the Northmen who had settled across the Channel a century before and were no longer heathen pirates. He cemented his treaty (991) by a marriage (1002) with Emma. She came to England with her Norman train but adopted an English name, Aelgifu. This union successfully closed the Norman ports as bases for Danish raiders, and Ethelred and Emma could go as refugees to the Norman court when Sweyn overran England (1013). Their sons, Alfred and Edward (later the Confessor), were accordingly educated in Normandy and made useful friends among the Norman nobles who later supported their hopes for the English crown. After this marriage Emma had many changes of fortune, but for fifty years her existence was a common factor in the shifting drama of English politics. Her marriage brought the histories of England and Normandy into closer connexion until in 1066 Emma's great-nephew, William, united the kingdom and the duchy. Whether or not it was Emma who defended London against Cnut (1016), Cnut secured himself against English and Norman intrigues on behalf of Emma's sons by marrying her himself (1017). Emma was ten years older than Cnut, but she came to love Harthacnut, the child of her second marriage, more than she loved her children by Ethelred. When Cnut died (1035) she was aged about forty-eight. With Godwin's help she tried to make Harthacnut king. She had Cnut's bodyguard, the 'huscarls', at Winchester, but her stepson Harold Harefoot secured Cnut's treasure and obtained the loyalty of Mercia and Northumbria (1035). Harthacnut made himself unpopular by remaining in his kingdom of Denmark. Emma's eldest son (by Ethelred), Alfred, came from Normandy to visit her. Harefoot seized him, blinded him, and left him to die, for fear of his superior claim to the throne. Emma believed, perhaps rightly, that Godwin had betrayed Alfred; and Godwin ceased to support her and Harthacnut against Harefoot.

Harefoot banished Emma (1037). She did not return to Normandy, where the claims of Edward, her neglected son by Ethelred, were preferred. She turned to the Count of Flanders, Baldwin V. Harthacnut joined her in Flanders (1037) to help plan an invasion of England; but the death of Harefoot (1037) enabled Harthacnut to land peaceably. Under him (1040–1) Emma returned to power. Harthacnut dug up and insulted Harefoot's body, but his reign was no restoration of the just administration of Cnut; and Englishmen welcomed the accession of his acknowledged heir, his step-brother Edward (1042). The Anglo-Saxon Chronicle says: 'Fourteen days before St. Andrew's Mass [16th Nov.] the king was advised to ride from Gloucester, and in his company the Earls Leofric [of Mercia, who had supported Harefoot], Godwin [of Wessex, whom Emma hated], and Siward [of Northumbria, a rival of Godwin] with their followers, to Winchester, came unawares upon the lady Emma. And they bereaved her of all the treasures that she possessed, which were incalculable, because before that she had done less for him than he would, both before he was king and also after'. Later experience of Norman rule caused men to look back at Edward the Confessor as a saint and at his rule as a golden age. The nobility approved of a purge of 'criminals' associated with the old régime, but at least Emma was allowed to live freely but obscurely for the rest of her life at Winchester. She had been queen in two reigns and queen-mother in two more reigns. She could hardly have guessed that her son would be a saint, regarded as a model of royal piety. See pedigree, p. 31.

Dorothy Whitelock, *English Historical Documents, c. 500–1042*, 1955, pp. 321–4 (Alfred's fatal visit from *Encomium Emmæ*).

GODWIN (d. 1053) enjoyed the favour of Cnut who gave him the earldom of Wessex (1020), an old kingdom which had never been an earldom before and was larger than any other earldom. Godwin accompanied Cnut to Denmark and in England was his greatest subject for fifteen years. His wife was Danish, Gytha, the sister of Cnut's brother-in-law Ulf, one of the most famous heroes in the history and romance of early

Denmark and described in legend as the son of a bear. The elder children of Godwin and Gytha were called Sweyn and Harold after Cnut's children. On Cnut's death (1035) Godwin tried to help the widowed Queen Emma to secure the accession of Harthacnut, but Leofric, Earl of Mercia, and the London merchants preferred Cnut's elder son by an earlier marriage, Harold Harefoot, and England was divided into two realms lying north and south of the Thames. This meant that Godwin's power no longer extended outside Wessex, and in Wessex itself the presence of Emma ceased to mean the presence of a friend, for Emma suspected Godwin of treachery (see p. 45). He decided to transfer his allegiance to Harefoot and Emma fled (1037). On Harefoot's death Emma returned and Harthacnut became king (1040). They thirsted for revenge. Godwin was tried but acquitted. He managed to retain his earldom. For this Godwin gave Harthacnut perhaps the most acceptable gift of the time, a costly ship with all accessories. She had a golden beak and eighty picked soldiers. Each wore a 16 oz. golden bracelet, a triple coat of mail, a helmet partly gilded, a shield with gilded boss and studs, a javelin, a sword with a gilded handle and a Danish battle-axe adorned with gold and silver. Harthacnut, Godwin's new master, was as cruel and unpopular as his enemy and step-brother Harefoot, in contrast to the great Cnut, their father. On Harthacnut's death (1042) Godwin helped secure the peaceful accession of Edward (the Confessor); and provoked the jealousy of Earls Leofric of Mercia and Siward of Northumbria by effecting a marriage between his daughter Edith and King Edward (1045) and by getting his sons Sweyn (1043) and Harold (1045) made earls of part of Mercia and of East Anglia. Godwin was rich and persuasive and he set himself to oppose Edward's Norman favourites; but he failed to stop the appointment of his Norman enemy, Robert of Jumièges, as Bishop of London (1044) and Archbishop of Canterbury (1051). Edward wanted to have Dover destroyed for having rioted against foreigners, but Godwin refused to obey the order and found himself in the position of a rebel. Queen Edith, his daughter, was sent into a nunnery, and

Godwin himself had to fly to his ally, Baldwin, Count of Flanders, father-in-law of Godwin's son, Tostig (1051). Thence he raided the Isle of Wight, Portland and the south coast (1052) and 'everywhere hostages were given and provisions, wherever he desired'. He sailed up the Thames under London Bridge in such force that, with the help of the men of Kent, Surrey and Sussex, he regained power. Edith returned from her nunnery as queen (1052). Godwin must then have been quite sixty-five. Soon afterwards he died of apoplexy (1053), when dining with Edward. Normans drew from folklore a tale to blacken his memory. Talk turned to the murder of Alfred; 'If I was an accomplice God choke me with this bread', said Godwin, and straightway it did choke him and he died (see p. 45).

EDWARD THE CONFESSOR (?1004–1066) was born at Islip (Oxon.), son of Ethelred II and Emma, and second cousin of William I. He was an albino, dignified, of medium height, and rather childish. Godwin helped to secure Edward's succession to Harthacnut (1042). Edward married Godwin's daughter, Edith, but politically he had a more European outlook and promoted a Norman, Robert of Jumièges, Bishop of London (1044) and Archbishop of Canterbury (1051). He built Westminster Abbey shortly before his death. The Bayeux tapestry portrays both the building and his deathbed. Harold, son of Godwin and brother of the queen, became king, a usurper in Norman opinion. Saxons looked back to Edward's time as to a golden age before the Norman age of iron, and all remembered his piety. From him English kings supposedly inherited power to heal the 'king's evil'. See plates 1 and 4.

Edward the Confessor (Seal)

Eleanor of Aquitaine
(Fontevraud)

Henry II
(Fontevraud)

Berengaria of Navarre, Queen of
Richard I
(L'Espan Abbey)

Plate 7

Richard I
(Fontevraud)

From effigies engraved by C. A. Stothard before restorations at Fontevraud.

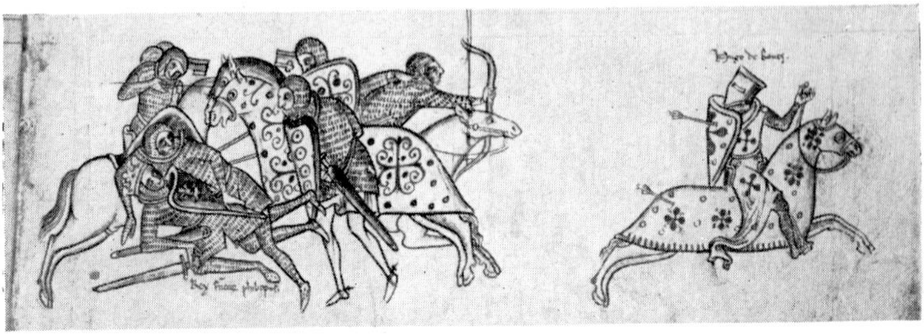

Battle of Bouvines

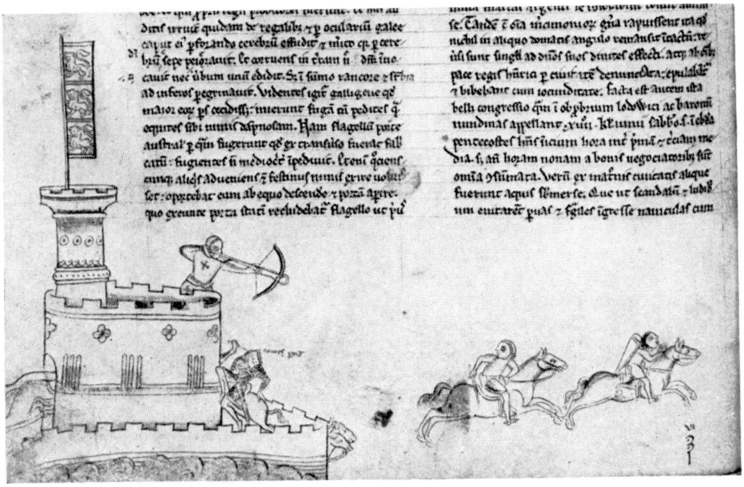

Siege of Lincoln

Plate 8

Henry III, as seen in procession

Drawings by Matthew Paris (Cambridge C.C.C. MS. 16).

Prof. D. Douglas, 'Edward the Confessor, Duke William of Normandy and the English Succession', *English Historical Review*, vol. 68 (1953), 526–45.

HAROLD (*c.* 1022–1066) was son of Godwin (d. 1053) and Gytha, Cnut's Danish sister-in-law. Edward the Confessor banished Godwin's family (1051) and Harold sailed with his brother, Leofwine, from Bristol to Dermot, King of Leinster and Dublin, to raise troops. He returned with nine ships, plundered Porlock, met Godwin at Portland, sailed to London, and was restored to his earldom of East Anglia. He was feasting with the king at Winchester at Easter, 1053, when Godwin died. Harold thus became Earl of Wessex, the mightiest subject in England. After repeated Welsh campaigns he crushed Gruffydd ab Llywelyn, by adapting his tactics to the terrain. He ravaged Wales and gave the Confessor Gruffydd's head (1063). He had been on pilgrimage to Rome, but a later journey (1064) ended in his capture and an enforced stay with Duke William in Normandy when he swore on holy relics to support William's accession on the Confessor's death (see p. 54). Harold had first opposed the Earl of Mercia but eventually married his daughter, Aldgyth, Gruffydd's widow. In 1065 Northumbria revolted against Harold's violent brother, Tostig, and elected Morkere as earl. Tostig believed Harold had instigated the rising and Harold granted the rebels' demands at Oxford; Tostig was exiled and Morkere was established as earl. In January, 1066, the Confessor died, commending the realm to Harold. The nobles elected Harold king and he was consecrated. Duke William required Harold to keep his oath, but in vain, and Harold guarded the south coast from invaders. Tostig made ineffectual raids and joined Harold Hardrada, King of Norway, whose great host suddenly anchored in the Tyne and sailed south to the Ouse. They beat Edwin and Morkere, Earls of Mercia and Northumberland, near York and the Northumbrians joined them; but Harold marched north and was victorious at Stamford Bridge (25th September, 1066). Both Harold Hardrada and Tostig fell, but English corpses covered the field for years. Harold was feasting at York when news came that William had landed. He hurried south and arrayed a great army in a good defensive position on the Sussex Downs where Battle Abbey was later built. On 14th October, 1066, Harold was killed by a Norman knight. Some say William buried him on the shore; others that Harold's former mistress, Edith of the Swan Neck, identified the remains and took them to his foundation of Waltham

Death of Harold (Bayeux Tapestry). He is falling on the right. The tradition that he was killed by an arrow appears first about 1100, based on a misunderstanding of this theme.

Abbey; and others believed that he survived as a hermit. Opinion then and later has differed about his merits. He was tall, strong, temperate, hardy, vigorous, ambitious and loyal, generally wise but sometimes rash, generally unreserved but sometimes crafty, and a good soldier. Opinion varies as to whether the Norman Conquest benefited England or not.

D. Whitelock, *The Beginnings of English Society*, Pelican History of England, vol. 2, 1952.

T.S.I.H., i, 39 (Battle of Hastings). See plates 1 and 4.

EALDRED (**ALDRED**) (d. 1069) was a monk of Winchester, Abbot of Tavistock, Bishop of Winchester and Archbishop of York (1060), friend of Godwin, and first English bishop to go on pilgrimage to Jerusalem (1058). He served on papal and imperial diplomatic missions (1054). He crowned Harold but later crowned William I and his Queen Matilda

(Christmas, 1066). His curse was said to cause William to tremble before him.

F. M. Stenton, *Anglo-Saxon England*, 2nd ed. (Oxford History of England), 1947.

HEREWARD (flourished 1070–1), hero of the Saxon resistance, is alleged to have been pardoned and either to have died fighting for William I abroad or to have died peacefully at home. If he is the same man as the Hereward described in Domesday Book as having land in Warwickshire and Worcestershire, he would have been still alive in 1086; but these places seem far away for one who was not a great landholder. The heroic Hereward was a tenant of the monks of Peterborough and held land in Lincolnshire. He was probably the son of Leofric of Bourn (Lincs.), though an impossible legend makes him son of Leofric, Earl of Mercia. He is first called Hereward 'the Wake' in a rhyming French chronicle written in the middle of the twelfth century by Geoffrey Gaimar, but the name Wake may have survived in unwritten local tradition. Up to the thirteenth century a wooden castle in the fens was called Hereward's Castle. Within sixty years of his death he was a hero of popular songs and legends. Some contain impossible details and some contradict each other, but all are witnesses to his fame. The one certain date in his life is 1070–1 when he sacked Peterborough and defended Ely. His heroic resistance in those years is what matters in history and what inspired the legends. In 1070 a Danish fleet in the Humber stirred a spirit of revolt. At Ely 'the English folk of all the Fenland came to them, weening that they should revolt'. Meanwhile the tenants of Peterborough Abbey revolted against the Norman abbot, Turold. Hereward, who is called nephew of the former Saxon abbot, Brand, led them and together with the Danes sacked and looted Peterborough 'from love to the monastery'. Then Turold came and drove them to their ships. The Danes sailed away, while 'Hereward and his gang' remained at Ely. 'Florence of Worcester' says that 'Morkere and Aethelwine, Bishop of Durham (the only Saxon bishop known to have rebelled against William I), Siward, surnamed Barn (a

Northumbrian thegn), and Hereward, a man of great bravery, with many others, took ship and went to the Isle of Ely, intending to winter there. The king, hearing of this, blocked up every outlet on the eastern side of the island by means of his boatmen, and caused a bridge, two miles long, to be constructed on the western side. When they saw that they were thus shut in, they resisted no longer, and all surrendered themselves to the king, except the brave Hereward, who escaped through the fens with a few others'. Legend has added to the list of those who joined Hereward people who were either dead or, like Stigand (see below), in prison; but it stresses a great truth of historical geography. Survivors of a conquered race can resist best not only in the 'Highland zone', in places like Wales and Scotland, but also in inaccessible marshes. William's combined operation succeeded, but his personal attention was needed at Ely. The Hereward story also draws attention to the geographical changes caused through cultivation for he lived as an outlaw in Brunswald, then a tract of ancient woodland along the Huntingdonshire and Buckinghamshire border.

E. A. Freeman, *History of the Norman Conquest of England*, 1887, iv, pp. 454–87. C. Kingsley, *Hereward the Wake*, 1866 (fiction). *T.S.I.H.*, i, 43 (Peterborough sacked).

STIGAND (d. 1072) was the chaplain of Cnut and the chief confidant of his Queen Emma. Like her he found the accession of Edward the Confessor an unwelcome change, for while the Confessor confiscated his mother's property Stigand lost for a while the see of Elmham (1043), of which he had recently become bishop. He became Bishop of Winchester (1047) and prevented bloodshed when Godwin returned from exile (1052, see p. 48). The Norman Archbishop of Canterbury (1051–2) fled, and Stigand offended the champions of church discipline at Rome, who wanted church laws properly kept, by unlawfully becoming archbishop himself. Worse still, Stigand kept his bishopric of Winchester. The rightful archbishop appealed to Rome successfully and Stigand was excommunicated by five consecutive popes. Papal dislike of Stigand was a reason for the pope's sending William of Normandy a special banner to symbolize St. Peter's approval of the invasion of England. It led English bishops to avoid consecration by Stigand while he was excommunicated and explains why Harold had himself crowned by the Archbishop of York and why William of Poitiers, the Norman propagandist, alleged that Harold had been 'ordained by the unholy consecration of Stigand', as shown in the Bayeux Tapestry (see p. 56). After Hastings, Stigand joined in electing Edgar Atheling to succeed Harold, but submitted to William at Wallingford (1066). William included Stigand in a group of Saxon notables whom he took to Normandy to keep out of mischief (1067). With them Stigand witnessed various royal charters in the strange company of Norman magnates like Odo. It is a tribute to William's respect for Stigand's influence with the Saxons that his just deposition from Canterbury was delayed until 1070. Domesday Book shows that he was allowed to keep his rich manor of East Meon (Hants.). See plate 4.

WILLIAM I (1027–87), the Conqueror, was the bastard son of Robert the Devil, and Harlotta, a tanner's daughter. She had attracted Robert by her dancing. Before William was born, Harlotta dreamed that her intestines stretched over Normandy and England. It was a time when Norman adventurers were gaining fame and authority in distant lands, and the gossips of Falaise noted as a portent the firm grasp with which little William's hands seized and held straws from the floor. The father became duke when William was one year old and he tried to invade England, but was thwarted by a storm. When Robert died (1035) William succeeded by Robert's wish, but the lawless barons saw in the ill-born child-duke no object for a common loyalty. They straightway fortified and victualled their castles; and fire and slaughter raged. The French king, Henry, became aggressive, relatives were treacherous and William's guardians were murdered. Osbern, father of William's trusted lieutenant in later years, FitzOsbern, was butchered when guarding William's bedroom door and an uncle hid William with some poor people. At twenty years of age William crushed rebels at Falaise and Val-ès-dunes (1047).

Then began a masterful and comparatively merciful establishment of order. Such boyhood experiences helped to mould William's attitude to problems of English government. Edward the Confessor regarded William as heir to the English throne, to balance the excessive power of Scandinavians abroad and the family of Godwin at home (1051). The French king was driven back (1054 and 1058) from the Norman borders; and over the border, Maine (1063) and Brittany (1064) were beaten. At Alençon the burghers insulted William's birth by hanging skins over their walls and shouting 'Hides for the Tanner'; when he took their town he cut off their hands and feet. It was probably in 1064 that a chain of events occurred, most fortunate for William and unfortunate for the rival claimant to the English throne, Harold. These events were portrayed at the time in a unique continuous historical strip, in the simple lines dictated by the use of embroidery, on the Bayeux 'Tapestry'. The first scene is a conversation between Edward the Confessor and Harold. Then Harold rides to his manor of Bosham (Sussex), with hawk on wrist. He prays in the church, of which parts of this period survive. After a meal in an upper room a messenger calls them and they wade to a boat which takes them aboard a ship. Shields hang along its bulwark. They sail across to France near St. Valéry. There Count Guy of Ponthieu takes Harold prisoner. He has to ride with no spurs, and with his reins lying on the French horse's neck to prevent escape, to Beaurain. A messenger tells Duke William and Duke William sends for Harold. They go to William's palace. The next scenes are in Brittany. The duke's army comes to Mont St. Michel. They cross the River Couesnon and Harold drags them with his great strength out of quicksands. They come to Dol, shown as a typical Norman castle standing on a mound or *motte* as is Rennes. Conan flees and William fights the men of Dinan and sets fire to their town. Conan hands over the keys on the end of a lance and William gives arms to Harold as his knight. Then comes a famous incident at Bayeux where Harold swears to help William to the English throne. The oath was taken on relics, perhaps more relics than Harold knew at the time, but Harold might well feel that he had no

NORMANS AND ANGEVINS

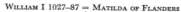

WILLIAM I 1027–87 = MATILDA OF FLANDERS

ROBERT D. of Normandy d. 1134
WILLIAM II RUFUS d. 1100
HENRY I BEAUCLERC 1068–1135 = MATILDA d. of St. Margaret
STEPHEN OF BLOIS = ADELA (See pedigree p. 31)

WILLIAM CLITO d. 1128
WILLIAM drowned 1120
MATILDA = Emperor HENRY V
= GEOFFREY OF ANJOU
ROBERT E. of Gloucester
THEOBALD
STEPHEN ?1097–1154 = MATILDA
HENRY of BLOIS

ELEANOR OF AQUITAINE d. of William X divorced from Louis VII = HENRY II 1133–89
EUSTACE d. 1153
WILLIAM

HENRY = MARGARET OF FRANCE
MATILDA = HENRY THE LION OF SAXONY
RICHARD I = BERENGARIA OF NAVARRE
GEOFFREY = CONSTANCE OF BRITTANY
JOHN = ISABEL OF GLOUCESTER
= ISABEL OF ANGOULÊME
JOANNA = WILLIAM II OF SICILY
= RAYMOND IV OF TOULOUSE

OTTO IV
ARTHUR

HENRY III 1207–72 = ELEANOR OF PROVENCE
RICHARD OF CORNWALL K. of the Romans
JOANNA = ALEXANDER II OF SCOTLAND
ISABEL = Emperor FREDERICK II
ELEANOR = WILLIAM E. of Pembroke
= SIMON DE MONTFORT

EDWARD I 1239–1307 = ELEANOR OF CASTILE
= MARGARET OF FRANCE
MARGARET = ALEXANDER III OF SCOTLAND
BEATRICE = D. of BRITTANY
EDMUND CROUCHBACK E. of Lancaster 1245–96

EDWARD II 1284–1327 = ISABEL OF FRANCE
EDMUND E. of Kent executed 1330
THOMAS E. of Lancaster d. 1322
HENRY E. of Lancaster d. 1345

EDWARD III 1312–77 (See ancestry p. 176 and descendants p. 178)
JOAN, 'FAIR MAID OF KENT' = SIR T. HOLLAND
= EDWARD 'BLACK PRINCE'
BLANCHE (See descendants p. 178) = JOHN OF GAUNT

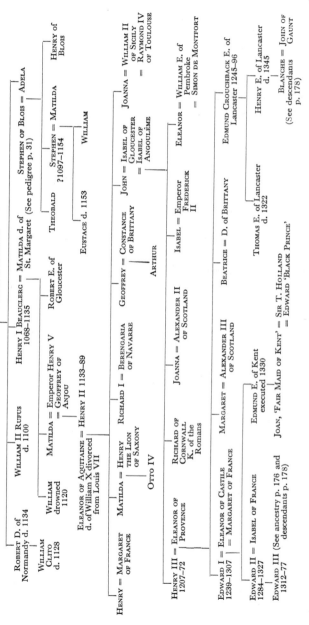

choice but to swear. Harold sails back to England, eagerly awaited by a look-out and with the heads of the harbour folk craning forward out of the windows to see him. Edward, whose infirmity is suggested by the stick in his hand, receives Harold.

Edward, on his deathbed, addresses his servants. Queen Edith weeps at its foot and Harold stands opposite a priest. Edward's corpse is shrouded (5 Jan., 1066). A procession of priests takes Edward in an open bier to his church of St. Peter, Westminster. It has been consecrated ten days before. A man is just setting up the weathercock and the hand of God is visible in heaven. They give Harold the crown and (6 Jan.) Harold is shown being crowned by Archbishop Stigand (but see p. 53). Men marvel at a portentous star, now identified as Halley's comet. It shone for seven days like a sign of God's wrath. Harold hears news, and a row of ships in the margin may portray what fears pass through his mind. An English ship crosses the Channel and William learns the news of what he counts as Harold's treachery. Advised by Odo (see p. 65), William gives orders for an invasion fleet to be built. Trees are felled, planks prepared and shipwrights work with adzes. Swords, chain mail, spears and helmets are brought to the coast and a wine-cart carries a huge barrel. The great fleet leaves St. Valéry (27 Sept.). The papal banner, or a lantern, marks the top of William's mast, and there is a figure supposed to represent the boy Rufus in the stern. The next morning the Normans land at Pevensey, the masts are unstepped and the horses leave the ships and are led ashore by their bridles. The soldiers hurry to Hastings to forage and English farmers have to slaughter and bring in their animals. One Wadward supervised the boiling of meat. Joints and fowls are on the spits for roasting. A baker minds his oven. Servants carry food to the board on spits and a horn sounds the summons to eat. Odo says grace at table and a page kneels with water and a napkin before William. William sits in council between Odo and Robert of Mortain, his mother's sons. An officer supervises the erection of a castle-mound at Hastings, while two diggers fight with their typical medieval lop-sided spades. A messenger comes with news of Harold (who is hurrying south from York). A mother and child are seen fleeing from a burning house. The soldiers leave Hastings (shown with tower and gate) and ride to battle. They have long kite-shaped shields, pointed helmets with nose-pieces, spears, spurs and chain-mail. The leaders have maces. William asks Vital, a mounted scout, if he had seen Harold's host. A mounted scout is on the look out at Telham Hill, a slope opposite that occupied by Harold. An English scout stands behind trees opposite shading his eyes with his hand. He reports to Harold. The duke, again shown with a mace, exhorts his men to fight well and the knights ride off in a line. There are some archers on foot with quivers (Sat., 14 Oct.). The English army (of scarcely 7,000 men) fights in serried ranks with spears and long-headed axes, without horsemen or archers. They form a wall of shields, but did not erect a palisade. The Norman lancers charge on every side. Arrows fly. The lower margin is full of the slain. Confusion grows and Leofwine and Gyrth, Harold's brothers, fall. English and French fall together. (The French retreated and the undisciplined English broke their ranks to pursue, though their only hope was to stand fast. William pretended to retreat again and lured more down the slope.) Odo holds a mace and rallies his men. Eustace (of Boulogne, whose sons later became kings of Jerusalem) cries: 'Here is Duke William', when he was thought to have fallen. The French rally. The margin is full of archers. They shoot arrows high (towards evening) so as to fall on Harold's bodyguard. Under the Dragon standard of Wessex, Harold is slain (but not as generally stated by an arrow) and falls dead. The English are routed. Stripped corpses cover the ground. At this point the 'tapestry' ends in rags. Such was the Battle of Hastings, which after two centuries came to be sometimes known as the Battle of Senlac.

The Pope regarded William as a crusader. Aristocrats have regarded him as one who founded an empire with the help of heroic companions from whom an alleged descent was an especial glory. Some historians have seen him as a leader who redeemed England from stagnation, and who imported a superior culture from the south. Others, of a liberal outlook sympathetic to nineteenth-century nationalism, have rather thought of him as a priest-ridden tyrant who destroyed the patriotic Saxon leaders and interrupted the flow of English national history. He may also be conceived of as the soldier whose prowess and military efficiency determined that England should be linked with the Latin instead of the Scandinavian world, and that its rulers should command a realm which straddled the Channel instead of one which straddled the North Sea. It is equally correct to call him a militaristic and piratical destroyer of a fine native culture or the creator of an efficient central executive—yet English literature and art re-emerged in due course, perhaps much as if William had never been, and who can tell that the English might not have evolved eventually a strong government of their own? After the victory at Hastings William punished his opponents at Romney as an example to others. He received, thereupon, the surrender of Dover, Canterbury and Winchester. He circled round London, crossing the Thames at Wallingford and following the line of the Chilterns along the Icknield Way.

At Little Berkhamstead the Londoners and Edgar Atheling came to submit. Stigand had crowned Edgar king, so this was almost as important for William as the fact that he himself was there offered the crown. William's coronation at Westminster (25 Dec., 1066) ended in panic, caused by his knights misinterpreting Saxon cries of acclamation. He gave the Londoners a charter, but built the Tower to overawe them. He pardoned all who had remained passive but made them pay a ransom for their lands. He accepted the tardy surrender of the Earls of Mercia and Northumberland, Edwin and Morkere; but he took them back, as possible leaders of resistance, when he returned to Normandy (1067). He left England in charge of Odo and William FitzOsbern. He suppressed a revolt at Exeter (1068), revolts by Edwin and Morkere (1068 and 1071), revolts in the North (1069 and 1070) and a revolt by Hereward the Wake at Ely (1070). He inspired terror by wasting every village from York to Durham (1070). He distributed lands, as and when they were confiscated from rebels, to chief supporters to be administered privately as great 'honours' or groups of manors. Half of the total went to ten great interrelated barons whom he trusted. These included Warenne, Montgomery and FitzOsbern, and, above all, Odo and Robert of Mortain.

Land was held in return for the service of so many knights. He summoned a great gathering of his tenants and their tenants on August 1st, 1086, at Salisbury and they took an oath that they would fight for William. That year commissioners methodically collected for William answers to sixteen detailed questions about the past and present capacity of each estate in different branches of production. These answers were digested under the names of the chief tenants in each shire in 'Domesday Book', now exhibited in the museum of the Public Record Office. A facsimile edition of the pages relating to each shire was published in the nineteenth century and translations for different counties are gradually appearing in the *Victoria County Histories*. Domesday Book shows that the Saxon nobility only retained one-eighth of the land.

On September 9th, 1087, at Mantes, William's horse trod on hot ashes when the town was sacked. He fell and was mortally hurt. He was sixty, having reigned twenty-one years as king and fifty-three as duke. A dispossessed knight interrupted his funeral and his body burst out of a stone coffin which had been too small for it. See plates 1, 4 and 5.

Bayeux Tapestry, Phaidon Press, 1958.
F. M. Stenton, *William the Conqueror*, 1915.
T.S.I.H., i, 39, 49 (character).

LANFRANC (?1005–1089), Archbishop of Canterbury (1070–89), was a scholarly lawyer who left his native Pavia and taught at Avranches (Normandy) (1039). Chance led him to Bec Abbey, then being built, and there he became a monk. When he was young, Lanfranc was so humble that he abandoned the correct pronunciation of a word which occurred in something which he was reading aloud at table, when an ignorant person had said that he was pronouncing it wrongly. When he became Prior, his unrivalled teaching (1045–63) drew from afar such famous students as Pope Alexander II, Anselm and Ivo of Chartres. In later life he did not hesitate to rebuke Rufus for breaking his coronation oath. Rufus replied that no man could keep all his promises, but thenceforth he could not look Lanfranc in the face. Lanfranc fought Berengar's heresy that the eucharist was only symbolic (1055 and 1059). He liked solitude, but had to exchange a contemplative for an active life by becoming adviser to William I. He dared to condemn William's marriage, and, as Justiciar, sometimes ruled England with royal authority of life and death. He became Abbot of St. Stephen's, Caen, and, when Stigand was deposed, Archbishop of Canterbury. As such he defended its lands against the encroachments of Odo and its rights against the rivalry of the Archbishop of York. Lanfranc rebuilt Canterbury Cathedral. It was he who crushed the rebellious Earls of Hereford and Norfolk and who assured the accession of Rufus. Lanfranc crowned him in 1087. In a lawsuit against Odo, Lanfranc's case had largely depended upon a statement of Saxon customs made by the old Saxon ex-bishop of Chichester, who had been specially driven up to the place of trial in a wagon drawn by four horses, yet in general Lanfranc disliked Saxon ways. He distrusted Saxon respect for some whom the Saxons regarded as saints. His legal mind felt that Alphege should not be regarded as a saint, as Alphege had died in order to save his tenants from oppression and not in order to testify to Christ. Anselm, with humane acuteness, argued to Lanfranc that a man who could welcome death for such an unimportant principle would certainly have been ready to die for something that really mattered, like the faith. Lanfranc saw this point and had Alphege's *Life* written and set to music. Thenceforth Alphege received, thanks to Lanfranc, more honour at Canterbury than any other martyr, until the death of Thomas Becket provided Canterbury with a popular local martyr who had died through clear-cut church principles. Lanfranc made rules for the English monks, minute but respectful of custom and adaptable. He continued Dunstan's struggle against clerical marriage. The *Acts of Lanfranc* show him in old age forcing the monks of St. Augustine's, Canterbury, to obey an unpopular abbot of his choice. Lanfranc fettered the disobedient and had one malcontent brought before him. 'Would you kill your abbot?' asked Lanfranc. 'Certainly I would if I could', replied the monk. Lanfranc thereupon caused him to be tied naked in front of the great door of St. Augustine's and there to be flogged in view of all the people. Afterwards his hair was shaved and he was driven from the city. Lanfranc died at Canterbury in the nineteenth year of his archbishopric. He was in possession of his faculties, and had been wont to pray that he would die of illness not of old age. His death was hastened because he would not drink until after Communion a draught of medicine which the doctor had told him to drink fresh. He drank it rancid. He was much interested in church ceremonial and vestments and favoured a movement for reform of the church led by a Cluniac monk, Hildebrand, who became Pope as Gregory VII (1073–85). No miracles were attributed to Lanfranc, and his reform of cathedral bodies, his replacement of Saxons by Normans as abbots and bishops, and his unsuccessful attempts to discourage the clergy from marrying did not make him beloved. He established the principle that the church should have its own law courts separate from those which the king had for laymen. He continued a policy which had been started whereby the see of the Bishop of Crediton had moved to Exeter (1050) because it was more populous. Under him the Bishops of Selsey, Sherborne and Dorchester moved to Chichester (1075), Salisbury (1075) and Lincoln (1086). Thus the relationship of church and state and the pattern of diocesan organization which lasted until Henry VIII's Reformation were a monument to Lanfranc, William I's trusted head of the English church.

A. J. Macdonald, *Lanfranc*, 2nd ed., 1944. This is full of useful quotations and includes chapters on Lanfranc's dispute with the archbishop of York, on the revival of church councils, diocesan life and monasticism, Lanfranc's restoration of Canterbury, Rochester and St. Albans, his friends, his prestige in Ireland, Scotland and Normandy, and his relations with Pope Gregory VII.

Prof. D. Knowles, *The Monastic Constitutions of Lanfranc*, Nelson, 1957.

T.S.I.H., i, 45 (Lanfranc's *Constitutions*).

ST. MARGARET (?*c.* 1045–1093), Queen of Scotland, was a Saxon princess (see pedigree, p. 31), who became daughter-in-law of Duncan whom Macbeth murdered (1040). The Anglo-Saxon Chronicle tells how Malcolm Canmore married her when she arrived with other Saxon refugees after the Conquest. She introduced the Use of the Roman church, fostered English and Norman influence, and reformed manners and customs in Scotland, founding many Augustinian monasteries. This influence shows in the architecture of Dunfermline which closely resembles that of Durham. She made the Scottish court more dignified, introducing a uniform, and more orderly, insisting that payment should be made for goods consumed as it moved from place to place. Her chaplain, Turgot, wrote her life at the request of her daughter Matilda, queen of Henry I. Her softening influence on the King by her example of piety seemed miraculous. 'Hence also the books which she used either in her devotions or for reading, he, though unable to read, used often to handle and examine, and when he heard from her that one of them was dearer to her than the others, this he also regarded with kindlier affection, and would kiss and often fondle it. Sometimes also he would send for the goldsmith, and instruct him to adorn the volume with gold and precious stones, and when finished he would carry it to the Queen as proof of his devotion'. One of her favourite volumes is still to be seen in the Bodleian Library, Oxford. It is one which was accidentally dropped into a river, but when it was found again and brought to her it was found to be miraculously undamaged. 'The Queen on the other hand, herself the noblest gem of a royal race, made the splendour of her husband's royal magnificence much more splendid, and contributed much glory and honour to all the nobility of the kingdom and their retainers. For she brought it to pass that merchants who came by land and sea from divers lands, brought with them for sale many precious kinds of merchandise which in Scotland were before unknown, among which, at the instigation of the Queen, the people bought garments of various colours, and different kinds of personal ornaments; so that from that time they went about clothed in new costumes of different fashions'. The palace 'was made resplendent with gold and silver; for the vessels in which the King and nobles of the kingdom were served with food and drink, were either of gold or silver, or gold or silver plated. And this the Queen did, not because the honour of the world delighted her, but because she felt compelled to do what the royal dignity required of her'. Malcolm was slain when raiding England by Robert Mowbray, Earl of Northumberland, and Margaret died soon after of grief. William of Malmesbury describes her devotion and says 'departing from the church, she used to feed the poor; first three, then nine, then twenty-four, at last three hundred: herself standing by with the King, and pouring water on their hands.' Three of her sons were kings, Edgar (1097–1107), Alexander I (1107–24) and David I (1124–53). Malcolm used to interpret Gaelic for Margaret, but some Celts disliked her policy and a temporary anti-foreign reaction followed her death.

Agnes Strickland, *Lives of the Queens of Scotland*, 8 vols., 1850–9.
T.S.I.H., i, 51.

ST. WULFSTAN (*c.* 1008–1095) was born at Itchington (Warwickshire) and was educated at Evesham and Peterborough Abbeys. His name is compounded from those of his parents, Aethelstan and Wulfgifu, both of whom entered monasteries at Worcester. Wulfstan entered the Bishop of Worcester's household, becoming a priest, then a monk, and later schoolmaster, precentor, sacristan and Prior at Worcester. He was consecrated Bishop of Worcester (1062) by Archbishop Ealdred of York, not Stigand, and later he had some trouble in shaking off the unjustified claims to authority of the Archbishop of York. He persuaded the turbulent Northumbrians to accept Harold as king (1066) but quickly submitted to William I and gained his favour. He helped suppress revolts against William I and II, presided with the sheriff in the shire court and was often at court where he witnessed royal charters with the other magnates. He travelled round his diocese, covering definite areas each year so as not to exhaust his retinue of clerks, and he kept in close touch with the vast crowds who assembled for sermons, mass, baptism and confirmation. He preached in Bristol against its slave-trade with Ireland, and he shared with Lanfranc the credit for its suppression; he forced priests to choose between their churches and their wives; he had more churches built; and he even accepted invitations to dedicate churches in other dioceses, as at High Wycombe. The Bishop of Coutances mocked his lambskin clothes and long drinking bouts were countenanced in his hall; but there is no truth in the report that Lanfranc wanted him to resign because of ignorance and that he was only saved by a strange miracle. Nobody except Wulfstan could lift up the ring and crozier of office which he had laid upon St. Edmund's tomb. The good order of Wulfstan's diocese before the conquest suggests, indeed, that the church reforms made by the Norman clergy were not really as necessary in all parts of England as their admirers have suggested. Even in Wulfstan's life sailors between Bristol and Ireland found him a better protector than St. Nicholas from storms and a notorious Lundy Island pirate. Before his canonization (1203) many miracles had been proved, especially cures of women and children. Some left crutches behind as a memorial. One man prayed to Wulfstan to heal his horse, bitten by a snake; the man repeatedly made the sign of the cross on its head with a penny 'vowed' to St. Wulfstan, until the swelling went. Among sufferers relieved was a boy whose tongue had been cut out by a stepmother who had murdered his father, a woman with a jaw displaced by yawning, a woman whose arm was broken by her husband, a mad potter who had been bound and had sticks placed near him so that passers-by could help beat the demons out of him, and a woman who had been miraculously blinded for working on the feast of SS. Philip and James (May 1st). In the rebellion of 1088 he helped the defenders of Worcester by weakening the arms and eyes of the attackers. A priest who doubted Wulfstan's miracles was, however, not alone and one magnate ridiculed a saint who could not protect pilgrims from pilferers. One of his last acts was to have the monastery chest brought. He examined its contents and tried to repair decaying documents and to recover missing

Plate 9

Henry III (1–4) and Simon De Montfort (5)
(Seals, British Museum)

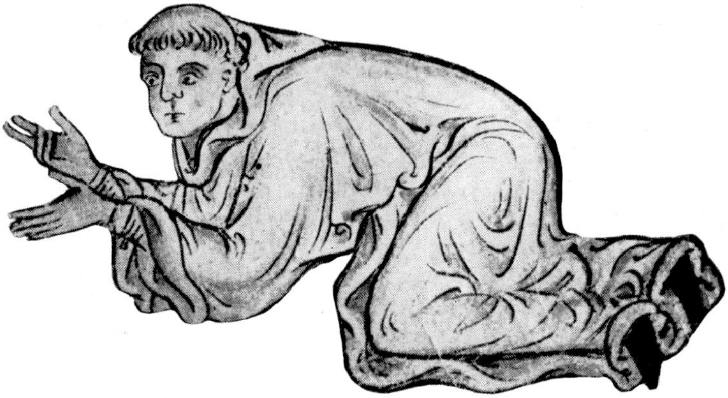

Matthew Paris (Self-portrait) (Cambridge C.C.C. MS. 16)

Plate 10

Friar Roger Bacon (MS. Bodl. 211, p. 5)

ones. Then he told Hemming, the subprior, to copy them all into a register. It still survives. Wulfstan is not to be confused with the Wulfstan who told St. Swithun's life in verse (*c.* 1000) or with Wulfstan II, Archbishop of York (d. 1023), who also acted as bishop of Worcester. There is a good biography, written by Coleman, his chaplain, and translated by William of Malmesbury. William thought it would be read as long as literature or the universe should last.

R. R. Darlington, *Vita Wulfstani*, Royal Historical Soc., 1928, Introduction.

ODO (1035–1097), Bishop of Bayeux, was half-brother (through his mother) of Duke William and brother of Robert of Mortain. The Duke made him Bishop of Bayeux (where he modernized the cathedral) at the age of fourteen or fifteen. He sent forty ships to invade England and wielded a mace at the battle of Hastings so as not to shed blood. He was rewarded with Dover castle, vast estates recorded in thirteen various counties in Domesday Book, and the Earldom of Kent. He became Regent (1067) but was imprisoned at Rouen (1082–7) 'on account of his overweening pride'. When the Conqueror was dying, as he hoped for mercy, he ordered the prison doors to be opened and all the prisoners, except Odo, to be released. Odo's friends persuaded William to set Odo free. They exhausted William with their prayers and Ordericus Vitalis puts words in his mouth which express adequately the views alike of William and of posterity: 'I wonder that your penetration has not discovered the character of the man for whom you supplicate me. Are you not making petitions for a prelate who has long held religion in contempt, and who is the subtle promoter of fatal divisions? Have I not already incarcerated for four years this bishop, who, when he ought to have proved himself exemplary in the just government of England, became a most cruel oppressor of the people and destroyer of the convents of monks? In desiring the liberation of this seditious man you are ill-advised, and are bringing on yourselves a serious calamity. It is clear that my brother, Odo, is an untrustworthy man, ambitious, given to fleshly desires, and of enormous cruelty . . . I imprisoned, not the bishop, but the tyrannical earl . . .' It was Lanfranc who made this distinction. Rufus restored Odo's earldom but he joined Duke Robert's revolt against his brother (1068), for he preferred to see the Duke of Normandy still the same man as the King of England, for barons with inherited land one side of the Channel and conquered land the other were liable to suffer loss with their divided loyalty in any conflicts. Rufus won and Odo was banished (see p. 69). His wealth and ambition enabled him to build a palace in Rome and aspire to be Pope. He accompanied Duke Robert on the first Crusade and died at Palermo (Sicily) in February, 1097, aged about sixty-four. There he is buried. As a patron of art as well as learning, he perhaps commissioned the Bayeux Tapestry. See plate 4.

H. W. C. Davis, *England under the Norman and Angevins*, latest ed.

WILLIAM II (*c.* 1060–1100), Rufus, was the third but favourite son of the Conqueror. Lanfranc educated him and secured his accession on condition that he took an oath to keep justice and defend the church, but powerful rebels including Odo of Bayeux, the Earl of Shrewsbury and the Bishop of Durham sought to make William's elder brother Robert King of England as well as Duke of Normandy. Rufus received effective English support, but after Lanfranc died (1089) he displayed uncontrolled tyranny aided by his Justiciar, Ranulf Flambard. Intelligent, cynical and greedy and unsoftened by any woman's love, he plundered bishoprics and abbeys as soon as they fell vacant, though it is only fair to note that Becket, when he was Chancellor of Henry II, did exactly the same, although Becket's sanctity is unquestioned. During one of William's periodical illnesses Anselm was nominated to the vacant see of Canterbury (1093) in spite of strenuous resistance. A Council at Rockingham failed to decide whether the King or the Pope should enjoy his undivided loyalty and he retired into exile until Rufus died.

William of Malmesbury says that he feared God but little, man not at all. In public he used to dart threatening glances at bystanders, putting on a fierce voice. He was cruel and avaricious. In private he was jocular, laughing at his own failings. At the beginning of his reign he feared disorder and soon spent his father's treasure on soldiers. He was no judge of value for money and tradesmen and soldiers could fleece him. He was angry if the price of his clothes was not high enough. One morning he had a pair of new boots. He asked the price and the chamberlain said they cost three shillings. Rufus swore at him, indignantly asking how long the King had been wearing such cheap boots. 'Go, and bring me a pair worth a mark of silver (13s. 4d.)'. The chamberlain brought a cheaper pair which he said cost that much. 'Aye', said the King, 'these are suitable to royal majesty.' The chamberlain thus used to charge what he pleased for clothes and managed to feather his own nest. His prodigality was even talked of in the distant East and soldiers came for what they could get. As his money was spent, so he began to double the taxes, to plunder the rich, to exterminate the poor and to confiscate men's inheritances. Discipline was relaxed. Courtiers wore long hair and extravagant dress. Shoes with curved points were invented. Young men became womanlike and minced in their gait. Anselm could not stop the rot and on his way into exile, while he was waiting for a favourable breeze, his bags and packages were brought out and ransacked. In London the Jews even had a debate with the bishops, because the king had said, in jest as Malmesbury liked to think, that if their reasoning prevailed over that of the Christians he would join their sect. The clergy dreaded this debate, but the Jews were put to confusion; though they would keep on saying that they were defeated not by reason but by force. Robert of Normandy pawned the duchy to Rufus to raise money for a crusade. When the bishops complained of the tax levied to collect the ten thousand marks needed for this, the courtiers angrily replied: 'Have you not shrines adorned with gold and silver, full of dead men's bones?' and the bishops accordingly melted this metal for the exchequer. Rufus so monopolized hunting that he inflicted the death penalty for killing a stag and this led to the nobles' plotting against him. As a result Robert de Mowbray, Earl of Northumberland, was imprisoned for life,

William de Hou was blinded and mutilated, and a friend of the King was scourged at every church in Salisbury and hanged . . . It was, however, possible to find examples of courage and magnanimity in Rufus such as might have led anyone who believed in the transmigration of souls to have said [according to Malmesbury] that 'Julius Cæsar's soul had migrated into Rufus'. He spared no expense on building Westminster Hall. He was well-set in person, florid, with yellow hair, open countenance, eyes of different colours, and was very strong, though not tall. His belly protruded. His speech was hesitant, especially in anger. Rufus survived various Scottish, Welsh, Norman and French campaigns to be slain by an arrow in the New Forest, said to have been accidentally shot by Walter Tirel. A memorial stone now marks the spot. The Anglo-Saxon Chronicle says that 'all that was hateful to God and just men was all customary in this country in his time: and therefore he was hateful to nearly all his people, and odious to God . . .' and when his bleeding body was carried to Winchester the clergy refused it religious rites. See plate 1 (coin).

The above account from Malmesbury is condensed.
E. A. Freeman, *Reign of William Rufus*, 2 vols., 1882.
T.S.I.H., i, 56 (his end).

GUNDULF (1024–1108), Bishop of Rochester (1077–1108). was born in the Vexin (Normandy) and educated at Rouen. He went on pilgrimage with William Goodsoul, future Archbishop of Rouen, and in Palestine they both vowed to become monks. Lanfranc's fame drew Gundulf to Bec, where he became a friend of Lanfranc and Anselm. He accompanied Lanfranc to Caen (1063) where he became prior (1063–70). He followed Lanfranc to Canterbury as his steward (1070–7) and succeeded another monk of Bec as Bishop of Rochester (1077), then closely linked to Canterbury. He administered the archdiocese of Canterbury while Rufus kept it vacant (1089–93) and during Anselm's exiles (1097–1100 and 1103–5). Gundulf suppressed a rebellion against the Abbot of St. Augustine's, Canterbury, by scourging the monks and dispersing them to other monasteries, and by blinding citizens who could not prove their innocence (1089). He championed Anselm's cause, resisted the encroachments of royal officials and used to deliver Anselm's letters to the King. In 1088 Odo of Bayeux and other supporters were besieged in the hot and crowded castle of Rochester, afflicted by swarms of flies, and at last allowed to depart to the sound of triumphant blasts of the royal trumpets and the cries of the Saxon loyalists, 'Halters, bring halters! Gallows for the Bishop'. Even at that time Gundulf managed to remain neutral and keep the friendship of all. Gundulf had built the castle for Rufus and Rufus gave him Lambeth to make up for expenses caused by the siege. For the thirty-one years of his rule at Rochester Gundulf retained the friendship of all three Norman kings, and of both their Archbishops of Canterbury. Contemporaries realized his skill as a builder, based on all his previous experience at Bec, Caen and Canterbury. He rebuilt Rochester cathedral, adapting the plans of Canterbury, and his constructional work elsewhere includes the White Tower at London. Though busy with commissions for the Archbishop, he often stayed at his episcopal manors, celebrated Mass twice daily, was peculiarly devoted to the Virgin, and was a wonderful preacher, dwelling much upon the Passion. He founded Malling nunnery (Kent) (1099–1100). Thirteen poor persons dined daily in his hall, and he settled poor people on land especially bought near Rochester. His admirer, Abbot Gilbert Crispin of Westminster Abbey, once had to rebuke his zeal in trying to pluck one hair from the sacred beard of Edward the Confessor. At the last at the age of eighty-five he had himself carried into the infirmary at Rochester so that he might die among his monks. His successor, Ralph, Abbot of Séez, was a pupil of Anselm at Bec.

R. A. L. Smith, 'The Place of Gundulf in the Anglo-Norman Church', *English Historical Review*, 1943, vol. 58, pp. 257–73.

For Bec, see D. Knowles, *The Monastic Order in England, 943–1216*, 1940, pp. 82–92.

ST. ANSELM (1033–1109) was an attractive character and an original thinker, forced to be Archbishop of Canterbury (1093–1109). As a boy he was glad to be ill so that his harsh father might let him study. Improved health and his mother's death made him more worldly for a time, but finally he left his home in Aosta (N. Italy) and followed Lanfranc to Avranches (1059) and Bec. He became a monk at twenty-seven (1060) instead of succeeding his father, and wrote two books to justify belief in God. He succeeded Lanfranc as prior (1063) and Herlwin as abbot (1078–93). He felt that Lanfranc's greatness left him no scope. Attentive to all, he encouraged his pupils with simple examples and words. His sympathy overcame the jealousy of disappointed rivals, and when business brought him to England his presence made even old William I gracious. At Canterbury (1071) he first met Eadmer, a monk of Christ Church who wrote his *Life* and a *Modern History* which give intimate details about Anselm. Once Anselm stopped a boy teasing a bird and another time sheltered a hunted hare. Anselm personally corrected the *Life* and tried to suppress it, making Eadmer promise to destroy it. Eadmer kept his promise but copied it out first. On his death-bed William I sent for Anselm, but Anselm was too ill to come. In order to keep the income of the archbishopric himself, Rufus appointed no one to succeed Lanfranc as archbishop, but when the King was ill fear of Hell made him repent and he was amazed to find that Anselm did not want to be archbishop. Anselm was dragged (6th March, 1093) to Rufus's bedside and Rufus tried to force open Anselm's clenched fist to press into it the pastoral staff of office. 'Long live the bishop', cried the crowd. 'It is naught what you are doing', said Anselm repeatedly. Anselm told Rufus that he would get well and would not be bound by what had been done; and he complained to the magnates, 'You have yoked together the untamed bull and the old and feeble sheep and what good will come of it?' A quarrel followed because Anselm recognized Urban II as the rightful Pope and Rufus did not at that time recognize him. The King and the Pope both had claims on Anselm's loyalty and a Council at Rockingham (1095) refused to please Rufus by condemning Anselm, though the bishops renounced their friendship with their archbishop. A later quarrel ended in Anselm's going abroad for the rest of Rufus's life (1097–1100). Henry I recalled Anselm, but as soon as Anselm returned (1100) he felt bound to refuse homage for land held of the crown and would not recognize new bishops invested with their insignia of office by Henry. This was because the church had made decrees against churchmen receiving such 'investiture' in their offices by laymen. Henry I and Anselm were personally friendly, but as the Pope held fast to his point of view Anselm went into exile again (1103–5). In 1106 Henry I agreed to stop investing prelates with the ring and staff which were symbols of office, but he was to receive homage for their lands. Thus the dispute about forms was outwardly settled, but the real aim of the Pope, the independence of bishops from worldly kings, was not achieved. Anselm died in 1109, and after a vacancy of four years, Henry I found a successor so cooperative that his name is almost forgotten, Ralph of Séez.

Over 400 of Anselm's letters survive, including a letter from Henry I apologizing for having been hurriedly crowned by someone else.

R. W. Church, *St. Anselm*, New ed. repr. 1905.

T.S.I.H., i, 54 (Eadmer on Anselm's election and Council of Rockingham).

EDITH, MATILDA or MAUD (1080–1118), Queen of Henry I, was the orphaned daughter of St. Margaret. She was educated at Wilton and Romsey Abbey where she said that her aunt, Christina, forced her to wear a black veil. She threw it on the ground whenever left alone, in spite of beatings. When her mother died she came to England to Edgar Atheling, her uncle. She was a sister of King David of Scotland; she was a correspondent of Anselm and Hildebert, Bishop of Le Mans, who wrote poetry about her; and she was mother of Matilda the Empress (see p. 88) and Henry I's only son William, who was lost in the White Ship (1120). She built a stone-arched bridge over the Lea at Bow and founded the leper hospital of St. Giles-in-the-Fields and (1108) the first Augustinian Priory in England, Holy Trinity, Aldgate (London); but her importance lies not in anything she did, but in her existence as a symbol of the union of Saxon and Norman. Stephen based his claim to the throne in part on a statement that Matilda the Empress was illegitimate because Henry could not legally marry Matilda (1100), because she was a professed nun; Anselm, however, had decided at the time that there was no objection to her marriage. Matilda once made an attempt to mediate between Henry and Anselm and she was worried that Anselm would make himself ill by unreasonable abstinence; she reminded him that St. Paul had exhorted to use wine for the stomach's sake. William of Malmesbury describes her uneventful domestic life: 'She stayed many years at Westminster content when the king and court were busy elsewhere. She did not lack royal estate and crowds of visitors and talebearers would visit the palace. She was very holy and her beauty was not despicable. In Lent she wore hair cloth under her royal habit and trod the churches barefoot. Nor was she disgusted at washing the feet of the diseased, handling their ulcers dripping with corruption, and, finally, pressing their hands, for a long time together, to her lips and decking their table. Through love of divine service she was thoughtlessly prodigal towards clerks with good voices. Her famous liberality attracted scholars, poets and singers and many foreigners, but at the expense of her grumbling tenants. She was Henry's Queen for seventeen years and six months, and died in her prime like most of her family. Her brother, Alexander the Fierce, King of Scotland, once found her on her knees attending to her beggars' feet. She begged him to help, but he went out of the room smiling quietly.' England remembered her as the good queen 'of England's right kingly kin' (see pedigrees p. 31 and 55).

Agnes Strickland, *Lives of the Queens of England*, 6 vols., 1864.

HERBERT LOSINGA (?1054–1119), first Bishop of Norwich, is the most attractive of Anglo-Norman scholars. Prior of Fécamp, Abbot of Ramsey (1087) and Bishop of Thetford (1090), he paid Rufus a 'relief' of £1,000 upon being admitted as bishop, just like a lay baron. He was a sensitive man and this was a practice which the church regarded as simony (see p. xxii). At his consecration he opened the Gospel at random, as was the custom, to see what the text thus found might portend; he found the passage where Christ asked Judas when he betrayed Him, 'Friend, wherefore art thou come?'. Losinga felt as if he too had sold Christ. He enraged Rufus and was deposed, for proposing to seek absolution in Rome from a pope whom Rufus had not recognized. When reconciled he moved his seat to Norwich (9th April, 1094) and began to build the Cathedral (1096). Losinga was a learned student of the theological writings of the Fathers of the Church, but his great love was the classics. He was apologetic about this and 'felt like a cock in a fable who found a pearl on a dunghill, for even in the classics thoughts of serious value could be found'. His correspondence with his pupils shows the nature of the classical teaching which was to become more self-confident with John of Salisbury and has in it a spirit like that of the revival of ancient learning in the fifteenth century.

Life, Letters and Sermons of Herbert of Losinga, translated (with notes) by E. M. Goulburn and Henry Symonds, 1878.

RANULF FLAMBARD (d. 1128) was an illiterate and coarse Norman priest, 'son of a one-eyed witch'. He established himself in William I's household by his malicious wit and became financial adviser of William Rufus (1093). He was perhaps the editor of Domesday Book. He ruthlessly exacted feudal dues. He had twenty thousand men assembled at Hastings each with ten shillings for expenses, but instead of embarking them to fight Robert, Duke of Normandy, he dismissed them having first collected all their journey money from them (1095). Rufus rewarded such unscrupulous and efficient loyalty with the important bishopric of Durham (1099). On becoming king, Henry I won popularity by imprisoning Flambard in the Tower. But a cask of wine to intoxicate the jailers and a rope for the window were smuggled in, and Flambard fled with his mother to Duke Robert. After Henry's victory at Tinchebray (1106) Flambard was pardoned and returned to Durham where he finished the stupendous Norman nave, demolished many hovels between the castle and the cathedral, rebuilt the city walls and built Norham castle (on

Tweed). His name means 'the devouring flame'. His last words were: 'I wanted to do more harm than I could'.

R. W. Southern, 'Ranulf Flambard and Early Anglo-Norman Administration', *Trans. Royal Historical Soc.*, 4th ser. 16, 1933.

ROBERT OF BELLÊME (*c.* 1057–*c.* 1131), Earl of Shrewsbury, was the younger son of Roger de Montgomerie. Roger was a trusted relative of William I. He contributed sixty ships to the invasion of England, built many castles on the Welsh border and died, a monk, in his own foundation of Shrewsbury Abbey (*c.* 1093). Robert was often at war with his neighbours in Normandy and rebelled with Robert Curthose against both Rufus and Henry I. He inherited Bellême, a feudal lordship strategically placed on the border of Normandy and Maine, from his mother, Mabel Talvas, and he kept it practically independent of Robert Curthose. (See p. 75.) He paid Rufus £3,000 for his dead brother's Earldom of Shrewsbury, built Bridgnorth and Tickhill castles, aimed at an independent tyranny and laughed while he indulged in his habit of roasting his victims. He was brave and intelligent as a diplomat and general. In 1102 he fortified the castles of Bridgnorth and Arundel against Henry I. Henry soon took Bridgnorth while Robert was at Arundel, for the townsmen were impressed by Henry's army. Robert was allowed to leave the country with his brothers, Arnulf of Pembroke and Roger of Poitou, and a contemporary song bade King Henry rejoice, for he could rule freely now that Robert of Bellême was driven abroad. Robert de Bellême fought against Henry I at Tinchebray (1106). Henry imprisoned him at Wareham (1112) and he was still a prisoner at least nineteen years later. William of Malmesbury thus describes this bad baron: 'He was a man intolerable from the barbarity of his manners, and pitiless to the faults of others; remarkable besides for his cruelty; and, among other instances, on account of some trifling fault of its father, he blinded his godchild, who was his hostage, tearing out the little wretch's eyes with his accursed nails. This civil and cunning hypocrite used to deceive the unwary by his serene face and charm of speech'.

ROBERT CURTHOSE (?1054–1134), Duke of Normandy, was the eldest son of William I. His parents intended him to inherit Normandy. He was regent when William was in England (1067). He was short and fat, with a pleasant face, chatty, generous and intelligent but frivolous. He quarrelled with his father and wounded him at Gerberoy (1079) but

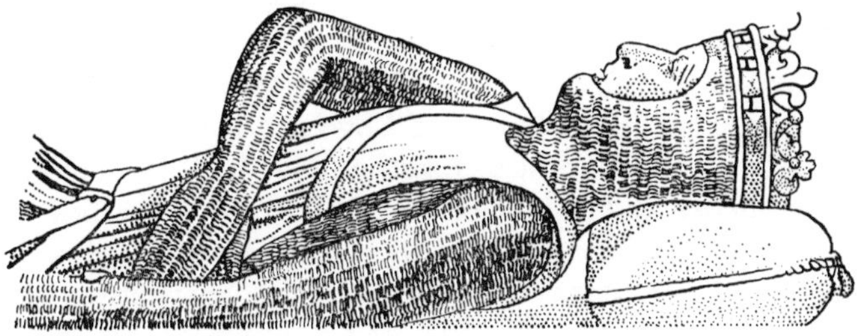

Robert Curthose (Gloucester Cathedral)

regained favour. He felt he, not Rufus, should have England (1087); and Odo and other barons would have preferred one man to rule both England and Normandy as they had lands both sides of the Channel (see p. 66). In 1096 Robert pawned Normandy to Rufus to raise money for a crusade and fought the Turks at Antioch (1098). Ranulf Flambard fled to Normandy (1100) and helped organize an attempt to take England from Henry I (1101). Robert and Henry made peace at Alton (Hants.) but soon quarrelled in Normandy. Henry captured Robert at Tinchebray (1106) and imprisoned him for life 'as a noble pilgrim, worn out with cares, to rest in a royal castle with every comfort'. He is said to have starved himself to death in disgust at being sent a mantle which did not fit Henry. His oaken effigy at Gloucester was made about 1200. See plate 4.

C. W. David, *Robert Curthose*, Harvard Hist. Studies, 1920.

ST. STEPHEN HARDING (d. 1134), co-founder of the Abbey of Cîteaux, was Abbot of Cîteaux (1110–33), and founder of thirteen abbeys, including Clairvaux (1115), of which he made St. Bernard the first abbot. The Cistercian order was strict. Its religious observances and architecture were simple compared with those of the Cluniacs, and its property tended to be derelict waste, reclaimed by the monks and lay brothers. The order was the most flourishing one in the twelfth century, especially in England, where the first house was founded at Waverley (1118). Of sixty-eight English houses founded before 1216 the greatest were those in the lands devastated by William I in Yorkshire, where Rievaulx was founded (1132) as what St. Bernard described to Henry II as a fortification of the soldiers from the Lord's army. Stephen Harding drew up a constitution for the order called 'Charter of Love' (*c.* 1117) on a uniform system for all houses, linked together on federal principles with various checks and balances. Stephen Harding's work was a natural source of national pride to William of Malmesbury, as Stephen was born and educated at Sherborne, of undistinguished parents. He founded a monastic order which played an important part in the spiritual and economic life of four centuries. Stephen wearied of being a monk there and travelled in Scotland and France, for in his youth he knew for a time worldly wishes. After studying in France he visited Rome with a fellow student, singing the whole psalter daily throughout the privations of a long and difficult journey. By then he was more mature and knew his aims. He became a monk in the fine new monastery at Molesme in Burgundy and his desire for a return to earlier simplicity affected the abbot, though many of the inmates preferred their existing ways. The abbot, Harding and seventeen others accordingly departed and settled at Cîteaux, a place then densely covered with woods, but soon transformed. The abbot was at first eager for the privations which contrasted strongly with the gluttony of Molesme, but at last the daily abstinence overcame him; and he welcomed a call to return to Molesme. Some went back with him, but eight stalwarts remained. These appointed Alberic as abbot and Harding as prior. Eight years later Alberic died and Harding 'though absent at the time, was elected abbot, being the original author of the whole scheme, the especial and celebrated ornament of our times . . . Thus by the resounding trumpet of God he directs the people around him, both by word and deed, to heaven, acting fully up to his own precepts, affable in speech, pleasant in demeanour and with a mind always rejoicing in the Lord. Hence, openly, that noble joy of countenance; hence, secretly, that compunction coming from above. For despising the state of a sojourner, he constantly yearns for a heavenly country. For these reasons he is beloved by all . . . A proof of his abstinence is that you see nothing there, as in other monasteries, gleaming with gold, blazing with jewels or glittering with silver . . . The Cistercians at the present day are a model for all monks, a mirror for the diligent, a spur for the indolent'.

Innocent II exempted the Cistercians from the control of bishops and payment of tithes (1132).

N. Hadcock and M. D. Knowles, *Medieval Religious Houses*, 1953.

T.S.I.H., i, 59 (translated from William of Malmesbury).

HENRY I (1068–1135), undeservedly nicknamed Beauclerc for imaginary scholarship, was the youngest son of William I. William of Malmesbury says: 'He was of middle stature . . . his hair was black and set back on his forehead; his eyes were mildly bright; his chest brawny; his body well fleshed. He was jocular in proper season', but after warring with his brothers in disorderly Normandy he learnt to rule by craft, promoting trustworthy subordinates. He was first to hear of Rufus's death and prudently left the hunt to seize the treasury at Winchester. His supporters elected him king the next day and the Bishop of London crowned him at Westminster. He then published in every shire-court a celebrated Coronation charter (a forerunner of King John's Magna Carta, promising redress of grievances), purged the court of vice, imprisoned Ranulf Flambard, invited Anselm to return and married Edith, daughter of St. Margaret. Saxons rejoiced whilst Normans nicknamed the pair by typical Saxon names, Godric and Godgifu. Flambard escaped (1101) and encouraged Robert Curthose to claim England, but a Treaty at Alton left Henry able to punish disloyalty with English help. The three powerful Montgomeries, Robert of Bellême and his brothers, resisted in vain (1102). At last, a year of war with Duke

Robert culminated in the conquest of Normandy at Tinchebray (28 September, 1106), where English soldiers felt that Hastings was avenged. Unfortunately Anselm's loyalty to the Pope (concerning investiture of bishops by laymen) clashed with Henry's attachment to his royal rights until a compromise was reached. With peace established in England Henry's court became a centre for laws, the same for all the king's subjects, and, however selfish his intentions were, Henry earned the title 'the Lion of Justice' and the Anglo-Saxon Chronicle reports 'In his days no man dared harm another'. Across the Channel the politics of Louis VI, the Fat, King of France, and of William Clito (son of Robert Curthose, d. 1128), meant trouble; and the accidental loss of the White Ship (1120), when Henry I's only heir was drowned, brought not only personal grief but a disputed succession. Henry remarried within three months, but though his bastards outnumbered those of any other king, Queen Adela of Louvain produced no son, and the Great Council (1125) recognized Henry's daughter Matilda as heir. He died because he ate lampreys when forbidden by his doctor. He was buried in Reading Abbey, which he had founded. His great work was the creation of a regular system of administration with the help of Roger the Great.

T.S.I.H., i, 63 (White Ship).

ROGER THE GREAT, or OF SALISBURY (d. 1139), was a priest of Caen who first gained Henry I's notice by his speed at Mass. He became Chancellor (1101), Bishop of Salisbury (1102), justiciar and regent of England. He rebuilt Salisbury Cathedral and reorganized the royal exchequer on lines which were continued by his nephew Nigel, Bishop of Ely, and his great-nephew, Richard FitzNigel (d. 1198). Roger caused another nephew, Alexander, to be made bishop of the vast see of Lincoln; but though he used his power to get his nephews promoted, he served Henry I, if not his God, well. He swore allegiance to Matilda (1126), but supported Stephen (1135). Stephen said that, if Roger wanted half the kingdom, he should have it in such troubled times. Roger had his son, Roger Poor, made Chancellor and Nigel made treasurer, and contented himself with the borough of Malmesbury, taking no regular office. William of Malmesbury says (1139): 'Alexander had built the castle of Newark, as he said, for the defence and dignity of the bishopric. Roger, who wished to manifest his magnificence by building, had erected extensive castles at Sherborne, and more especially at Devizes. At Malmesbury, even in the churchyard, and scarcely a stone's throw from the principal church, he had begun a castle. He got custody of Salisbury castle, and surrounded it with a wall. Some powerful laymen became jealous. They said that the Bishops of Salisbury, Ely and Lincoln intended treason, from love of the Empress Matilda's father, and would support her when she arrived. They advised Stephen to take the bishop's castles before it was too late. Stephen pretended not to listen, but at last he decided to act at the first excuse. There was to be an assembly at Oxford. The Bishop of Salisbury set out for this expedition with great reluctance; for I heard him say "By my lady St. Mary, I know not why, but my heart revolts at this journey; this I am sure of, that I shall be of much the same service at court, as a foal is in battle". His forebodings were justified; for his servants were involved in a quarrel in which the Bishop's retainers left their meal unfinished and many were wounded. The king, seizing the opportunity, ordered the bishops to give satisfaction to his court, as their people had infringed his peace: that this satisfaction should be the delivery of the keys of their castles, as pledges of their fidelity. Though prepared to make compensation, they hesitated at the surrender of their fortresses; and in consequence he ordered them into close confinement. He therefore conducted bishop Roger, unfettered, but the chancellor (the nephew, or as it was reported, more than the nephew, of the bishop) in chains, to Devizes . . . At the first summons, the castles of Salisbury, Sherborne, and Malmesbury were yielded to the king. Devizes surrendered after the bishop had refused to eat anything for three days. Roger's mistress, Maud of Ramsbury, was inside, and his sufferings made her insist on surrender'. This incident hastened Roger's death, but Stephen's violent action, though successful, was fatal to his cause, for the leaders of the church, including his brother Henry of Blois, were thrown into horrified opposition. Roger is an outstanding example of a medieval clerical statesman whose main service lay in administering worldly affairs for the king rather than in saving souls for God.

T.S.I.H., i, 88 (the Exchequer).

WILLIAM OF MALMESBURY (1090–6–*c.* 1143) was of mixed English and Norman ancestry and was educated at Malmesbury Abbey, of which he became librarian. He was an intelligent and voluminous historical writer, though not equal to his model, Bede. His *Chronicle of the Kings of England* is a true history as opposed to a mere chronicle. It is interesting in the earlier part because it uses lost poems, while the part just before its conclusion is based on personal knowledge. It was finished in 1125. Malmesbury's other works include *Lives* of Wulfstan, Dunstan and Aldhelm, *The Antiquities of Glastonbury* (1129–39), *Chronicles of the English Bishops*, finished in 1125, and a *Modern History* (up to 1142) dedicated to his hero and patron, Robert, Earl of Gloucester (d. 1147). His works seem to show a personal familiarity with Glastonbury. They contain fine character studies, intimate personal details, revealing legends and penetrating observations. His actual handwriting has been identified.

N. R. Ker, 'William of Malmesbury's Handwriting', *English Historical Review*, vol. 59, 1944.
T.S.I.H., i, 37, 41, 56, 59.

GEOFFREY DE MANDEVILLE (d. 1144), first Earl of Essex, followed a consistent policy of self-interest during the wars of Stephen and Matilda. According to his lights, perhaps, he was a good knight, for he enjoyed the respect of the chronicler of Holy Cross, Waltham; but his name has become a byword of lawlessness, for his career shows how an ambitious baron might behave when there was no strong king to enforce obedience to a central government. Mandeville's inherited lands in the eastern counties earned him the Earldom of Essex as the price of supporting Stephen (1140). When Stephen was captured

Armorial Glass, Dorchester (Oxon.), *c.* 1300

Plate 12

Seals, John De Warenne (*Checkered Gold and Azure*) with sword. Aymer De Valence (*Burelly Silver and Azure with an Orle of Martlets Gules*). Roger Bigod (*Party Gold and Vert a Lion Gules*). Humfrey De Bohun (Bohun Swan. *Azure with a bend of Silver and Cotises of Gold between six Golden Lioncels*). 1301.

Matilda confirmed Mandeville's earldom and ensured his support by making him keeper of the Tower of London and hereditary sheriff and justiciar of Essex. When Matilda fled from Winchester Stephen confirmed the position which Matilda had given Mandeville; Stephen also made him the representative of the crown as sheriff and justiciar in London, Middlesex and Hertfordshire. While Matilda was at Oxford, she pursued her usual policy of buying the powerful, while ignoring people with no military importance, by buying him back. This was detected and Stephen seized Mandeville at a council at St. Albans (1143), but released him in return for the surrender of his castles, 'to the ruin of the realm'. Mandeville then turned the monks out of Ramsey Abbey and made it a headquarters, whence he issued forth to sack Cambridge and St. Ives and to devastate the country round the fens. He was slain by a chance arrow in 1144. His greatest coup was the capture in London of Stephen's queen with Constance, sister of Louis VII, who was on her way to marry Stephen's son, Eustace. Mandeville let the queen go, but kept Constance with a view to a large ransom. Mandeville's son, William, loyally served Henry II during the revolt of 1173–5, became a Justiciar of Richard I and founded several monasteries.

These Mandevilles have no connection with a popular book of travels written by one who was buried in Liège in 1372 under what was probably the assumed name of John Mandeville.

J. H. Round, *Geoffrey de Mandeville*, 1892, a model piece of detective work, but hard reading.

ROBERT, EARL OF GLOUCESTER (d. 1147), was the eldest (bastard) son of Henry I who gave him in marriage Mabel, heiress of the earldom of Gloucester and a great group of manors called the honour of Glamorgan. These her father, Robert FitzHamon (d. 1107), had conquered from the South Welsh. In order to preserve his property he accepted the rule of King Stephen, when he first seized the crown (1135), but Robert's heart was with his step-sister, the Empress Matilda. Robert was patron of William of Malmesbury. In his works more space is devoted to Robert than to any other baron and not only his actions but his motives are described with sympathetic knowledge. Stephen soon attacked Robert's castle; 'Bristol alone remained, which not only expelled the enemy, but even harassed the king by frequent incursions', says Malmesbury. Robert's enemies said that it was jealousy of William of Ypres, Stephen's mercenary captain, which led him to plot against Stephen in Normandy (1137). Two years later he landed with the Empress and 140 knights, and rode to his headquarters at Bristol, leaving her at Arundel. Malmesbury says 'did it not look like flattery, I would say that he was not inferior to Julius Caesar. Julius attacked the world with few troops, trusting to fortune and courage; but Robert relied on the Holy Spirit and the lady St. Mary. Julius had many partisans, but Robert found the nobility hostile "except a very few who regarded their plighted oath" '. Robert burnt Worcester and won a great victory at Lincoln (1141): 'The earls, to a man, for six of them had entered the conflict, together with the king, consulted their safety by flight. A few barons, of laudable fidelity and valour, who would not desert him, even in his necessity, were made captive. The king, though he by no means wanted spirit to defend himself, being at last attacked on every side by the Earl of Gloucester's soldiers, fell to the ground by a blow from a stone; but who was the author of this deed is uncertain. Thus, when all around him were either taken or dispersed, he was compelled to yield to circumstances and became a captive. On which the truly noble Earl of Gloucester commanded the king to be preserved uninjured, not suffering him to be molested even with a reproach; and the person, whom he had just before fiercely attacked when dignified with the sovereignty, he now calmly protected when subdued: that the tumults of anger and of joy being quieted, he might show kindness to his relation, and respect the dignity of the diadem of the captive. The citizens of Lincoln were slaughtered on all sides by the just indignation of the victors, and without commiseration on the part of the conquered, as they had been the origin and fomenters of this calamity'. The same year Robert was himself captured, at

Stockbridge, covering the Empress's retreat from Winchester, and was exchanged for Stephen. His death at Bristol (1147) deprived Stephen's enemies of their best leader. It was to Robert that William of Malmesbury dedicated his 'Chronicle of the Kings of England'.

William of Malmesbury's *Chronicle of the Kings of England*, ed. and translated by J. A. Giles, Bohn's Antiquarian Library, 1866.

DAVID I, King of Scotland (1080–1153), was the youngest son of St. Margaret. He shared his mother's wisdom and love of civilization. He continued to found Augustinian monasteries, to strengthen Roman Christianity, and he much favoured the Cistercians. He founded burghs of independent townsmen; and bishoprics; established the office of chancellor to issue official documents bearing the royal seal, and he made Norman feudal law apply to Scotland. His education and his favourites were English; but politically he aimed not merely at independence of the English king, but at control of the Northern shires of England. He gained control of Cumberland and Northumberland and the tyrannous William Comyn, bishop of Durham. He became Earl of Huntingdon and Northampton and acquired a dangerous claim to Northumberland by his marriage (1114). When Stephen usurped the English crown, David had a good excuse for repeated invasions on the pretext of supporting his niece Matilda the Empress. William of Malmesbury wrote that he was more courtly than his two brothers who were kings before him, 'polished from boyhood by familiarity with us which had rubbed off all the rust of Scottish barbarism. He remitted three years' taxation for those who improved their houses, their dress and their table manners. No three royal brothers were ever so holy and chaste'. Richard of Hexham, living near the border, however, tells how David exulted when he heard how his countrymen had carried off women from Yorkshire: 'these they drove before them naked, fettered and herded together, lashing them with whips, and goading them with their spears. Such atrocities occur in all wars but very seldom to such an extent'. The

Archbishop of York, old Thurstan, rallied the countryside and won a victory at Northallerton over David's undisciplined hordes (1138). It was called the Battle of the Standard because the English erected in a frame the mast of a ship on which they hung the banners of St. Peter the Apostle, St. John of Beverley and St. Wilfrid of Ripon (1138). David accompanied Matilda on her flight to Winchester (1140) and it was from him that his great-nephew, the future Henry II, received knighthood at the age of sixteen. See plate 6.

R. L. G. Ritchie, *The Normans in Scotland*, 1954.
T.S.I.H., i, 66 (Battle of the Standard).

STEPHEN (1097?–1154) was son of Stephen, Count of Blois, and the Conqueror's daughter, Adela. He was knighted at Tinchebray (1106) and became a favourite companion of Henry I. He became Count of Boulogne through marrying Matilda, daughter of the crusading count Eustace and Mary of Scotland, the sister of Henry I's queen. They lived in London at the Tower Royal, says the Anglo-Saxon Chonicle. Stephen was 'a man of great resolution and audacity, who had sworn an oath of fealty to the daughter of King Henry, the Empress (Matilda). Trusting in his own strength shamelessly he seized the crown'. A truer account is that he was a mild man whom the church and baronage supported, partly because he was soft and good and partly because they disliked the idea of a woman on the throne. The Londoners received him and sent for the archbishop, William of Corbeil, who consecrated him on Christmas Day (1135), for Stephen, like his uncle Henry before him, lost no time in getting himself proclaimed king and seizing the royal treasure. He was the first king to allow tournaments and he appealed to the romantic chivalrous ideals of an age which cherished the memory of King Arthur; but 'in this king's time there was nothing but disturbance and wickedness and robbery' and the chronicler has painted an appalling picture of anarchy with wicked men building castles as centres from which to rob their neighbours. At a council at Oxford (1137) Stephen seized Roger, Bishop of Exeter, Alexander, Bishop of Lincoln, and the Chancellor Roger, his

KINGS OF SCOTLAND

DUNCAN I murdered by Macbeth 1040

MALCOLM CANMORE = ST. MARGARET sister of Edgar Atheling
k. 1057–93 (See pedigree p. 31)

EDGAR k. 1097–1107

ALEXANDER I 'The Fierce'
k. 1107–24

DAVID I k. 1124–53 = MATILDA COUNTESS OF NORTHAMPTON

HENRY Earl of Carlisle, Doncaster, Huntingdon and Northumberland d. 1152

MALCOLM IV 'THE MAIDEN'
k. 1153–65

WILLIAM THE LYON
k. 1165–1214

JOANNA sister of Henry III = ALEXANDER II
k. 1214–49

MARGARET daughter of Henry III = ALEXANDER III
k. 1249–86

MARGARET = ERIC OF NORWAY
d. 1283

MARGARET 'MAID OF NORWAY'
1286–90

ALEXANDER
d. 1283

DAVID Earl of Huntingdon

MARGARET

JOHN BALIOL = DEVORGUILLA

JOHN COMYN = MARGARET
The Black

JOHN COMYN
The Red
murdered 1306

JOHN BALIOL
k. 1292–6

EDWARD BALIOL
Nominal
k. 1332–8

ROBERT BRUCE = ISABEL
Lord of Annandale

ROBERT BRUCE VI
Claimant
d. 1295

ROBERT BRUCE VII
Earl of Carrick
d. 1305

ROBERT I BRUCE
k. 1306–29

ADA = HENRY HASTINGS

HENRY HASTINGS

JOHN HASTINGS
Lord Abergavenny
Claimant

JOAN sister of Edward III = DAVID II BRUCE k. 1329–71

MARJORY = WALTER THE STEWARD

ROBERT II k. 1371–89

ROBERT III k. 1390–1406

JOAN BEAUFORT grand-daughter of John of Gaunt = JAMES I k. 1406–1437

MARIE DE GUELDRES = JAMES II k. 1437–60

MARGARET OF DENMARK = JAMES III k. 1460–88

MARGARET = LOUIS XI
k. of France

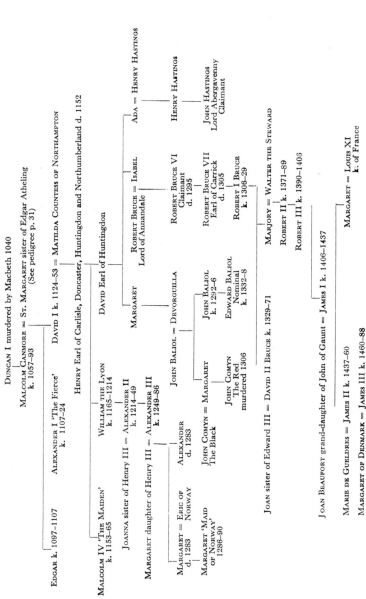

nephew, and imprisoned them until they surrendered their castles (see pp. 79). The Earl of Gloucester championed the cause of his sister the Empress Matilda and captured Stephen at Lincoln (1141). The Earl was himself soon captured in turn and his countess, who had custody of Stephen at Bristol, agreed with Stephen's queen, Matilda, to an exchange. At last, after the devastation of much country, especially in the south and south midlands, Stephen made a treaty at Wallingford (1153) whereby he might reign for life, but his family lost all claim to the succession in favour of the Empress's son, Henry, later Henry II. Stephen died at Dover on 25 October, 1154, aged fifty-one, after reigning for 'nineteen long winters', and was buried beside his queen, Matilda, and their son Eustace, at their own foundation of Faversham Abbey. See p. 55 and plate 1.

Gesta Stephani, translated by K. R. Potter, Nelson's Medieval texts, 1955 (contains many facts narrated in a manuscript recently discovered by Professor Mynors).

T.S.I.H., i, 64 (anarchy), 70 (scorched earth).

ADRIAN IV (NICHOLAS BREAKSPEAR) (d. 1159), born at Langley, was elected Pope (4th December, 1154) less than a week before Henry II's accession. He was the only English Pope ever elected. It was a time when lay rulers were challenging the power of churchmen and Adrian, though born of humble origin, maintained the papal point of view against the Holy Roman Emperor, Frederick Barbarossa, whom he crowned on 18th June, 1155. He granted Ireland to Henry II.

The 'bull *Laudabiliter*' by which he did so has been called a forgery, and in 1318 Irish kinglets complained to a later Pope that his predecessor Adrian was even more an Englishman by affection and condition than by birth. An account of this grant was made by John of Salisbury, a friend of Adrian, in a book written within a year of Adrian's death, at latest: 'The death of our lord, Pope Adrian, which has dismayed all Christian peoples and nations, has brought especially bitter grief to our country of England, whereof he was a native. He is to be lamented by all good men, but by no one more than myself, whom, though he had a mother and a brother living, he loved with a more intimate affection than he bestowed on them. Alike in public and in private he made no secret of the fact that no one was so dear to him as I; and he had come to think so much of me that he never missed an opportunity of gladly opening his inner thoughts to me. While he was Pope, he took pleasure in inviting me to his table and in making me, against my will, eat from his plate and drink from his cup. It was at my request that he granted to the illustrious King of the English, Henry II, the hereditary possession of Ireland, as his letter bears witness to the present day; for all islands are reputed to belong by a long-established right to the Church of Rome by the Donation of Constantine, who instituted and endowed it. Moreover, he sent to the King through me a golden ring, adorned with a fine emerald, in token of his investiture with the government of Ireland; and this ring is still by the King's command preserved in the public treasury. Were I to enumerate all the virtues of the late Pope, this topic alone would fill a large volume'. In another book John of Salisbury reports a long conversation in which Adrian discussed the worry and overwork of being Pope and how he would rather never have left England.

E. M. Almedingen, *The English Pope*, 1925.
W. Ullman, 'The Pontificate of Adrian IV', *Cambridge Historical Journal*, vol. 11 (1955), pp. 233–52.

THEOBALD (d. 1161), Archbishop of Canterbury, was born of a knightly family which came from the same part of Normandy (Thierceville) as Becket's family. Like Anselm, he became a monk and then Abbot of Bec (1137) and Archbishop of Canterbury (consecrated 8th January, 1139). For this appointment he was indebted to Stephen. As archbishop he resisted the attempts of monks to get free from the control of bishops and he had disputes with the monks of St. Augustine and of Christ Church, Canterbury. His relations with Stephen varied; but, when Stephen made government impossible and alienated the church by arresting the bishops (see p. 79), the organization of the church became more powerful although it became more dependent on Rome. Theobald's household was a school for future leaders of the church and included John of Salisbury, as 'official', and Becket, as archdeacon. In it church law was first seriously studied in England and indeed there were the beginnings of a university at Canterbury. Theobald was a rival of Henry of Blois, who had hoped to become archbishop, but who had been allowed to become papal legate, to Theobald's annoyance, instead. Stephen exiled Theobald for some months, for having secretly crossed the Channel in a fishing boat (1148) to attend a Council at Rheims, although he had defended Stephen at that Council. Theobald refused to crown Stephen's son Eustace (1153) and secured the accession of Henry II. Henry accordingly treated Theobald with respect and accepted Becket as Chancellor on his recommendation. Becket's conduct as Chancellor was not what Theobald expected, but it was in accordance with Theobald's wish that Becket succeeded him as archbishop.

A. Saltman, *Theobald, Archbishop of Canterbury*, 1956. This is largely an edition of charters but there is a good historical introduction.

MAUD or MATILDA, THE EMPRESS (1102–1167), was left the sole legitimate child of Henry I by the loss of his son in the White Ship (1120). She married the Emperor Henry V and was crowned at Mainz (1114), but was widowed in 1125 and remarried (1129) Geoffrey le Bel, Count of Anjou. Her first husband was thirty years older, her second one ten years younger than herself. Henry made the barons recognize the Empress as his heir (1126, 1131 and 1133), but when he died Stephen ignored her claim to rule England by hereditary right. The Normans preferred his chivalrous geniality to her haughtiness and they disliked the House of Anjou as much as they did the House of Blois, into which Stephen's mother, the Conqueror's daughter Adela, had married. The Empress appealed to the Pope in vain (1136) and Archbishop Thurstan of York defeated her uncle and champion, David I, King of Scotland (1084–1153) at the Battle of the Standard (1138); but at last she landed in England. At first her rank made Stephen hesitate to make her prisoner, though he might have done so at Arundel, but in 1141 he brought her captive to Gloucester. Yet the same year fortune changed, she won recognition from a council at Winchester (which included even Stephen's brother) as 'Lady of England and Normandy'. 'But', says Henry of Huntingdon, 'she was swollen with insufferable pride by her success in war, and alienated the affections of nearly everyone. She was driven out of London. With a woman's anger she forthwith ordered the King, the Lord's anointed, to be bound in fetters.' Stephen's queen (called Matilda, like the Empress and the Empress's mother and the Conqueror's queen) organized resistance with William of Ypres. The capture of the Empress's illegitimate brother, Robert of Gloucester, made possible the liberation of Stephen. Soon the cause of the Empress was hopeless and she fled, escaping from Oxford Castle over the snow, camouflaged in a white cloak (1142). The attacks of Geoffrey of Anjou on Normandy (1135–9) so prospered that Rouen fell (1144) and with the capture of Arques King Stephen's last Norman castle was taken (1145). Normandy was ceded to Henry, son of the Empress, later Henry II (1150), and by the Treaty of Wallingford (1153) he was recognized as Stephen's sole successor to the throne. After Geoffrey's death (1151) Matilda lived in Normandy, charitable and respected. Her seal shows a majestic queen. Her epitaph in Bec Abbey ran 'Here lies Henry's daughter, wife and mother; great by birth—greater by marriage but greatest by motherhood'. See p. 55 (genealogy).

Lord Onslow, *The Empress Maud*, 1939.
T.S.I.H., i, 70 (flight over snow).

THOMAS BECKET (1118–70), Archbishop of Canterbury, was educated at Merton Priory, in his native London, and in the law schools of Bologna and Auxerre. A romantic tale that his mother was a Saracen is false; his parents were Norman by birth, and settled in London to trade. Becket's training was so secular that as archbishop he kept an instructor to explain the Scriptures for him and he knew so little Latin that he avoided preaching at the Council of Tours (1163). He became a priest only three days before his enthronement (3rd June, 1162) and like Reginald Pole (see vol. ii) before he was archbishop he never celebrated Mass. Entering the household of Archbishop Theobald (1143) he became (1154) his loyal and efficient Archdeacon of Canterbury, and his administrative reputation earned him transfer into royal service (1155). He became Henry II's Chancellor, serving the king devotedly, fighting in Toulouse, fleecing the clergy to finance the French wars and working harmoniously with Henry for seven years. Thomas then laid the foundations on which Chancery became the greatest office of state. Henry felt that ecclesiastical independence made government inefficient, so on Theobald's death (1162) he made Thomas archbishop, wanting a loyal friend to be both chancellor and archbishop. To his dismay Thomas resigned the chancellorship, determined to serve the church whose devoted servant he had become. Besides many small points, the inevitable clash involved the standing of church courts and the sixteen 'Constitutions of Clarendon'. To Henry these 'Constitutions' were necessary reforms. To Becket acceptance was treachery to the freedom of the church. In an undignified and bitter quarrel (1163) Henry removed his son from Becket's charge, confiscated certain manors and made Becket promise to 'obey in good faith' 'ancient customs'. Becket fled from a hostile council in Northampton Castle, without a safe-conduct, to France (1164) and Henry exiled four hundred of his connexions. Henry proposed to crown his son Henry and encouraged Roger, Archbishop of the rival see of York, to affront Canterbury by performing a coronation. A reconciliation allowed Thomas to return, but he excommunicated or suspended bishops who had assisted the coronation.

Three of them complained to Henry in France, provoking an outburst which led to Becket's murder before the High Altar (29th December, 1170), eight days before his fifty-second birthday. Of nine contemporary accounts four are by eye-witnesses. Christendom was aghast and Pope Alexander III canonized Thomas (1173). Miracles occurred and Henry did penance (1174). Every art celebrated his cult and his shrine became the most popular in Europe, churches were dedicated to him, and the greatest English hospital still commemorates in London the name of England's greatest saint. His morals were exemplary, he was generous and talented, but aggressive, ambitious and uncompromising. One of eleven contemporary biographers declared 'he was ever a fool and ever will be'. He was a martyr for his idea of the freedom of the Church. Henry VIII strove unsuccessfully to efface his memory, destroying his shrine at Canterbury and having his name struck out of books (1538). It was Becket who instituted Trinity Sunday, and though the Roman calendar calls Sundays between Whitsun and Advent Sundays after Pentecost, the Anglican church, in its twenty-five Sundays after Trinity, pays him an abiding if unconscious tribute.

T. F. Tout, *St. Thomas of Canterbury*, 1921.
W. H. Hutton, *Thomas Becket*, New Ed., 1926.
T.S.I.H., i, 78 (Becket as chancellor), 82 (his martyrdom).

HENRY OF BLOIS (d. 1171) was Abbot of Glastonbury (1126–71) and Bishop of Winchester (1129–71). He was educated at Cluny Abbey, of which he became the greatest benefactor, and was a rival of Archbishop Theobald. He secured the accession to the throne for his brother, Stephen of Blois (1135) (see pedigree p. 55), and his support only wavered in 1141 when he admitted Matilda to Winchester and accompanied her to London. He helped to engineer the Treaty of Wallingford (1153) although it meant the accession of Henry of Anjou. Anjou and Blois were neighbouring counties on the river Loire and their rulers were hereditary rivals, but the action of Henry of Blois debarred his own house from ever ruling England. Henry consecrated Becket as archbishop. In the dispute with Becket he sought peace and was a moderate supporter of Becket. As legate (1139–43) he had represented the Pope and had encouraged appeals to Rome, but later, when he was no longer legate, he came to resist them. On his deathbed he received a visit from Henry II at Winchester (6 August, 1171) and rebuked him as the real murderer of the archbishop, with threats of Divine vengeance. Like his uncle,

Henry I, the bishop collected rare animals. He bought statues in Italy like the collectors of centuries later. Alms are still distributed at St. Cross, a hospital which he founded at Winchester. In his day he was hailed as an outstanding example of a warrior monk.

JOHN OF SALISBURY (*c.* 1120–80) was born at Old Sarum and became one of the greatest medieval thinkers, and the greatest scholar of his day, but he was no pedant in his humane love of the writings of the past. He studied under famous teachers at Paris, Rheims and Chartres, including Peter Abelard at Paris, and would have liked to see Latin literature taught in English schools in preference to Law and Logic, as it was at Chartres. His writings reveal current enlightened opinion on many topics. His *Policraticus, on the Frivolities of Courtiers and the Traditions of the Learned* (1159) recommends classical moderation to Becket and the actual copy which John gave to Becket is still preserved at Corpus Christi College, Cambridge. It criticizes the dazzling court of Henry II, illustrates Christian morals with examples from ancient history and the Bible and is the first study of the State since St. Augustine's *City of God.* John says that a knight should defend the Church and the poor; he deplores the dirt, downcast heads, affected pale faces and sighs of the monks and he speaks out against executing poachers. John's *Metalogicon* (translated, 1955) shows how in the twelfth century there was a brief flowering of a re-born classical culture like the 'Renaissance' three centuries later. Some of John's letters show how the Church was governed under Archbishop Theobald, to whom St. Bernard introduced him (1148) and whose secretary he became. Others were written to Becket, whose exile John shared, whose murder he saw, and whose biography he wrote. We can still see art and architecture inspired by the directing brain of John in the choir of Canterbury and in the cathedral of Chartres, where he returned as bishop (1176).

John of Salisbury, *Letters* ed. W. J. Miller and H. E. Butler, revised by C. N. L. Brooke (with a charming introduction), Nelson's Medieval Texts, 1955. In the same series is

Marjorie Chibnall's edition of *Historia Pontificalis*, 1956, describing events of 1148–52.

BARTHOLOMEW (d. 1184), Bishop of Exeter for twenty-three years, is one of the six most praiseworthy bishops of his age selected as subjects for biography by Gerald of Wales; Gerald says he was gloomy and nervous, but learned and religious. It is fortunate that a modern life has been written of Bartholomew just because he was a normal person who as such did not acquire notoriety in the headlines of history. He was able and conscientious and did his duty on the fringe of the great events of Becket's dispute with the King. He was of Breton origin, studied in Paris, served in the administrative machine of the great international organization of the Catholic Church as a 'papal judge delegate', was an authority on church law and wrote a penitential or manual on penances. A year after he had become Bishop of Exeter Henry II sent him to Canterbury to help arrange the election of Becket as archbishop (1162). He then attended Becket's ordination as priest. At the Council of Northampton (1164) he begged Becket to yield to Henry II, as the king had denounced all Becket's supporters as traitors. Becket replied 'Get thee hence, for you do not know the things that are of God'. He was one of those sent with Gilbert Foliot to win over Pope Alexander III to Henry II's side; they reached St. Omer the same day as Becket, but reached Rome a day after the archbishop's case against the king had been explained to Alexander. When John of Salisbury followed Becket into exile he corresponded with his friend, Bartholomew, and the correspondence shows that Bartholomew became a champion of the archbishop and thereby incurred royal anger. Bartholomew took part in the coronation of Henry's son (1170) in Becket's absence. The Pope suspended all bishops participating, but Becket asked him to exclude Bartholomew from the sentence. It took seven days for news of Becket's murder to reach Exeter, but it was to Bartholomew that William de Tracy, a rich Devon baron who was one of the murderers, made confession. It was Bartholomew whom the Pope instructed to provide suitable penances for those involved in proportion to their guilt. While lamenting the murder Bartholomew had a vision of one who told him 'Truly is he dead, but his power lives on'. His hundred surviving sermons show him as a simple and sincere preacher, full of tender devotion to the Virgin, telling the laity stories of saints' lives and explaining the meaning of saints' days. They contain homely allusions, such as to the danger of life in a dry-stone house with no mortar. Once when visiting a parish he woke up at midnight intending to say matins. His light had gone out and he sent his servant to get another. While he was gone the bishop heard voices: 'Woe to us! Who will pray for us, and give alms and celebrate masses for our salvation'. Meanwhile the servant found a house with a light at the far end of the street. When he went in he found the priest and some mourners round a dead man. Bartholomew heard about this and asked the priest the next day about the deceased. The dead man had been accustomed to pay a chaplain to say masses for the dead. The bishop then earmarked part of the village church income for the dead man's chaplain to continue saying mass daily for the souls whom he had heard grieving in the graveyard. In 1184 Walter Map says he was still busy at literary work though very old.

Dom S. A. Morey, *Bartholomew of Exeter, Bishop and Canonist*, 1937 (the first serious attempt to make the dry bones of one of Becket's bishops live).

GILBERT FOLIOT (*c.* 1108–1187), a relation of the Earl of Hereford, was Prior of Cluny, Abbot of Gloucester (1139), Bishop of Hereford (1147–63) and Bishop of London (1163–87). He was a vegetarian, a total abstainer and a scholar, but a very active man. He was the only bishop to oppose the election of Becket. Gilbert disliked Becket and regarded him as a persecutor of the clergy, the appointment of one who was neither monk nor priest (1162), and when he became Bishop of London he had a further quarrel with Becket for he wanted to make London independent of Canterbury and claimed that it had been pre-eminent even in Roman times. This aroused the sarcasm of John of Salisbury. At the Council of Northampton (1164) Foliot said that Becket was always an idiot; and after Becket's flight he received the administration of Canterbury and incurred blame for his supposed harsh treatment of Becket's relations. Becket excommunicated Foliot in 1167, 1169 and again, for consecrating Henry II's son and heir as king, in 1170. In a sermon at Canterbury itself Gilbert argued that Henry was innocent of Becket's murder (1174). His influence on Henry was great right up to his death, at the age of eighty, two years before that of the king. His letters have been printed.

ST. GILBERT OF SEMPRINGHAM (before 1089–1189) died at Sempringham aged over one hundred, having founded the only English monastic order. He was son of a rich Lincolnshire Norman knight and a Saxon woman of 'lower rank' and suffered from a deformity which made him unfit for arms and such that 'even the serving men would not sit at meat with him'. At first 'learning, which is wont heavily to afflict boys, frightened his tender years', but study in France gave him such a love of letters that when he came home he started a school to teach even girls Latin, assembling the children in dormitories and curbing their liberty of playing and wandering at will. His father gave him the living of Sempringham, but successive Bishops of Lincoln kept him with them (*c.* 1122–1134) awhile. He was ordained priest unwillingly and built a place for maids to live together on the quiet north side of Sempringham Church. Food was supplied through a window and poor village women were organized as lay sisters to serve them. Poor parishioners, fugitive villeins and city outcasts were made lay brothers to do rough outdoor work, and finally learned priests were added to complete a 'double monastery' such as those which flourished in the seventh century. Knights gave endowments (*c.* 1139) and by the end of Stephen's reign (1154) there were thirteen 'Gilbertine' houses of which nine admitted women. St. Bernard helped compile rules on Cistercian lines and the Pope approved. Gilbert supported Becket and his houses helped Becket escape after the Council of Northampton (1164), but Henry II protected Gilbert when his lay brothers revolted for more food and less work and slandered him to Pope Alexander III (1170). Later the severity of diet and dress was relaxed (1187), though Gilbert abstained even from fish in Lent. He used to ride from house to house, with a lay brother and one or two canons, in his dark grey tunic, never chattering on the way but praying or singing psalms. In old age he entered his own Order. He became blind, but continued his rounds in a litter, always eating and sleeping with the others in the refectory and dormitory. His biography said the Order 'is the chariot of Aminadab, that is of a willing people, of the voluntary poor of Christ. It has two sides, one of men, another of women; four wheels, two of men, clerk and lay, and two of women, lettered and unlettered. Two oxen draw the chariot, the clerkly and monastic discipline of the blessed Augustine and the holy Benedict. Father Gilbert guides the chariot over the places rough and smooth, over the heights and in the depths. The way by which they go is narrow, but the path is eternal life'. By 1189 the thirteen houses contained 700 men and 1,500 women, a number reduced to 143 canons and 139 nuns at the dissolution of the monasteries. Gilbert's successor collected witnesses to his many miracles when Archbishop Hubert Walter wanted him canonized. But Gilbert appeared in a dream and said it was unnecessary. He was canonized in 1202 and Hubert Walter remitted forty days' penance for all visitors to his shrine.

Rose Graham, *S. Gilbert of Sempringham and the Gilbertines, A History of the only English Monastic Order*, London, 1901.

HENRY II FITZEMPRESS (1133–89), the eldest son of Geoffrey of Anjou, was born five years after his father had married, at the age of fifteen, Henry I's daughter Matilda 'the Empress' to unite the rival houses of Anjou and Normandy. Gerald of Wales describes him 'of reddish, freckled complexion with large round head, grey eyes which glowed fiercely and grew bloodshot in anger, a fiery countenance and a harsh, cracked voice. His neck was somewhat thrust forward from his shoulders, his chest was broad and square, his arms strong and powerful. His frame was stocky with a pronounced

Robert Bruce (Seal, British Museum)

Plate 13

Edward I (Seal, British Museum)

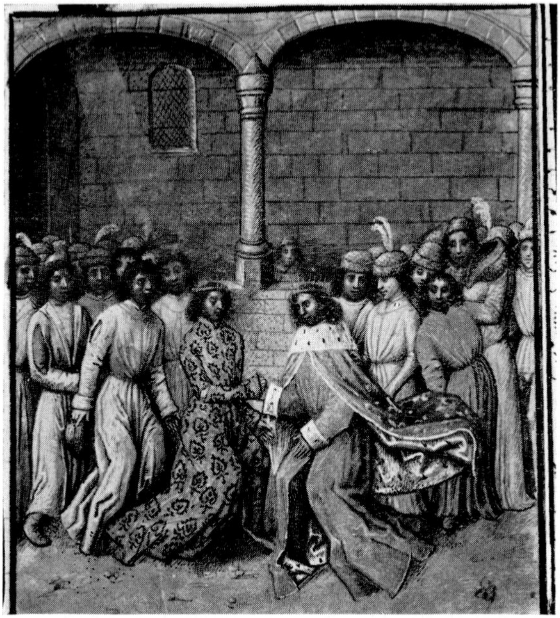

Edward III as Prince does homage to Charles IV of France, 1325

Plate 14

Queen Isabel, 1327 (Holkham MS. 659)

tendency to corpulence . . . which he tempered by exercise'. He never spared his courtiers from continual travel and was ever restlessly busy, even during Mass.

During Stephen's reign Henry visited England to study (1142–6) and fight (1149 and 1153); and before he became king (1154) in accordance with the Treaty of Wallingford he had succeeded Geoffrey (d. 1151) in Anjou, Maine and Touraine and had acquired Normandy, conquered from Stephen, and Aquitaine gained by marriage with Eleanor the Duchess (1152). He expelled Stephen's Flemish mercenaries, thereafter using mercenaries only abroad, and destroyed unauthorized castles, so that the Anglo-Saxon Chronicle recorded that 'he did good and made peace'. Henry fought continental wars and negotiated to preserve wide territories from his brother Geoffrey and from the King of France; he strove to extend his influence to Brittany and Toulouse and knew something of every tongue from Biscay to the Jordan; yet he found time to improve financial and judicial machinery, substituting the verdict of neighbours for ordeal by battle, and perfecting work which his grandfather had begun. He was disappointed to find that his appointment of his friend and chancellor, Thomas Becket, as Archbishop of Canterbury (1162) was a terrible mistake, for it gave the church a champion against his desire to punish criminal clerics. Thomas fled from a hostile council at Northampton (1164) to France, and Henry enforced his policy of curbing ecclesiastical power as formulated in the 'Constitutions of Clarendon' (1164) to the horror of orthodox Europe. Churchmen regarded as persecution limitations on the independence of the church which Henry regarded as essential for orderly government. Henry made in the Assize of Clarendon (1166) the first real attempt at making law as opposed to defining custom and he caused juries to 'present' or report crimes in the county courts. He was determined that his death should not lead to disorder such as that which followed the death of his grandfather, Henry I; so on 14 June, 1170, he made a further fatal mistake, having his son Henry actually crowned king; though he himself was in his prime and had no intention of giving up any real power. Such an action was not unusual abroad. The coronation was performed, to the vexation of the Pope and Becket, by the Archbishop of York. After a hollow truce with Becket some angry royal words encouraged four knights to murder Becket in Canterbury Cathedral on 29 December, 1170. Henry invaded Ireland (1171) but had to return (1172) because of intrigues around young King Henry which broke into widespread revolt (1173). On 7 June, 1174, he allowed all 70 monks of Canterbury to scourge him for Becket's martyrdom and at once the tide miraculously turned with news of the capture of the Scottish king at Alnwick. Everywhere Henry triumphed and he continued his reforms with such measures as the Assize of Northampton (1176), which reserved certain pleas for the royal courts, and the Assize of Arms (1181), which assessed liability according to the amounts of personal property held. However little appreciated by some contemporaries, Henry was assured an important place in books on constitutional history, but his latter years were full of real tragedy for his quarrelsome sons rebelled again (1183). After receiving the kiss of peace from Henry, Richard his son heard him mutter 'God grant I die not before I have worthily avenged myself on thee'. Henry saw his authority destroyed by his rebellious sons, and himself defeated; 'Shame, shame on a conquered king', were among the sad words he uttered in his last illness at Chinon (1189). His attendants, as usual, took everything when he died, but a lad covered his nakedness with a short cloak, which seemed to Gerald of Wales to fulfil a nickname given him when young, 'Curtmantle', for he had first introduced into England the short cloak from Anjou, whereas in Henry I's time only long cloaks were worn in England. Richard came and gazed on the body, and blood flowed from the king's nostrils as long as he remained there. At its height, Henry's power had been greater than that of any other European ruler and his position was comparable to that of such 'Holy Roman Emperors' as Charlemagne and Frederick Barbarossa. His tireless energy had built up law courts, a central chancery to administer the issue of official documents throughout his wide dominions, a central exchequer for the collection of money, and a carefully devised military system. Not even continual neglect in the time of his successor, Richard, destroyed Henry's work.

L. F. Salzmann, *Henry II*, 1917.
T.S.I.H., i, 72 (Henry's character by Walter Map), 86 (penance). See p. 55 and plate 7.

RANULF GLANVILLE (d. 1190), fighter, diplomat and lawyer, was sheriff of Yorkshire (1163–70 and 1174), Justice in Eyre, and Chief Justice of England (1180–9). He used always to be called the author of the most important 'Treatise concerning the Laws and Customs of the Kingdom of England', though it may be the work of his protégé Hubert Walter. This treatise describes in detail the King's Court in which Glanville served. It explains the different methods of trial, ancient and modern, central and local, and the conditions under which tenants held their land of the King or of others under the King. Glanville is little influenced by Roman Law, which was being then carefully studied abroad, except perhaps in his love of precise definitions. As sheriff of Lancashire at a time of general rebellion against Henry II he captured Henry the Lyon, King of Scotland, at Alnwick (1174). As Justiciar (1180) Glanville received an important judicial office which Richard de Lucy 'the loyal' had held for twenty-five years. He was to preside over the legal side of the King's Court as it had been reorganized (1178) after the unsuccessful revolt of Henry's sons (1173) had made royal confidence in them impossible. He founded Butley Priory (Suffolk) but, as Justiciar, remarked that in all his long experience he had never seen such shameless forgeries as those by which the Cistercians buttressed bad titles to their estates. He was 'the eye of King Henry' and had custody of his prisoners, including Queen Eleanor of Aquitaine, until her release on Henry's death (1189). At Richard's coronation Glanville tried in vain to reason with the mob which sacked the London jewry (1189). His power, but not his activity, was over. Richard I ruined him by excessive exactions of money and he resigned. He preceded Richard I on the Third Crusade (1190). Richard of Devizes says that in Palestine extremes of temperature by day and night killed thousands monthly. Local victuallers could not believe their eyes when a small army consumed three times as much bread and a hundred times as much wine as whole nations. When scarcity came (1192), the victims of famine could hardly restrain themselves, he says, from eating their own fingers. The *Itinerary of Richard I* describes the high prices during a famine in 1190. Then soldiers would rush to get even the intestines of a dead horse. Anybody who had any food hid it. Men were glad to eat grass. Heavy rain increased a pestilence which caused bodies to swell as with dropsy and teeth to fall out. Starving men fought for bread if it was known that an oven was baking. Men sucked dirty bones that had been gnawed by dogs for days. Even noblemen stole bread, and some fled to the Turks and abandoned Christianity in order to get food. At last a food-ship arrived and prices fell. Glanville was one of many victims in this outbreak of pestilence in the unhappy army at Acre (1190).

F. W. Pollock and Maitland, *History of English Law (-1272)*, Cambridge, 2nd ed., 1898, vol. 1, chapter 6.

HUGH DE PUISET (1125–95) was Bishop of Durham for forty-two years, longer than any other of the great medieval bishops of Durham. His uncle, Henry of Blois, made him Archdeacon of Winchester (1142), his cousin, the Archbishop of York, made him treasurer of York (1143), and his uncle, King Stephen, made him Bishop of Durham (1153), although he was under age and of worldly tastes and morals. He adorned the cathedral with imported marble and inserted stained glass round the altar. He restored Durham and Northallerton castles and was active locally, but despite his outstanding magnificence he remained relatively remote from royal business and for a time lost Henry II's favour by letting the Scots through in 1173. At the price of money raised for the Third Crusade Richard I made him Earl of Northumberland, justiciar of England and vice-regent. 'Behold', said Richard, 'how out of an old bishop I have made a new earl.' He tried unsuccessfully (1190–2) to make Durham independent of York. A survey of his episcopal estates is called the Boldon Book.

He was tall and handsome. He died of overeating at a Shrovetide feast.

G. V. Scammel, *Hugh de Puiset: a Biography of a Twelfth Century Bishop of Durham*, 1956.

WILLIAM LONGCHAMP (d. 1197) was lame and short. He stammered. Gerald of Wales hated him and called him deformed and hairy, with a low forehead. He was an arrogant Norman, of such humble origin that his enemies said that his grandfather had been a runaway serf of the Bishop of Beauvais. He became a very loyal servant of Richard I and served him as Chancellor, first of Aquitaine and then of England (1189). He became Bishop of Ely (1189) and finally (1191) Richard's ruthless and vigilant Chief Justiciar, wielding royal power in his master's absence. Longchamp despised Englishmen and he had noble pages to wait upon him. He even managed to thwart the ambitions of his noble rival, Hugh de Puiset. Longchamp seemed to have attained complete control of the Church as well as of the State, for the Pope made him legate for England (5th June, 1191). There was, however, considerable opposition to him and Richard's brother John put himself at the head of this movement. Longchamp arrested John's half-brother, Geoffrey, Archbishop of York, but had to flee to the Tower of London. The London mob rose against him, but he continued to defy John, 'as pale as one who treads upon a snake with his bare feet'. He was forced to give up the keys of the Tower and of Windsor Castle. After two unsuccessful attempts to escape, he was allowed to leave the country and went to Paris. In spite of these misadventures he retained the confidence of Richard I as his 'dearest chancellor'. Richard was then imprisoned and Longchamp served him well, getting him moved to more accessible strongholds in Germany. He was able to return to England to arrange about the collection of his ransom and the assembling of the noble hostages who were demanded to ensure its payment (1193–5). While Richard's chivalry touched the imagination of all, it was Longchamp's task to do the necessary, unspectacular and unpopular work of ruling a neglected kingdom and extracting money from it.

Even if his manner had been attractive, he could hardly have been an efficient royal agent, without making himself hated. He was travelling to Rome on a diplomatic mission when he fell sick and died at Poitiers. He was buried at Le Pin Abbey. At his death a crucifix in Poitiers was said to weep; but England rejoiced. Longchamp was a man devoted to Richard's interests. In Poitiers, perhaps, this virtue was appreciated, for Richard was the beloved Count of Poitiers. In England it was not.

K. Norgate, *John Lackland*, 1902.

RICHARD I, COEUR-DE-LION (1157–1199), was taller than his father, Henry II, though stocky. He was bold and strong with a ruddy complexion and furious eyes. Though born in Oxford, he was brought up as a Poitevin, like his mother, Eleanor, and only returned to England twice (Aug.–Dec., 1189 and March–May, 1194). Historians may think his crusade and his Norman border wars less important than the charters he gave to towns; but he remains a hero of romance such as impressed Walter Scott and even Saracens. His need for cash enabled towns to buy grants of freedom. Third but favourite son of Eleanor he became Duke of Aquitaine (1170) and was soon involved in plots with the King of France against Henry. On becoming King of England (1189) he raised funds for the Third Crusade. On his way to the successful siege of Acre he married Berengaria of Navarre (d. 1230) at Limasol (Cyprus). This queen never visited England. Dissension in England made Richard return when he was only twelve miles from Jerusalem, but the Archduke of Austria captured him in disguise, at a wayside inn cooking chickens, to avoid the many enemies whom he had made. Blondel the minstrel discovered where he was imprisoned, at Durrenstein (Styria), by singing a song which they had composed together. Hubert Walter visited Richard; and a ransom of 100,000 marks had to be raised (1193) to secure Richard's release (1194). The Normans welcomed Richard and he displayed his interest in fortification (1196–7) by building at Les Andelys Château Gaillard (or 'saucy'), perched on a crag overlooking French territory. From here in rage he cast to death French prisoners. He died before his forty-second birthday after a reign of ten years. A peasant near Châlus (Limousin) when ploughing found ancient coins and 'an Emperor and his family in gold seated round a table'—presumably figures surrounding the boss of a shield buried in the Dark Ages like the Mildenhall treasure. The overlord of the lord of Châlus claimed this interesting and valuable hoard. So did Richard. Richard besieged Châlus to get it. He rejected the surrender of the garrison and swore to hang all in Châlus castle. One defender stood on a bastion nearly all day watching the besiegers. He had a cross-bow in one hand and a frying-pan for shield in the other. At last he saw Richard unarmed save for shield and helmet. Richard heard the bolt coming, applauded his foe, but ducked too late. It struck his shoulder and pierced his side. When he tried to pull it out in his tent it broke, and a surgeon of Mercadier, Richard's ruthless captain, could hardly find it and extract it from the fat flesh by candle-light. While the wound festered Mercadier took Châlus, and all the defenders were hanged except the sniper. Richard asked why he slew him and he replied that Richard had killed his father and brothers: 'freely will I suffer the greatest torments thou canst think of, now that thou, who hast brought so many to so great evils on the world, art stricken to death'. Richard gave him 100s. Richard died on April 6th and on Palm Sunday, April 11th, Bishop Hugh of Lincoln buried him at his father's feet at Fontevraud; but his great heart joined the other relics in Rouen Cathedral.

K. Norgate, *Richard the Lion Heart*, 1924.
P. P. Henderson, *Richard Coeur de Lion*, 1958.
T.S.I.H., i, 98. See p. 55 (pedigree) and plate 7.

ST. HUGH OF AVALON (*c.* 1135–1200), Bishop of Lincoln for fourteen years, is not to be confused with Bishop Hugh de Wells (d. 1235) who built the nave of Lincoln or with little St. Hugh of Lincoln said to have been crucified by a Jew (1255). Hugh was son of a Burgundian knight and both father and son became monks. Henry II brought him from the Grande Chartreuse to set on a sound basis a Carthusian monastery at

Witham. It was founded as part of the royal penance for Becket's murder and had fallen into difficulties. Hugh was a very practical and upright man and after Witham was established Henry II made him (1186) Bishop of Lincoln in face of opposition from the Cathedral Chapter. Hugh refused to accept office until he was freely elected. Then he rebuilt the Cathedral, of which the tower had fallen, in the latest Early English style of architecture, of which he was a pioneer. Hugh resisted three kings over forest law, appointments of courtiers to sinecures and the use of churchmen for civil purposes, but kindness replaced severity when he was dealing with children, animals, swans, lepers or Jews and he refused to oppress his tenants. He loved relics but disliked talk of miracles. He was auburn haired, blue-eyed and strong, though he suffered from a puffiness which sometimes comes from fasting. He regarded Henry II's marriage with Eleanor of Aquitaine as invalid, but indignantly turned out of the choir of Godstow nunnery the tomb of Fair Rosamund, mistress of Henry II. Henry II took his reproofs in good part, but John was bored by a long sermon on bad kings. Hugh died after a sickness contracted abroad, whither he had gone to make peace for King John. The Kings of England and Scotland bore his pall.

R. Thurston, *St. Hugh of Lincoln*, 1898.

ELEANOR, DUCHESS OF AQUITAINE (1122–1204), was charming and lively, the inspiration of troubadours, patroness of fashionable social gatherings called courts of love, and the richest lady in Europe. She accompanied her first husband (1137–52), Louis VII, King of France, on the unlucky Second Crusade, but after a divorce she married Henry II (1152), though he was eleven years her junior, and helped him to win the English throne (as Henry II) (1154). There is no truth in the belief that she murdered Henry's mistress, Fair Rosamund, at Godstow nunnery; but she did incite Henry's sons against him and was consequently imprisoned for eleven years (1173–84). She supported her son Richard I against his brother John, and King John against her grandson Arthur (born 1166), and Arthur besieged her in Mirebeau castle

(1202). Three weeks after John lost Château Gaillard, the key to Normandy (1204), she died, aged about eighty-two, and was buried at Fontevraud Abbey. There, when once in temporary retreat, she had built the kitchen and there the nuns recorded in the list of departed souls for whom they used to pray that 'she enhanced the grandeur of her birth by the honesty of her life, the purity of her morals, the flower of her virtues; and in the conduct of her blameless life she surpassed almost all the queens of the world'. There she lies between Henry II and Richard I with her daughter Joanna, Queen of Sicily, and her daughter-in-law Isabel of Angoulême. Her effigy represents her as smiling, book in hand. The sculptured heads of Henry II and Eleanor are to be seen at Oakham, near Saintes, and (from near Bordeaux) in New York.

Amy Kelly, *Eleanor of Aquitaine and the Four Kings*, Harvard University Press, 1950. See p. 55 and plate 7.

HUBERT WALTER (d. 1205) was nephew and chaplain of Ranulf Glanville and was perhaps the real author of Glanville's monumental treatise on English Law and Custom. He was Baron of the Exchequer (1184) and Dean of York (1186) and Richard I made him Bishop of Salisbury at the same time that the vacant sees of Winchester, London and Ely were given to Godfrey de Luci, Richard FitzNeale and William Longchamp (1189). With Baldwin, Archbishop of Canterbury (1180–90), who died in Palestine, Bishop Hubert Walter left England with Richard I on the Third Crusade (1190–2). He organized charity during the famine which tormented the army (1190); and negotiated the final truce with Saladin. Richard of Devizes says: 'Hubert, Bishop of Salisbury, and Henry, Captain of Judæa, together with a numerous band, went up to Jerusalem to worship in the place where the feet of Christ had stood. And there was woeful misery to be seen—captive confessors of the Christian name, wearing but a hard and constant martyrdom; chained together in gangs, their feet blistered, their shoulders raw, their backsides goaded, their backs wealed, they carried materials to the hands of the masons and stone-layers to make Jerusalem impregnable against the Christians. When the captain and bishop had returned from the sacred places, they endeavoured to persuade the king to go up; but the worthy indignation of his noble mind could not consent to receive that from the courtesy of the Gentiles which he could not obtain by the gift of God'. Hubert led the army homewards, but turned aside to seek Richard when he heard of his capture. He visited him in prison and was one of those who stood by him in the Emperor's court at Speyer and Worms. Richard was put on trial by his enemies, although his person should have been protected as he was a crusader. Richard was charged with having insulted the Duke of Austria, with being an accomplice in the murder of Conrad de Montferrat, with being a friend of the leader of the Guelf Party which opposed the Emperor and with being an ally in Sicily of the usurper, Tancred. Hubert was a commissioner for the collection of Richard's ransom, and as justiciar (1193) he suppressed the treason of Richard's brother, John. His authority became yet greater in 1195 when he became papal legate, having already become Archbishop of Canterbury (1193). He improved local administration by the use of coroners and juries (1194) but the vast taxation needed for Richard's ransom made him personally unpopular; and when he suppressed William FitzOsbert, leader of the London poor, (1196), he violated sanctuary in the church of St. Mary-le-Bow, Cheapside. The monks of Christ Church, Canterbury, generally hostile to their archbishops, complained to the Pope; and Innocent III successfully protested against Hubert's retaining his office as justiciar and head of lay legal administration to the neglect of his duties as head of the church. As archbishop Hubert Walter had officiated at a second coronation of Richard I after his return from captivity (1194); and at the coronation of John he insisted on the principle that the monarch is elected. Under John he was chancellor (1199) and had such a moderating influence upon him that John said that only after Hubert Walter's death did he feel a real king. He began the practice of systematically enrolling copies of all charters and writs issued in the king's name in three series of rolls. These are preserved in the Public Record Office, and summaries, or 'calendars' of their contents provide an important source for later English medieval history. His bones were identified at Canterbury in 1890.

C. R. Cheney, *From Becket to Langton: English Church Government, 1170–1213*, 1956, chapter 2, on bishops.

MAP, WALTER (*c.* 1140–*c.* 1205), Canon of St. Paul's Cathedral, Lincoln and Hereford, was a lively and satirical courtier and poet who retailed much gossip of Henry II's court. He was an Anglo-Norman aristocrat from the Welsh Marches on the Herefordshire border, he accompanied the court abroad (1173 and 1183) and he hoped in vain to become Bishop of Hereford. He reveals the prejudices of his circle, praising Henry II's treasonable son, Henry, for reviving chivalry by his example, although he was most undutiful to his father and king; and he declared 'My soul loathes villeins (*servi*)'. More personal is his prejudice against monks, especially Cistercians, including St. Bernard, a saint who only bore with jokes if made by one in authority. As ex-itinerant justice and ex-clerk of Henry II's household, Walter knew his facts when he said that Minos was more merciful than forest justices. As one who attended a Church council in Rome (1179) and became Archdeacon of Oxford (from 1197) he admitted to Ranulf Glanville, the justiciar and legal writer, that the king's courts compared favourably with church ones, but suggested that it might be because the king was nearer than the Pope. Gerald of Wales, his friend and 'fellow-countryman', records specimens of Walter's wit, but Walter is best known for a racy collection of anecdotes and legends called 'Of Courtiers' Trifles'. The only surviving copy is in the Bodleian Library. It contains a penetrating character of Henry II which ends with an example of unusual royal generosity to sailors who lost twenty-four ships in a stormy Channel crossing which he made with the king.

W. Map, *De Nugis Curialium*, translated by M. R. James, Cymrodorion Record Soc., 9, 1923.

WILLIAM THE LYON (1143–1214) succeeded his brother

Malcolm IV 'The Maiden' (1141–65) as King of Scotland. William supported a general revolt against Henry II (1173) in the hope of winning back Northumberland for Scotland; but Ranulf Glanville and the men of Yorkshire defeated and captured him near Alnwick. He was led captive to Henry II at Falaise and a treaty was made there (1174). Jordan Fantosme, a poet, has described the battle:—

'The fighting of the King and his troops was very vigorous;
Everything would have gone on well, to my knowledge,
Had it not been for a serjeant who rushed up to him,
With the lance which he held rips up his horse . . .
The King lay on the ground, thrown down, as I tell you,
Between his legs lay the horse upon him;
Never will he rise from it for relation or for friend,
If the horse is not drawn from him with which he is encumbered,
He will always be humbled and disgraced.
He was soon taken, with my two eyes I saw it,
By Ranulph de Glanville, to whom he then surrendered,
And all his boldest knights are taken . . .'.

After another 132 lines Jordan tells how the news came to Henry as he leant on his elbow and slept a little in his own chamber while a servant was gently rubbing his feet. The chamberlain refused to let the messenger disturb Henry, but Henry heard the noise and said the messenger was to come in. He feared ill news but when he heard of the victory:—

'Then says King Henry, "God be thanked for it,
And St. Thomas the Martyr and all the saints of God" . . .
And the King is so merry and joyful that night
That he went to his knights and awoke them all.
"Barons wake up. It has been a good night for you,
Such a thing I have heard as will make you glad,
The King of Scotland is taken, so it has been told me for truth,
Just now the news came to me when I ought to have been in bed".
And the knights say, "Now thank the Lord God,
Now is the war ended, and your kingdom in peace".'

The treaty defined for the first time the relations of Scotland with England; and William had to do homage for his kingdom to Henry, 'as the other men of my lord the king are wont'. William had to surrender Roxburgh, Berwick, Jedburgh, Edinburgh and Stirling castles; and had to cause his bishops and barons to swear fealty to Henry. William promised that the Scottish church should be subject to the English, 'as it ought and is accustomed', but he later persuaded the Pope to declare the church of Scotland independent of York. Fifteen years after this humiliation at Falaise William bought back both castles and independence for 15,000 marks from Richard I (1189). He failed to make a purchase of Northumberland because the offer did not include its castles. William tried in vain (1199–1212) to recover Northumberland from John, but John's enemies were ready to let it pass to William's son, Alexander II (1198–1249). As a Scottish king, William's authority was mainly confined to Lothian and Strathclyde. He had a hard struggle to subdue the Celtic and Norwegian provinces of Scotland, but he conquered the Moray highlands, Caithness and Sutherland. He was seventy years old when he died, and old age made him content to enjoy an alliance which he had bought with King John.

Sir A. C. Lawrie, *Annals of the Reigns of Malcolm and William, Kings of Scotland, A.D. 1153–1214*, 1910. See plate 5 (seal).

JOHN (1167–1216) was the favourite son of Henry II who nicknamed him Lackland because he was his youngest son. He declared John king of recently conquered Ireland (1177), but John's presence there (1185) was short and disastrous. John fought his brother Richard (1184) for refusing him Aquitaine and hastened the death of Henry by grief at his treachery (1189). While Richard I was abroad John won the support of the barons and the Londoners against Longchamp (1191), allowing London to elect its first mayor. He would like to have prolonged Richard's captivity, but their mother, Eleanor, made a reconciliation and John was crowned at Westminster as Richard's successor (27th May, 1199). The general belief in John's superhuman wickedness is based on dubious statements by Roger of Wendover. He was able and intelligent and in his reign the Exchequer, the Chancery and the Law Courts became more efficient. He could be generous to inferiors and

King John. Head from Effigy. (Worcester Cathedral)

Enthroned and on horseback (from Seal)

merciful in court and he knew England better than any king since 1066. Others could be more cruel. Henry's death in defeat and misery through openhearted trust in unworthy sons may have made John's nature arbitrary and suspicious, and this led to such unpopularity that Matthew Paris said: 'Foul as it is, Hell itself is defiled by the presence of John'. He divorced his first wife, Avice of Gloucester, but kept her dowry; and abducted his second wife, Isabel of Angoulême, when scarcely fifteen (1200). He probably murdered his nephew and heir, Arthur (1203). He lost his continental possessions including

Oppression in the reign of John (Matthew Paris)

Battle of Sandwich (Matthew Paris)

Normandy (1204–5). and through his refusal to accept Archbishop Langton and his expulsion of the monks of Canterbury, England was laid under an interdict (see p. xxi). He oppressed the clergy and took hostages from the barons; but he managed to make peace with the Pope and to build up an alliance against France only to see it ruined at Bouvines (1214). He had to seal the Great Charter of Liberties called Magna Carta at Runnymede (15th June, 1215). This event was important for itself, but perhaps even more important for the inspiration which it gave to later generations, who regarded it as a symbol of freedom, although it was largely intended to protect the privileges of the nobility. John fought on, getting his foes excommunicated and hiring mercenaries. Louis of France landed by invitation of John's foes (1216) and took most of England. The barons and citizens led by FitzWalter and Mayor Hardel did homage to Louis in Paul's churchyard and John fled. Hubert de Burgh and Nichola de Camville held Dover and Lincoln for John and some of his enemies wavered. On leaving loyal Lynn John's baggage train and treasure, including some of the regalia, were lost in fording the Welland where it reaches the Wash. John was sick and on reaching Swineshead Abbey regaled himself excessively with new cider and peaches. He reached Newark with difficulty, partly in an 'accursed ill-made litter' and partly on an ambling nag and retired to bed. In dying he found it hard to forgive his enemies. He made those present swear fealty to his little heir Henry and he died on 18th October, 1216, shortly before his forty-ninth birthday. The servants stole everything portable and he was buried, as he had wished, at Worcester, near St. Wulfstan, a saint whose loyalty had attracted John. There can be seen his effigy. None of the barons was great enough to stand up to him, save William Marshal, Earl of Pembroke, and Ranulf, Earl of Chester. John was exhumed in 1797 and found to measure five feet five inches in height.

S. Painter, *The Reign of King John*, 1949.

A. Bryant, 'King John and the Charter', *History Today*, vol. 3, 1953.

T.S.I.H., i, 106. See p. 55 and plate 8 (Bouvines).

ALEXANDER NEQUAM (1157–1217) was born on the same night, 8th September, 1157, as Richard I. Alexander's mother, Hodierna, a woman of St. Albans, was employed to nurse Richard I. Just as Richard I grew to sum up within

Battle of Crécy

Plate 15

Before the Battle of Poitiers (Holkham MS. 659)

Edward III (Sixth Seal, 1340–72, British Museum)

himself the courageous chivalry of the age, so Nequam, who was a scholar, gathered within himself the learning of his day. He was fortunate in his place of birth, for a school in the town of St. Albans was then the best in England. He wrote a treatise on natural science which is remarkable, not so much for original contributions to thought, as for showing the encyclopædic nature of his mind. He was a famous teacher at Paris and Oxford and in 1213 became Abbot of Cirencester. Dante represented him as being in the same part of Hell as his own old tutor was, where vices considered characteristic of schoolmasters were punished. There was not any suggestion of his being really guilty, but Dante was led by Nequam's fame to regard him as an outstanding example of the grammarian's profession. The word *Nequam*, presumably a nickname, happens to be the Latin for 'naughty', and, as medieval minds loved puns, the name had suggested verbal jokes during his lifetime.

J. C. Russell, 'Alexander Neckham in England', *English Historical Review*, vol. 47 (1932), pp. 260–8.

WILLIAM MARSHAL (1146–1219) was younger son of a minor baronial supporter of Matilda. He was a hostage in Stephen's hands (1152). He was a guardian of Prince Henry (1170); but until he was forty years old he was little more than a knight-errant, busy with the brutal tournaments of the time. These had not yet degenerated into courtly pageants. He unhorsed Richard I, when he was a young rebellious prince, and remained faithful to Henry II until the end; but Richard I pardoned him and made him a Justiciar (1191). He opposed Longchamp and fought John (1193), but on Richard's death he helped Hubert Walter to strengthen John's position (1199). He succeeded his brother, John, as Marshal in 1200. His surname was taken from this important office. It meant that he had to play an important part in war and at court. William's five sons inherited the office which then passed through a daughter to the Bigods and Mowbrays and to the present Duke of Norfolk. His marriage with Eva, daughter of Richard de Clare, Strongbow, the conqueror of Ireland, gave him wide estates, for she was heiress of Pembroke and Striguil; and King John, after his coronation, invested him as Earl of Pembroke. He opposed the French expedition of 1205 but was left in charge of England's defence (1206). He became John's chief adviser (1213) and guardian of his heir, Henry, and of England (1214). He became regent when John died (1216) and during the last three years of his life he was the central figure in England's history. One can know William Marshal as no other baron is known, for a nameless troubadour made a rhymed biography for William, his son. His last days show that this man, who beat the French at Lincoln (1217), was kindly and thoughtful in peace, alike as lord, husband and father. He was taken from the Tower by river, followed by his countess, to die at his manor of Caversham. He called the great council to Reading to witness his resignation. They sat round his bed, while he addressed Henry: 'Your barons must choose someone to care for you and your realm to the satisfaction of God and man. May He give you a guardian who will do you honour'. Then he realized no such guardian was possible, and entrusted Henry to the Pope's legate, Pandulf. 'Sire', he said, 'I pray God that if ever I have done anything pleasing to Him, He will give you grace to be a gentleman. If it should happen that you follow the example of some evil ancestor, I pray God not to grant you a long life'. William asked his wife for a kiss 'but it will be for the last time'. Then he was admitted by the Master of the Templars to that crusading order, for William had secretly prepared a Templar's mantle for this a year before. The Master said, 'In the world you have had more honour than any other knight for prowess, wisdom and loyalty. When God granted you His grace to this extent, you may be sure that He wished to have you at the end'. He wondered how the clergy could teach that none could be saved without having restored anything that he had taken from another, for how could knights restore the armour, horses and ransom that they had taken from the conquered? Once he felt a desire for three days to sing, and when he was advised to do so, as it might help his digestion, he said it would be crazy; so his daughters sang to him awhile. Day and night three knights watched over him. He had many fine scarlet robes, at least eighty of which were adorned with costly fur. These were to be left to the knights of his household. At last the Abbot of Reading came to say that Pandulf had seen a vision of William and had sent him absolution of all his confessed sins. His bier was taken to Reading Abbey, thence to Westminster and finally to the Temple. Langton buried him and said, 'Behold all that remains of the best knight who ever lived'. He was tall and dignified with brown hair. For fifty years he was the finest friend to four successive English kings. See plate 8.

S. Painter, *William Knight Errant, Baron and Regent of England*, Baltimore, Johns Hopkins Press, 1933.

T. L. Jarman, *William Marshal first Earl of Pembroke and Regent of England* (*1216–1219*), 1930.

GERALD OF WALES (*c.*1146–*c.*1220), author of a *History of the Conquest of Ireland*, topographies of Ireland and of Wales and of the earliest medieval autobiography, was born at Manorbier Castle, Pembrokeshire. He was the youngest son of a Norman, William de Barri, but his mother was Nesta, a famous Welsh princess, and his origin caused him to be fair to Welshmen and Normans, but to despise Saxons. When he went to Ireland (1184), Gerald's racial or social pride was such that he regarded the Irish as hardly human. In childhood he tells how he used to build monasteries instead of castles in the sand and was afraid of war. His father used to call him 'his little bishop', but Henry II refused to make him Bishop of St. David's (1176) because of his royal Welsh blood. He was educated at Gloucester Abbey and studied in Paris, where he saw two old hags in the street celebrating the birth of Philip Augustus by capering round with lighted tapers, as 'now we have a good stout boy for king who will put your king to shame and loss, you Englishman!' About 1186 he came to Oxford, 'because there were more clerks and more clerkly clerks there' than elsewhere, and he gave three days' public readings of his book on Irish topography. His study of Wales gives wonderful portraits of the Welsh as warriors, hosts and patriots. He knew the great men of his time and gives a rather hostile picture of Henry II in his book *Concerning the Instruction of a Prince.*

The Historical Works of Giraldus Cambrensis, ed. by T. Wright, 1905.

The Autobiography of Giraldus Cambrensis, ed. and translated by H. E. Butler, 1937.

T.S.I.H., i, 89 (boyhood), 90 (description of Wales).

PANDULF (d. 1226) was Papal Legate and one of the most important people in England for ten years following his arrival as Nuncio in 1211. To him King John surrendered his realms. The Pope gave them back to him as to a subject and John was to pay annually a tribute of 1,000 marks (1213). Pandulf had excommunicated John for excluding Archbishop Stephen Langton from England (1211); but later it was Pandulf who excommunicated the Magna Carta Barons and suspended Langton (1215). During Henry III's minority he did not abuse his power by enriching friends or relations, though of course he sometimes rewarded his subordinates. William Marshal realized his worth and when dying (1219) entrusted Henry III to him. Archbishop Langton and Justiciar Hubert de Burgh resented the interference of a Roman and Langton obtained his recall (1221). When he died (16th August, 1226) his body was brought for burial to Norwich Cathedral where he was Bishop (elected 1216, consecrated 1222).

WILLIAM LONGSWORD (d. 1226), natural son of Henry II, became Earl of Salisbury by marrying the countess Ela, then aged about twelve (1198). He was a councillor of John and commanded the English part of the army which Philip Augustus of France beat at Bouvines (1214). He supported John at Runnymede (1215), fought for Henry III at Lincoln and Sandwich (1217), and served with Hubert de Burgh as 'ruler of the King and kingdom' (1222). In 1225 he suffered severely in a stormy voyage home from Gascony but the Virgin appeared as a light at the masthead and saved him. When he died (7th March, 1226), as a sign of his salvation, driving rain failed to extinguish the light of his funeral procession as it went towards the unfinished cathedral of Salisbury. His widow became Abbess of Lacock (Wilts.) and in a vision saw her son, killed on crusade, enter heaven in full armour (1250).

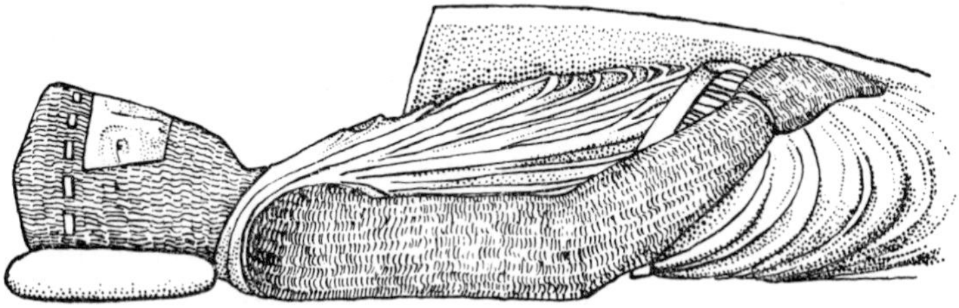

William Longsword (Salisbury Cathedral)

STEPHEN LANGTON (d. 1228) was an Englishman by birth and sentiment, who studied under Peter Lombard, and became Doctor of Theology at Paris. Pope Innocent III made him a cardinal, and when Hubert Walter died (1205) summoned him to Rome (1206) and consecrated him Archbishop of Canterbury at Viterbo (17th June, 1207). King John would not accept him and remarked unkindly and untruthfully that he had never heard anything about him except that he had lived in the realm of his enemy, Philip Augustus, the King of France. England was laid under a strict interdict and the dead could not be buried by priests or in consecrated ground; John retaliated by telling his sheriffs to confiscate church lands and letting his servants persecute the clergy. Meanwhile Langton lived at Pontigny until a threat of deposition by the Pope (1211) frightened John into allowing Langton to land (1213). John submitted to Rome, thereby converting the papacy from an enemy into an ally. Langton gave John the kiss of peace on 20th July, 1213, but on 4th August was co-operating at the Council of St. Albans in a demand for the restoration of the laws of Henry I. He was an active intermediary between John and the opposition in the Magna Carta crisis, being gradually drawn into greater hostility by John's vacillation, and it was he who read the barons' demands to him. The papal commissioner, Pandulf, suspended Langton from office for objecting to the public denunciation of 'disturbers of the King and kingdom', and Innocent III confirmed this suspension and almost deprived him when he went to Rome to attend the Fourth Lateran Council and to explain his attitude. Langton disliked John's acceptance of the Pope as overlord and this made him unpopular in Rome. Innocent III said he was not to revisit England while trouble continued. The general support accorded to young Henry III (1217) let Langton return with the favour of Honorius III (1218). He supported the regency against any papal or baronial threats, alike from Pandulf and from John's former mercenary captain, Falkes de Breauté. He persuaded Honorius not to send a resident legate to succeed Pandulf in England (1220). In 1222 at Oseney (Oxon.) he promulgated various laws for the English church, under one of which Jews were to wear a special badge, and he condemned to the flames a deacon who had become a Jew. In 1224 he was taken ill, and he died at Slindon, Sussex, after successfully obtaining a new reissue of the Great Charter. He may have been England's greatest archbishop, but it is unfortunate for his memory that he lacks a thirteenth-century biographer. He was the greatest English commentator on the Bible (except Bede) and divided it into chapters. His brother Simon, archdeacon of Canterbury, shared his exile and return. Simon supported the barons and became Chancellor of Louis of France (1216) when England experienced a French invasion at the invitation of the barons. After ten years' exile (1217–27) Simon obtained the favour of Henry III.

F. M. Powicke, *Stephen Langton*, 1928.

ROBIN HOOD (alive 1230) has a famous name which is connected with various places and plants and is derived from a forest-elf called *Hodeken*. Little is known of him as a historical character, although he had become a popular hero even before the *Lytell Geste of Robyn Hoode* was printed in the late fifteenth century. Ballad-writers popularized folk-tales about an attractive leader of a merry band of outlaws who lived in the greenwood and robbed the rich to help the poor, and, as in the story of King Arthur, fact is hopelessly mingled with fiction. If he lived in the reign of Richard I it is certain that he could not have had Friar Tuck for a follower, for the Friars did not come to England until after Richard's death. One solid fact is that the sheriff of Yorkshire, a county with which Robin is especially linked in legend, in 1230, was responsible for 32s. 6d. This sum is recorded in the records of the Exchequer and was due from the sale of the belongings of Robin, seized and sold when he was an outlaw. A namesake occurs at Wakefield in the early fourteenth century when one account makes him a supporter of Thomas of Lancaster. He is sometimes called Earl of Huntingdon, but the real earl was William the Lyon, King of Scotland (1143–1214). A slothful secular priest in Piers Plowman did not know the Lord's Prayer properly, but he knew 'rymes of Robyn Hood and Randolf Erle of Chestre'. The latter was Ranulf, who flourished from 1181 to 1232 and was a leading baron, besieging Nottingham for Richard I in 1194 and supporting John against other barons.

PETER DES ROCHES (d. 1238) began life as Treasurer of St. Hilary's church at Poitiers and served in the household of Richard Coeur-de-Lion, the Count of Poitou. As a trusted servant of King John he became Bishop of Winchester (1205); and although Pope Innocent III laid England under an interdict (1208–13) and Peter des Roches was then a bishop, he loyally stayed with John. When old Geoffrey FitzPeter, the justiciar, went, as John put it, to join his predecessor in Hell (1214), des Roches succeeded him. The barons disliked this, as des Roches was more sympathetic to foreign soldiers hired by John than to themselves. The crafty and warlike bishop's successful hold on the mercenaries led to his appointment as Henry III's tutor (1216–27), though Hubert de Burgh obtained his office of justiciar. He played an active part at Lincoln (1217) in the royalist victory over Prince Louis of France, whom he had previously excommunicated, but with the Earl Marshal he refused to fight at Sandwich as they were not 'pirates and fishermen' (see fig. p. 111). When Henry III renounced his guardianship, he joined the crusade (1227) of the Holy Roman Emperor, Frederick II, and he helped to mend a quarrel between Frederick and the Church (1230). He returned to England (1231), won Henry's confidence and engineered the fall of Hubert de Burgh (1232); but Peter fell from favour (1234) and spent his exile helping Pope Gregory IX fight the Romans at Viterbo (1235). He died at Farnham, the manor of the bishops of Winchester. He founded many churches.

LLYWELYN AB IORWERTH (1173–1240), 'the Great', was Prince of North Wales (Gwynedd). A poet no doubt exaggerated when he wrote that 'at ten he was the bold darling of fortune, the terrible Llywelyn', but by 1188 he had certainly begun to harass two uncles who were occupying most of his inheritance. Gerald of Wales was in North Wales at the time and noted the fact. He wrongly supposed that Llywelyn was then only twelve, though he was actually fifteen. Landmarks in the rise of Llywelyn were the expulsion of his uncle Davydd ab Owain (1197), a treaty with a rival ruler, Gwenwynwyn of Powys (1202) and marriage with King John's illegitimate daughter, Joan (1206). John was well informed on Welsh affairs. Throughout his reign John and Llywelyn were friends or foes according to the dictates of intelligent self-interest. Llywelyn aimed at uniting Wales under himself and resisting the threat to local independence offered by the increasing royal power of the kingdom of England. John wished to keep Wales divided and powerless. In 1210 John prevented Llywelyn absorbing the principality of Powys and in 1211 he made him do homage and promise to pay tribute annually. In 1212 the Welsh princes united to help Llywelyn expel the English, though the south and central Welsh principalities had never before united under the lead of Gwynedd. Llywelyn was fortunate in being in his prime, and in having little fear of trouble at home, when Henry III was crowned King of England as a minor. The Earl Marshal decided to appease Llywelyn with concessions. With characteristic public spirit he damaged his own interests as lord of Pembroke by putting the royal castles of Cardigan and Carmarthen into Llywelyn's hands in order to cement a peace made at Worcester with him (1218). Llywelyn even managed to make alliances with the Anglo-Norman lords of the Marches, not only with his old friend the Earl of Chester, but also with the Mortimers and the Braoses. With these families Llywelyn had personal links, as his daughters married members of all of them. These alliances enabled him (1220) to make raids in Pembrokeshire on the lands of the royal representative William Marshal the Younger, his chief foe. In 1223 his successes forced the English to retaliate. He received the only real setback of his career, losing Cardigan and Carmarthen. One of the charges made against Hubert de Burgh (1232) was that he had sent Llywelyn a magic ring. This was a tribute to Llywelyn's reputation as a continual thorn in the side of the English authorities, for to him the discontented could always turn for sympathy. In 1224 Llywelyn openly expressed sympathy for Falkes de Breauté when in revolt; and when Richard Marshal was leading a movement against Peter des Roches (1233–4) it was natural for him to make an alliance with Llywelyn. Llywelyn and Richard were so successful that they captured Shrewsbury and drove Henry III's forces out of the Marches. During Llywelyn's lifetime the internal strife of the Welsh was so far stilled that occasionally Councils were held under his presidency. This unaccustomed unity, combined with Llywelyn's political skill, gave to the Welsh an unusual influence in English affairs.

Llywelyn, Prince of North Wales, never called himself 'Prince of Wales'. In 1230 he adopted the title 'Prince of Aberffraw and lord of Snowdon' because Aberffraw, though only a hamlet, had been since the time of Cadwaladr (d. 664) a 'principal seat' of Gwynedd and its possession was held to confer much dignity. His bard proudly sang 'The South—dost thou not rule it as rightful lord?'. Llywelyn's wife, Joan, was his active helper, and she mediated between Wales and England in 1230. Shortly after, she was imprisoned and disgraced (1230–1), because Llywelyn was horrified to discover that she had allowed herself to be carried away by affection for William de Braose, but she regained his trust.

When she died on 2nd February, 1237, Llywelyn built over her grave a Franciscan friary at Llanvaes (Anglesey). Her stone coffin is now in Beaumaris church.

Llywelyn wished his only son by Joan, Davydd, to succeed him; but there was an elder son, Gruffydd, born of a Welsh mother before Llywelyn had married Joan. A disputed succession, with Gwynedd divided between rivals, meant that Henry III could seize the south and east of Wales and Llywelyn's grandsons were left with only Anglesey and Snowdon (1247) until one, Llywelyn II, conquered his brothers (1254) and headed a Welsh revival. Under the rule of Llywelyn I the unusual peace and prosperity in Wales enabled literature to flourish. The poetry of ten bards, whose names are known, survives. Among others, Llywelyn's kinsman, Einion ab Gwgon, declares 'He to me as the crystal mind; I to him as the hand and the eye'. When he was sixty-five Llywelyn had a slight stroke. He died on 11th April, 1240, at Aberconway Abbey. There he took the monastic habit and was buried:

Gruffydd (Griffin) and Davydd (David) at deathbed of Llywelyn (Matthew Paris)

> 'Lord of nought but the piled up stones of his tomb,
> Of the seven-foot grave in which he lies.'

The illustration is a copy of a sketch by Matthew Paris of the death of Llywelyn. His two sons Gruffydd and Davydd are with him.

Sir J. E. Lloyd, *History of Wales*, 3rd ed., 1939, ii, pp. 587–90, 612-93.

Powys and Gwynedd: see end-paper.

ST. EDMUND RICH OF ABINGDON (*c.* 1170–1240) was a generous and attractive scholar who recruited for a crusade (*c.* 1227). After three elections had been quashed he became Archbishop of Canterbury (1233). He was the chief opponent of royal and papal demands for money, but he gave way to despair and left his friend Robert Grosseteste to continue the struggle. He withdrew to Pontigny and there died (1240). His biographers give details of the novel forms of self-torture which Edmund learned from his pious mother, Mabel, as moral discipline. In 1247 his body was 'translated' in the presence of King Louis IX of France and his mother, Blanche (King John's niece). 'His body', says Matthew Paris, 'was found entire, uncorrupted, and bearing a sweet smell; and, what is more wonderful in a dead body, flexible in all limbs, as is the case with a person sleeping; and his hair and clothing were untainted in colour and substance. . . . Earl Richard (of Cornwall) said "Alas! that it was not ordained on high for us, that is, the King my brother and myself, to have been present at this glorious and solemn translation. For he was our saint by birth, education and promotion, although owing to our sins, he withdrew from England. However, what I was not present to do there, I will do absent,—I will pay reverence and honour to him". And from that time he began to love the saint more sincerely, and to honour him more devoutly. Happening to be oppressed by a severe and secret illness, which endangered his life, he invoked his assistance with confidence, and was happily freed from his disease; whereupon, in his gratitude to God and the saint, he took upon himself to build the front part of the shrine'. English women flocked to the tomb and in 1250 the monks of Pontigny 'horrible to relate, with rash presumption cut off the right arm of the saint . . . and . . . from want of faith presumed to embalm in oil the body of the saint, which the Lord had hitherto preserved entire; and whatever part of the body was so embalmed, was turned to a most foul colour'. Thereafter miracles occurred less frequently. The remains of the miraculous body survived the ravages of French Protestants and French revolutionaries. The site of St. Edmund's house at Oxford is commemorated in the name of St. Edmund Hall.

T.S.I.H., i, 117 (his hair shirt).

HUBERT DE BURGH (d. 1243) came of a respectable Norfolk family. His brother, William, accompanied Prince (later King) John to Ireland (1185), built castles and founded a family, destined to be Earls of Ulster. Robert served John faithfully and is remembered, thanks to Shakespeare, perhaps correctly, as the gaoler of John's nephew, Arthur, at Falaise (1202). He served in France, was made justiciar at Runnymede (1215) and defeated the French fleet at Sandwich (1217). There he blinded the French by discharging quicklime (fig. p. 111). After William the Marshal died (1219) and Pandulf departed (1221), Hubert 'had the realm of England in his hand'. His fourth marriage, to a daughter of William the Lyon called Margaret, like all her sisters, made Hubert brother-in-law to Alexander of Scotland. As Justiciar Hubert controlled royal castles like the Tower and built up a strong position in the Welsh Marches. Through the hostility of Peter des Roches and the unjust suspicions of young Henry III he was dismissed in 1232. He was accused of incredible crimes; of poisoning young William the Marshal, of witchcraft, of seducing the King of Scotland's daughter and of substituting stones and sand for money sent to pay for an expedition to Poitou; but nonetheless his reputation was such that when he was seized in sanctuary at Brentwood, a smith refused to clamp on his fetters (1232). At a trial on Cornhill (London) the charges were not proved, but he was imprisoned at Devizes (1233). He escaped. Two guards dragged him out of sanctuary to be triply chained in a vault. His friends, the bishops, insisted on his being returned again to sanctuary. From there he was rescued by Gilbert Basset, a Wiltshire magnate whose name is commemorated in several Wiltshire place-names. Henry III pardoned him on condition that he did not use his right to manage the affairs of his important ward, Richard of Clare. Clare's marriage, like other important marriages, was a centre of political intrigue and Henry was furious when Hubert's

Hubert de Burgh in sanctuary
(Matthew Paris)

daughter, Meggotta, secretly married Clare (aged sixteen, 1236); for the marriage seemed to be the work of Hubert and an interference in Clare's affairs. Meggotta died the next year and Clare married again within three months. Henry again forgave Hubert. He died, a disappointed man, at Benstead (Surrey), and was buried in the Black Friars' convent, London. His widow, who had been responsible for Meggotta's brilliant but unhappy marriage, died in 1259.

F. M. Powicke, *Henry III and the Lord Edward*, 1957.

ISABEL OF ANGOULÊME (*c.* 1187–1246) was daughter and heiress of Aymer, Count of Angoulême (d. 1213) and Alice, granddaughter of King Louis VI of France. She was betrothed to Hugh de Lusignan the Younger, Count of La Marche, a county strategically situated on the borders of Poitou where the interests of the Angevin Kings of England clashed with those of France. After a divorce King John took Isabel for his second wife (1200). In this John has usually been blamed for passionate and criminal irresponsibility, perhaps with injustice. Isabel was then aged twelve or thirteen. Hugh rebelled (1201) and war followed (1202). Isabel's son, Henry III, was born in 1207 and Richard, Earl of Cornwall, two years later (see pedigree, p. 55). A daughter was betrothed to Hugh, son of Hugh the Younger, as part of a peace treaty (1214). Isabel's father died three years after her husband, and the widowed countess (1219–1220) was harassed by the attacks of Hugh in her attempts to rule Angoulême. She found a solution by marrying her turbulent neighbour, although she had been betrothed to his father and he was betrothed to her daughter. This was Hugh X of Lusignan, not her first love, as is generally stated. He tried to keep Isabel's dower, and her daughter Joanna's dowry, to neither of which he had a right. War followed and he helped King Louis VIII of France to attack Aquitaine (1224). Sick of French rule (1241) Isabel goaded Hugh into rebellion against France. In outraged dignity she left him for Angoulême, crying: 'Get out of my sight! Am I a waiting maid to stand while they sit at ease?'. This rebellion encouraged Henry III to make a campaign in

Gascony, but he was nearly captured at Taillebourg (1242). Hugh quickly made peace with France and Henry was forced to accept defeat (1243). Isabel died at Fontevraud (1246). Dislike of French authority drove Isabel's children by Hugh de Lusignan to seek refuge at the court of their half-brother Henry III (1247), and it did not make him popular with the barons when he befriended his foreign relations.

H. S. Snellgrove, *The Lusignans in England*, University of New Mexico Press, Albuquerque, 1950.

La Marche and Angoulême: see end-paper.

RICHARD OF WYCH (?1197–1253) was named after his birthplace, Droitwich. His youth was impoverished by his father's death. His elder brother advised him to make a prudent marriage. He was then studying at Oxford, where a priest wasted his savings, and he had to share a gown with two undergraduates and live on bread and vegetables. He proceeded to Paris and Bologna universities, refused his tutor's daughter in marriage, and became Chancellor of Oxford University and Chancellor of Archbishop Edmund Rich. He remained with Edmund until death separated them in 1240 and gave Matthew Paris material for a biography. In 1244 he became Bishop of Chichester, to the rage of Henry III who kept the temporal properties of the see until 1246. Henry's annoyance was due to Richard's opposition to absolute royal rule. Richard travelled busily round his diocese winning general affection. He dressed simply but decently, wore a hair shirt and was a vegetarian out of humanitarianism. He died at Dover (3 April, 1253) while preaching a sermon to arouse enthusiasm for a crusade, and was buried in his cathedral. The omission of his festival at Droitwich in 1646 was followed by the failure of a local well. The well ceased being dry, it was said, when the festival was restored.

W. R. W. Stephens, *Memorials of the South Saxon See and Cathedral Church of Chichester*, 1876.

ROBERT GROSSETESTE or GREATHEAD (1175–1253) was the greatest Bishop of Lincoln, and such a great scholar that his name is quoted in almost every book written within two centuries of his death. He was born at Stradbroke (Suffolk) of stock humble enough for the fact to be cast in his teeth by the canons of Lincoln; and his brother never left husbandry.

Grosseteste and Pope Innocent IV at Lyons, 1245 (Matthew Paris)

Henry III marries Eleanor of Provence (Matthew Paris)

He admired the friars when they came to England (1221 and 1224) and was the first Reader of the Oxford Franciscans. Their historian, Brother Thomas of Eccleston, says they soon progressed under him in scholastic discussion and subtle moralities suitable for preaching: he was a voluminous writer and was most unusual for his period in that he studied Greek. A great library which he left to the Oxford Franciscans is scattered, but nine books from it have been identified by his autograph notes in them. As an old-fashioned biblical scholar he did not stir his contemporaries, but our generation has come to realize that he was an originator of experimental science of great influence on science in Oxford, especially through his pupil and admirer, Roger Bacon. He regarded the shrinkage of the power of the bishops as evil and resisted the encroachments of popes, archbishops, abbots and King Henry III. Though theoretically the most fervent supporter of the papacy, he objected to popes 'providing' nominees to vacant livings, and indeed in the last year of his life refused to obey a papal mandate on behalf of a nephew of the Pope. His hand was so much against every man that Matthew Paris compared him with Ishmael; yet his personality and charm delighted the Earl of Gloucester and he knew Simon de Montfort so well that he not only influenced him for good but was free to borrow his excellent cook for an excessively long period. As a man of principle he resigned the archdeaconries of Wiltshire, Northampton and Leicester, because he thought pluralism wrong (1232); yet his moderation made him tell a Dominican that food, sleep and good humour were necessary for temporal salvation. He liked to see friars' clothes patched, but he was able to prescribe wine to a melancholy friar. He lectured at Oxford as early as 1200–9 and his writing covered husbandry and French poetry as well as Greek translations and theology and philosophy; but his hardest work was done as bishop (1235–53) when he was over sixty-five during the last twenty years of a full life. In these years he visited the papal court and did much of his writing, though he had begun as early as 1200. Robert Marsh, Archdeacon of Oxford, has recorded how Grosseteste, when an old man, made the most vehement sermon against abuses ever heard by a pope (13 May, 1250) (see picture by Matthew Paris, p. 127). A list of Grosseteste's works would occupy twenty-five pages. His letters have been printed. In 1253 he fell ill at Buckden (Hunts.), a manor of the Bishops of Lincoln, and sent for his friend John of St. Albans, a doctor who had saved him from being deliberately poisoned sixteen years before. He was buried in his cathedral. Bells

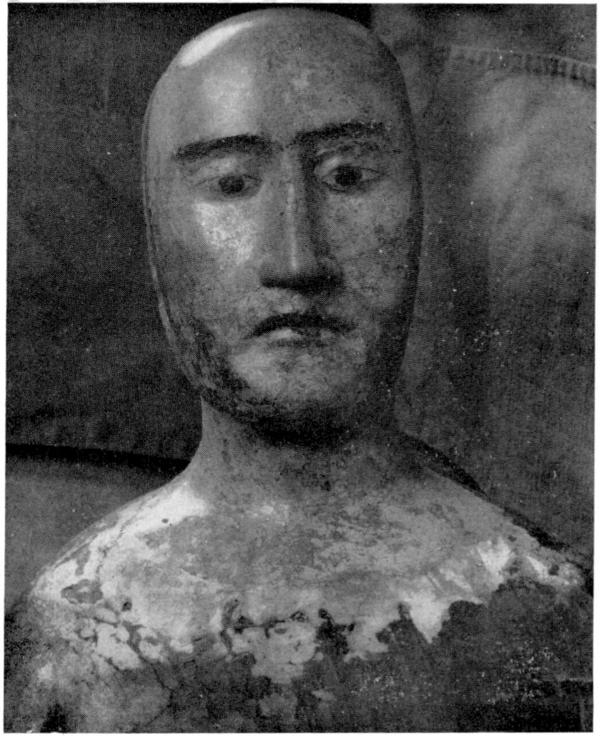

Edward III, Death Mask

Plate 17

Edward III, Effigy, Westminster Abbey. (Photo, Warburg Institute.)

Edward III and his sons. (From the Society of Antiquaries' copy of a wall painting in St. Stephen's Chapel, Westminster. The original is destroyed.)

Plate 18

rang in the sky when he died, and miracles occurred at his tomb.

Robert Grosseteste Essays, ed. by D. A. Callus, 1955, discusses episcopal administration, relations with King and Pope, attempts at canonization (1280 and 1307), and the opening of his tomb.

See end-paper for the vast Lincoln diocese.

T.S.I.H., i, 116.

MATTHEW PARIS (*c.* 1200–59) became a monk of St. Albans (1217). Its position on the great north road attracted many important visitors and the guests' stables could accommodate 300 horses. Matthew learnt much about the world from such visitors, including Henry III who was a frequent visitor, often for a week at a time; and he saw such events outside as the Translation of St. Thomas Becket at Canterbury (1200) and the marriage of Henry III and Queen Eleanor (1236) which he describes in sumptuous detail. Indeed he went as far as Norway on papal business (1247 or 1248); and he says that at the feast of St. Edward the Confessor (always especially honoured by Henry) at Westminster (1247) 'the king was seated on his throne, noticing the writer of this work, he called him to him, made him sit down on a step between the throne and the rest of the hall, and said to him: "You have noticed all these things, and they are firmly impressed on your mind". To which he answered: "Yes, my lord, for the splendid doings of this day are worthy of record". The king then went on: " . . . write an accurate and full account of all these events . . . lest in the future their memory be in any way lost to posterity"; and he invited the person with whom he was speaking to dinner, together with his three companions'. Between about 1245 and 1259 he wrote many diligent, entertaining and intelligent, though unsystematic works, largely based on personal knowledge. His strong prejudices reflect the dislike for foreigners and friars and tyranny of an English Benedictine with a dislike for authority; they have influenced later opinions on the relationship between king and barons. Though he loved malicious gossip and was unjust to friars he was prepared to modify some earlier criticisms of Archbishop Boniface of Savoy. Henry III personally gave him facts, and Matthew did not hesitate to argue with him about hunting rights (1251) or speak up to him on behalf of Oxford University. He enlivened his manuscripts with original drawings, verses and eye-witness accounts. His *Chronica Majora* is the first illustrated chronicle of current affairs. His wide interests included natural history and prompted him to include drawings of cannibal Tartars and an elephant, and his maps are a landmark in the history of cartography.

For his drawings, see plates 8 and 10. See also pp. 111, 122, 124 and 127.

T.S.I.H., i, 110, 112, 120 (extracts).

R. Vaughan, *Matthew Paris*, Cambridge Studies in Medieval Life and Thought, New Series, vol. 6, 1958, contains many facsimiles and prints long lists of people known to have visited St. Albans and to have given Matthew information.

V. H. Galbraith, *Roger Wendover and Matthew Paris, 1944*.

PETER DES RIVAUX (before 1190–1262), was born in Poitou, a kinsman, perhaps the son, of Peter des Roches. He came to England in youth, was actively concerned with the finances of the royal household (1218–23) and gained many preferments. After a period of eclipse (1223–30) he gained great power (1232–4) after the fall of the justiciar, Hubert de Burgh, overhauling local and central government finance, having custody of King Henry III's small seal and of many castles, and controlling all important sources of revenue. He was for a while sheriff of twenty-one shires at once and controlled all the other sheriffs; and it was his control of all royal rights to arrange marriages and wardships which aroused the frightened hostility of Henry's vassals. Peter des Rivaux fell out of favour (1234–6), but he was later Keeper of the Wardrobe (1258).

Sir M. Powicke, *The Thirteenth Century 1216-1307* (The Oxford History of England. Ed. by Sir G. Clark), 1953, especially pp. 48–9, 51–2 and 60–5.

SIMON DE MONTFORT (1208–65) was rightly regarded as a hero in his own day. His place in history books has been large because his acts made a most important contribution to the history of Parliament. The tyrannous incompetence of Henry III made the barons determined not to lose the benefits secured by their fathers in Magna Carta. The outstanding ability and lofty character of Simon made him their natural leader in an opposition which culminated in civil war. Simon's government did not last long enough for it to become unpopular, as the Commonwealth government of Cromwell became unpopular four centuries later. Simon was not only an outstanding personality in an age of great personalities, but he is one of the most memorable characters in English constitutional history, even though he would not have understood the ideas of democracy and toleration now associated with representative government. He began life as a French adventurer and was the second son of Simon of Montfort L'Amaury (Ile de France) who had led a crusade against heretics in Toulouse. His elder brother was Constable of France. Simon 'the Righteous' shared his father's hatred of Jews and heretics and was intolerant of everything which he thought evil. Through an English grandmother Simon had a claim on the Earldom of Leicester. He first figures in England as one of the unpopular foreigners who landed with Eleanor of Provence (1236). At her coronation he acted as Grand Seneschal, an office attached to his earldom. He shocked Richard Earl of Cornwall by marrying Eleanor, sister of Richard and Henry III, without the Council's consent and although she had vowed to remain a widow (1238). The next year Simon had the first of many quarrels with Henry. A crusader like his father (1240–2), he fell under the saintly influence of the scholarly Franciscan, Adam Marsh, and of Bishop Grosseteste, and settled quietly at Kenilworth Castle (1243–8). He was preparing to join King Louis IX on another crusade when Henry III asked him to pacify Gascony (1248). There he inevitably made enemies, he was recalled and was put on trial (1252). Henry called Montfort a traitor and Montfort called Henry a liar. Eventually Montfort withdrew to the kingdom of France in vexation and there the French barons wanted to make him seneschal and regent. Henry III went to Gascony, and, when he saw the actual situation, he persuaded Simon to return (1253); but cooperation between Henry and Simon had become impossible and the latter emerged as the leader of the barons in opposing foreign favourites at court, in spite of his own French origin.

William of Valence, Earl of Pembroke, suggested that those who blamed foreigners for setbacks in Wales were really allies of the Welsh. He called Simon a traitor and they nearly came to blows (1258). That year the barons' party rallied round a league formed between the Earls of Gloucester, Hereford, Leicester and Pembroke, and drew up 'Provisions' at Oxford to subject the King to a Council and a 'Parliament' consisting of fifteen and twelve barons each.

In 1260 Simon held a parliament and transacted important business in it contrary to Henry's orders; but Henry regained power, and, although Simon rebutted a charge of treason, he withdrew temporarily to France. Gloucester's death (1262) and a visit abroad by Henry encouraged Simon to return (1263). Simon declared war on the enemies of the Provisions of Oxford, captured castles, arrested the Savoyard Bishop of Hereford on the steps of his own cathedral altar, and forced the royal family to seek refuge from the riotous Londoners in the Tower.

Again Henry asserted himself with the help of the Lord Edward, and Simon had to accept the arbitration of Louis IX. By the 'Mise of Amiens' (1264) Louis cancelled the Provisions of Oxford. Simon rebelled against this decision saying: 'I have been in many lands and nowhere have I found men so faithless as in England; but, though all forsake me I and my four sons will stand for the just cause.' Simon was not however alone. The Franciscans, the Oxford students and town poor were for him; and at this juncture he had the support of Gilbert de Clare, the new Earl of Gloucester. The ensuing civil war reached a climax at Lewes where Simon's men wore white crosses on their breasts and backs like crusaders. Simon's generalship gained in a few hours the ground lost in three years and Henry III had to accept Simon's terms in the 'Mise of Lewes' (1264). Simon was supreme. He called a parliament (1265) which included two citizens from every borough in addition to the usual churchmen, barons and knights. This is the basis of his fame with those who see history as the story of the detailed development of modern parliamentary arrangements; but it was only mentioned by one writer at the time, as the importance of this step did not then strike observers. Simon's rule was imperilled by a quarrel with young Gilbert de Clare which led to renewed war (May, 1265). Prince Edward was kept for safety with Simon but he managed to escape, with the help of Gilbert's brother Thomas, who was then with Simon at Hereford and apparently still loyal to him.

Edward and Simon went out as if to hunt; and in pursuing the deer they eluded the Prince's keepers. Edward outdistanced pursuit and reached Wignore Castle. There Gilbert and others joined him. They cut off Simon from his main support which lay far away beyond the Severn. Simon summoned the help of his son, young Simon, from Sussex. Young Simon's men reached Kenilworth and were resting in the village and priory on August 2nd, when Margot, a female spy in male attire, brought in the Lord Edward and Gilbert de Clare to surprise them. Many were taken prisoner in their beds. On August 3rd, Simon reached Evesham and heard the bad news. He knew he would be surrounded. Though Henry III was his enemy, Simon had Henry with him in the anti-royalist army; and in the morning of August 4th the two hostile brothers-in-law had Mass together. When Simon saw Edward's well-ordered army he remarked that the prince had profited from lessons learnt of himself. The royalists charged with the cry 'Death to the Traitor'. Simon was unhorsed and fell. His mutilated body was thrown to the dogs, but the monks of Evesham brought the remains to their church on an old ladder, covered by a torn coat. They buried the corpse decently, but it was disinterred and thrown into the sewer. Thus Simon, unlike Cromwell, who killed his king, won a martyr's crown, and the fact helped sanctify the memory of his work. Simon died in a hair shirt and was reputed to have kept vigil longer than he slept at night. A monk of Evesham recorded over two hundred of his miracles. Some of them were associated with the Earl's Well (also called Battle Well or de Montfort's Well) on the battlefield. Here the water cured a horse of the Countess of Gloucester, though it had been broken-winded for two years. These miracles had to be kept secret because of the government's disapproval. One sick woman sent a girl for a pitcher of water. Some castle servants asked her what she was carrying; and when she said it was beer, they suspected that it was water from the Earl's well. They looked in the pitcher and saw beer there, so they let her go; but when she reached the sick woman the liquid was water again, and it healed her.

Such stories show the affection felt for Simon by his supporters. A window at Chartres shows Simon as a young knight with prominent eyes. See plate 9.

C. Bémont, *Simon de Montfort Earl of Leicester, 1208–65*, New Ed., translated by E. F. Jacobs, 1930.

T.S.I.H., i, 121.

E. F. Jacob, *Studies in the Period of Baronial Reform and Rebellion, 1258–1267* (Oxford Studies in Social and Legal History, vol. 8), 1925.

C. E. Petit-Dutaillis, *Feudal Monarchy in France and England from the 10th to the 13th century*, 1936.

HENRY DE BRACTON (d. 1268) wrote an important, though unfinished, study of the law, 'On the Laws and Customs of England'. He is first mentioned in 1240, when he had apparently recently become a royal clerk. His name often occurs in the public records between 1245 and 1267. A serious consideration of the meaning of law and custom foreshadowed the important legal activity of Edward I. It was reflected locally in manor courts for which written records of proceedings begin in the second half of the thirteenth century.

H. G. Richardson, two articles on Bracton in *English Historical Review*, vol. 59 (1944).

F. Schulz, 'Bracton on Kingship', *English Historical Review*, vol. 60 (1945).

RICHARD EARL OF CORNWALL (1209–72) was second son of King John. In addition to the earldom of Cornwall with its rich tin-mines (1225) he received the castles of Berkhamstead and Wallingford, each the centre of a great 'honour', or group of dependent manors. In the year in which he acquired Wallingford (1231) his position as a leading baron was confirmed by a marriage with the widowed Countess of Gloucester, daughter of old William the Marshal. But in spite of a fierce little quarrel about a manor with his brother, Henry III, and popularity earned by his opposition to foreigners at court, Richard developed into a loyal brother and a steadying influence. His sympathy for Queen Eleanor of Provence was fostered by his second marriage, which was with Sanchia, her sister (1243). He recovered Gascony (1225–7); and gained a great European reputation by leading a crusade (1240). He was the friend of the Holy Roman Emperor, Frederick II, and of Pope Innocent IV. He refused the Crown of Sicily (1252), but, as the Emperor's intended successor, was crowned at Aachen 'King of the Romans' or 'Kyng of Alemaigne' (1257). As such he was recognized in the Rhineland, but the honour caused a considerable drain on his purse, although he had one of the biggest fortunes in Europe. In 1263 Richard supported Simon de Montfort against the violators of the 'Provisions of Oxford' but the threat of violence drove him back to Henry III's side, and when his attempts at mediation failed he led the left wing for the royalists at the 'detestable Battle of Lewes' (1264). There he was captured in a windmill on the Downs to the delight of popular song-writers. Most wrote rhyming Latin verses like the *Song of Lewes*, a defence of de Montfort, but this occasion produced the earliest surviving political verses written in English. He remained captive in de Montfort's castle of Kenilworth until after the Battle of Evesham (1265). Then he was freed and he agreed to be the loyal friend of his sister Eleanor, whose marriage (1233) to de Montfort he had hated. If he had been an unscrupulous leader of the opposition to his brother, he would have been a hero to the monastic chroniclers. He shared Henry's piety and was especially devoted to the new cult of the Archbishop of Canterbury, Edmund Rich of

Abingdon (1231–40). Regarded as unreliable in England and as an object of scorn in Germany, Richard was heartbroken by the murder of his son by the sons of de Montfort (1271). Richard died a soured and prematurely old man in the same year as his brother. He was buried in his own foundation, the Abbey of Hailes.

N. Denholm-Young, *Richard of Cornwall*, 1947.

HENRY III (1207–1272) was a 'pretty little knight' aged nine when, on October 28th, 1216, he did homage to Guala as the papal representative, and was crowned at Gloucester with his mother's circlet by his tutor, Peter des Roches. The enemies of Henry's father King John were in revolt and Prince Louis of France held London and all the Channel ports except Dover. Next day the Earl of Chester, Randulf de Blundeville, the greatest baron in England, arrived and helped John's executors to persuade old William the Marshal to become *rector* of the king and kingdom. In November they renewed the Great Charter at Bristol. This meant leaving their opponents with no distinct political principles and eased the military task of John's ruthless captain, Falkes de Breauté, in the south Midlands in the seven shires of which he was sheriff. The king's mother, Isabel of Angoulême, left England and married again (1220), the Marshal died (1219), Guala's successor Pandulph departed (1221) and Hubert de Burgh ruled undisturbed until 1223. Then Henry, aged sixteen, became fully responsible for the disposal of his seals, castle, lands and wardships. He actually resumed control of several scores of castles with the aid of Archbishop Stephen Langton in spite of rebellion by Falkes de Breauté at Bedford.

Henry III
(Matthew Paris)

In 1227, when nineteen, he declared himself of full age. He had a drooping eyelid and his forehead became lined with care. His life fell in a period when there were many great men, but his only great achievement was the completion of Westminster

Abbey (1269). Expenditure on such luxuries combined with a costly foreign policy forced Henry to make extraordinary demands for money. He is memorable because he showed himself unfitted to exercise supreme power (1234–58). By acting as if Magna Carta had never been, he provoked the opposition of the barons and made possible the rise of Simon de Montfort.

Dante represents him in Purgatory among those punished for being negligent rulers. A favourite theme painted on the walls of his palaces was Fortune with her wheel, raising kings up from nothing and casting them down again. The metaphor of this wheel is much used by Matthew Paris in his account of the events of this reign. Unsuccessful in war, whether in Wales (1228) or Gascony (1242–3), he was equally unsuccessful at home, and the defeat of Simon de Montfort's baronial rebellion was due not to Henry but to his son, later Edward I. His generosity to guests, his cosmopolitan tastes and his family feeling led to love of foreigners, his greatest sin in the eyes of his English bishops and barons. The Lusignans, children of his mother's second marriage, arrived in 1246 to increase the unpopularity which he had earned by his encouragement of his wife's family in 1236. Henry's personality was completely overshadowed by his brother and his brothers-in-law (see plates 8 and 9 and pedigree, p. 55).

A political song runs:

> "The king that tries without advice to seek his people's weal
> Must often fail, he cannot know the wants and woes they feel;
> The Parliament must tell the king how he may serve them best,
> And he must see their wants fulfilled and injuries redressed.
> A king should seek his people's good, and not his own sweet will,
> Nor think himself a slave because men hold him back from ill;

For they that keep the king from sin serve him the best
of all,
Making him free that else would be to sin a wretched
thrall."

His death-bed, on November 16, was disturbed by the cries of rioting Londoners, "We, we are the commune of the city."

F. M. Powicke, *King Henry and the Lord Edward*, 2 vols., 1947.

LLYWELYN AB GRUFFYDD (d. 1282) was son of Gruffyd ab Llywelyn, who broke his neck trying to escape from the Tower of London (1244), and grandson of the greatest of all Welsh rulers Llywelyn ab Iorwerth, who married a daughter of King John. He succeeded his uncle Davydd II as Prince of Gwynedd, in north-west Wales (1246) and did homage (1247), as his grandfather had done (1216), to Henry III. He was helped, as his grandfather had been, by English dissensions, and he supported Simon de Montfort (1262). He fought Prince Edward and forced him to make a truce (1263), and was eventually (1267) recognized as Prince of Wales, a unique honour, though subject to the English crown. He thus became overlord of the other Welsh princes and became himself the only Welsh tenant-in-chief of the crown. On the accession of Edward I (1272) Llywelyn stopped certain promised annual payments to England, absented himself from the coronation and refused homage. He refused to attend Parliament as he said he would be unsafe in England. He quarrelled with his brother Davydd III and Gruffydd ab Gwenwynwyn, Lord of

Gruffydd ab Llywelyn falls from the Tower, 1244 (Matthew Paris)

Cveiliog or Upper Powys, and drove them to England (1274). Edward I took advantage of the legal right which Llywelyn had given him to make war (1277). Edward soon confined Llywelyn's power to the north, built a military road along the coast and cut off corn supplies from Anglesey. Llywelyn surrendered at the Treaty of Aberconway (1277), and Edward I attended his marriage with Eleanor, daughter of Simon de Montfort (1278). Edward's contempt for Welsh customs united Llywelyn even with his hated brother Davydd and goaded them into rebellion. Edward soon drove the Welsh to Snowdon, but Llywelyn himself was actually in Radnorshire when he was killed (1282). His head, crowned with ivy, was set on London Bridge and thus was fulfilled a prophecy that Llywelyn would wear his crown in London. Davydd was betrayed and executed after six months (1283). Edward divided Wales into counties, and built strategic castles with great curtain walls and gatehouses. In this formative period of Welsh history Llywelyn was the last great champion of Welsh liberty, but, though he fell, a rebellious love of freedom remained and the bards sang of his generosity.

J. G. Edwards, *Littere Wallie*, University of Wales, 1940. This register of documents (1217–92) has an introduction which discusses Llywelyn.

ALEXANDER III (1241–85), 'the peaceable king' of Scotland, was son of Alexander II (1198–1249) and Mary, the daughter of Engelram de Couci, a French magnate. He was crowned king at Scone when aged eight or nine. At his coronation a venerable Highlander recited in Gaelic the royal descent from heroes of Celtic legend, thereby flattering the Celts at the expense of the English. Alexander married Margaret, a daughter of Henry III, and received knighthood at the hand of Henry III (1251). He did homage to Henry III for Lothian and for lands in England, but not for the kingdom of Scotland (1251). Alexander aided Henry against the barons (1264) and Henry in turn aided Alexander against the Scottish barons. Alexander did homage to Edward I (1278) and his relations with England were always friendly. A great event of his reign was the defeat of Hakon of Norway at the battle of Largs (1263) whereby he obtained the Isle of Man and the Hebrides from Norway. Hakon's son, Eric, married Alexander's daughter, Margaret, who had a daughter, also called Margaret. This daughter was born at Windsor during one of Alexander's frequent visits to Henry's court. She became famous under the name of the Maid of Norway (1283–90); for when Alexander was killed by a fall from his horse, she was recognized as his heir, at the age of three (1285). Her death at sea when crossing from Norway prevented a marriage between her and the Prince of Wales (later Edward II) which was intended by Edward I to unite England and Scotland under a single crown.

Hume Brown, *History of Scotland*, 1911. See p. 85 and plate 1.

MARGARET, THE 'MAID OF NORWAY' (1283–90), was the daughter of Eric II of Norway and of Margaret, daughter of Alexander III of Scotland. In 1284 the nobles acknowledged the baby as heir to the Scottish throne. Edward I arranged a marriage between her and his son Edward (1287). A treaty reserved all the rights and laws of Scotland; but Margaret died in the Orkneys on her way to England from Bergen. This marriage was intended to unite England and Scotland under one crown, as was achieved in the person of James VI of Scotland and I of England over three centuries later. If it had been successful, Edward I would not have conquered Scotland and Robert Bruce would not have liberated it; thus generations of unneighbourly strife might have been avoided.

ELEANOR OF CASTILE (*c.* 1245–1290), daughter of Ferdinand III of Castile, was less than ten years old when she married (1254) the Lord Edward, aged fifteen, at Las Huelgas. Eighteen years later her husband became King Edward I. This marriage brought to a conclusion a war in Guienne between Eleanor's father-in-law, Henry III, and her brother, Alphonso the astronomer. Alphonso renounced his claim to Gascony and Henry III made Edward Lord of Gascony and the Channel Isles and Earl of Chester. He gave costly wedding feasts. So many kings attended a feast in Paris that it was called the Feast of Kings. Henry gave Eleanor Guildford Castle, her favourite seat. In 1264–5 Eleanor fled to France from Simon de Montfort and in 1266 she bore her first child, John, who died young. In 1270 Eleanor accompanied Edward on a crusade. An attempt was made to assassinate Edward with a poisoned dagger. Hearsay, repeated fifty years later in the *Ecclesiastical History* of Ptolemy of Lucca, is the sole basis for the story that Eleanor sucked out the poison from the wound. The romantic incident is one of the best remembered stories of the later crusades, though it seems not quite in keeping with the story that Edward had her carried out shrieking so that she should not see the surgeon cut away the flesh. Her kindly deed is attributed a few years later by a Flemish writer, John of Ypres, to someone else, Otto de Grandison. John of Ypres was unfamiliar with English history and wrote in ignorance of the fact that Grandison was in fact the trusted friend and secretary of Edward I, facts which suggest that the incident may have occurred, but that Grandison, not Eleanor, may have been the central figure in it. Eleanor was crowned Queen at Westminster with great festivities. The conduits ran with wine. Llywelyn refused to attend. War with Wales followed and Llywelyn's wife, Eleanor de Montfort, was captured and placed in the kindly care of Eleanor of Castile. All Eleanor's previous sons had died when, on 25 April, 1284, she gave birth at Caernarvon to Edward of Caernarvon, later Edward II. The baby was married by proxy to the Maid of Norway, heiress of Alexander III of Scotland. She was to be placed in

Eleanor of Castile
(Westminster Abbey)

Eleanor's charge, but died on the voyage. Eleanor fell ill with a fever when following Edward I to Scotland. She died on 29 November, 1290. The journey of her coffin to Westminster was marked by the erection at all the halting places of 'Eleanor Crosses'. Perhaps Charing Cross is the most famous. The others were built at Lincoln, Grantham, Stamford, Geddington near Kettering, Northampton, Stony Stratford, Woburn, Dunstable, St. Albans, Waltham and Cheap. Those at Northampton and Geddington still stand. A groundless tradition derived the name *Charing* from *chère reine*, because the Cross commemorated the dear queen. There is a beautiful effigy of Eleanor in Westminster Abbey (see fig. p. 141). She left seven daughters.

For the story of the poisoned wound see C. L. Kingsford, 'Sir Otho de Grandison, 1238(?)–1328', *Royal Historical Society Transactions*, 3rd series, 125–95, vol. 3 (1909).

ELEANOR OF PROVENCE (d. 1291), Queen of Henry III, was one of the beautiful daughters of Raymond Berenger, Count of Provence, and of Beatrice, daughter of the Count of Savoy. Eleanor was important because of the high stations occupied by Raymond's distinguished sons-in-law. Her marriage (1236) was celebrated with splendid ceremonial, described by Matthew Paris. Her eldest son, Edward I, was born three years later. Her daughter, Margaret, married King Alexander III of Scotland when ten years old (1251). Eleanor accompanied Henry III to Gascony (1243), was joint regent (1253) and collected mercenaries to fight the barons (1264); but she is especially memorable for the unpopularity brought on the royal family by the arrival of her uncles who were resented as foreign adventurers. Of them, Peter of Savoy became Earl of Richmond (1241). His house in the Strand is still commemorated by the name of a hotel on the site. William Bishop of Valence and his high-handed dependents were here for only three years but that was enough. Boniface of Savoy succeeded Edmund Rich as Archbishop of Canterbury (1241–70), and ruled conscientiously. Eleanor was personally unpopular in London because she had a right to dues on cargoes landed at Queenhithe. This unpopularity flared up during Simon de Montfort's rebellion (1263). The royal family fled to the Tower and Henry III tried to send her up the Thames by barge to Windsor. The London mob on London Bridge pelted the barge with blocks of stone, rotten eggs and sheep's bones, crying 'Drown the Witch! Drown the Witch!'. Her son, Prince Edward, was incensed, and the following year lost the Battle of Lewes (1264) by indulging in a running slaughter of the routed London contingent when his men were desperately needed on the Sussex Downs. Eleanor was less than half Henry III's age, and her widowhood lasted nineteen years (1272–91). The last eleven years were spent in retirement at Amesbury Abbey. There she became a nun at the same time as her granddaughter Mary (1284), and there Edward I built her a tomb, on his return from the crusade.

F. M. Powicke, *King Henry III and the Lord Edward*, 2 vols., 1947.
T.S.I.H., i, 112 (marriage).

JOHN PECHAM (*c.* 1225–92) was the first Franciscan friar to become Archbishop of Canterbury and he succeeded Kilwardby, the first Dominican to hold that office. The register of his official acts is the first to survive for Canterbury and gives a detailed account of his activities. Pecham was born at Patcham (Sussex), became a Franciscan about 1250, and studied at Oxford and Paris. At the latter his teacher was the famous visionary Bonaventura. Pecham was an authority on optics as well as theology. He became Provincial Minister in 1276 and in 1277 went to Rome as Lector in Theology. In 1278 Nicholas III nominated him to succeed Kilwardby as Archbishop of Canterbury. Nicholas made Kilwardby Cardinal Bishop of Prato, which meant that he would have to leave Canterbury for Rome, and there Kilwardby died the following year. When Kilwardby first became archbishop Edward I was disappointed as he would have preferred Robert Burnell, his legal adviser. In 1278 the monks of Canterbury acted as Edward wished and elected Burnell, but the Pope appointed Pecham, for Burnell, though a bishop, was not a good man. The multifarious activities of Pecham as archbishop included holding fifteen councils in twelve years. He struggled to improve the secular clergy and to combat ignorance, absenteeism and pluralism. He encouraged preaching, and though loyal could speak plainly to Edward I. When he became archbishop he offended Edward I by having Magna Carta posted up on all the cathedral doors, as if it was being ignored by the king; and he quickly aroused the opposition of the bishops under the leadership of St. Thomas of Cantilupe, Bishop of Hereford, a good man with whom Pecham failed to see eye to eye. On the one hand Pecham wanted to see rights of church courts protected from the encroachments of royal courts, and on the other hand he wanted to assert the rights of the archbishop's court against the rights of bishops' courts. His attitude towards monastic houses under his jurisdiction may have seemed to their heads one of fussy interference, animated by a friar's prejudice against monks, but his practical financial advice was invaluable. He always retained his personal simplicity and friendliness, and as a good friar he used to travel on foot instead of on horseback when making his frequent visitations. He wrote to Edward I on behalf of the safety of the conquered Welsh clergy and he told him that Cistercians were the hardest neighbours that bishops or parsons could have. Modern Franciscans praise his writings. His letters have been printed and reflect his opinions. Most of England and all of Wales would have seen this outspoken, argumentative, and conscientious man. He died on 8 December, 1292 at Mortlake, ill and, according to the letters of his chaplain, very irritable. He is buried at Canterbury. His effigy shows a tall man with a broad face and high cheekbones, dignified and serene, but with an ill-tempered mouth.

Decima Douie, *Archbishop Pecham*, 1952.

ROGER BACON (*c.* 1214–94) was born in Somerset. When Henry III came to Oxford (1233), at a time when Peter des Roches was very unpopular, Bacon asked him a pointed political riddle, 'What do sailors fear most?' 'Stones (*pierres*) and rocks (*roches*)'. In spite of this criticism of a royal favourite the only fact known about Bacon's family is that his

Plate 19
Thomas de la Mare, Abbot of St. Albans (brass)

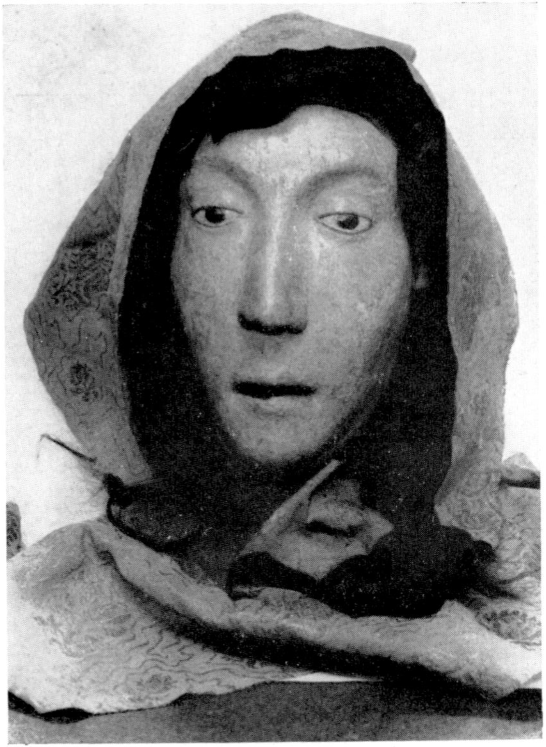

Anne of Bohemia, Death Mask

Plate 20

Richard II, Effigy (Westminster Abbey)

brother had to go into exile for supporting Henry III against de Montfort (1258-67); and that they were evidently not poor, as Bacon says he spent heavily on books and scientific instruments. He was a vigorous genius who insisted on observation in science and on combining the study of science with that of languages. He believed that learning should be concerned with the actual world, the things known to laymen, old women, soldiers, ploughmen, metal-workers and miners, and was not just an affair of ingenious verbal quibbles. He became a Franciscan and worked alternately at Oxford and Paris, where his lecture on Metaphysics (*c.* 1245) opened a new field. The range of his interests was enormous and he studied optics, anatomy, medicine, mathematics, the formula for gunpowder, Greek, Latin and Hebrew. He was much influenced by Grosseteste (d. 1253) but said 'I have learned more important truths beyond comparison from men of humble station, who are not named in the schools, than from all the famous doctors'. He was impatient, not only with pedants, but even with the truly learned, like the Dominicans, Albert the Great and Thomas Aquinas, and his fellow Franciscan, Alexander of Hales. The Franciscans came to suspect him, either because his thought was too daring, because his experiments savoured of magic, because of his exposure of pretentious pedants, or because his matter-of-fact approach would be unsympathetic to the lofty mysticism of St. Bonaventura, the new general of the Franciscan order (1256). On papal orders (1266) he submitted to the Pope his *Opus Majus*, *Opus Minus* and *Opus Tertium* (1268). He said he had then been studying for forty years. His purpose was the glory of the Catholic Church and his outlook was intensely papal; but his desire to learn by experiment could not but seem a challenge to some supporters of ecclesiastical authority, even if he had not deplored the crusades through belief in the force of persuasion. In 1278 the Bishop of Paris seized him and he was imprisoned apparently until 1292 when he returned to Oxford to die. The cause of the imprisonment was 'his suspicious novelties'. In our generation the history of science has become an important part of historical study and therefore Bacon is receiving ever greater recognition; but his ideas, hailed with enthusiasm in Elizabeth's reign by her scientific adviser, John Dee, had borne mighty fruit before the end of the fifteenth century by contributing to the discovery of America (1492). Columbus wrote a famous letter to his patrons, the Catholic monarchs of Spain, Ferdinand and Isabella. He quoted the opinion of a geographer that India could be reached by sailing westwards from Spain. It was not realized that the geographer's opinion, with all its revolutionary consequences, was in fact a word-for-word quotation from Roger Bacon. See plate 10.

J. H. Bridges, *Life and Work of R. Bacon*, 1914.

WILLIAM DE VALENCE (*c.* 1230–96), called de Valence from his birthplace is to be distinguished from the equally unpopular William Bishop of Valence, uncle of Eleanor of Provence, who left Dover with his saddle-bags stuffed with valuable presents (1237). He was the fourth son of Isabel of Angoulême by her second husband, Hugh X de Lusignan, the gay troubadour and untrustworthy lord of La Marche on the borders of France and Poitou. The Lusignans provided kings of Cyprus, Jerusalem and Armenia, and in William they produced one of the worst advisers of Henry III and one of the best generals of Edward I. When William's parents died Henry welcomed his step-brothers and sister 'with every sign of joy, and rushed to give them the paternal embrace and kiss, promising them handsome presents and ample possessions' (1247). William de Valence was knighted (1247) on the occasion when Matthew Paris saw Henry carry some of Christ's blood from St. Paul's to Westminster, and Henry III asked him to record the occasion carefully (see plate 8). Henry excited the jealousy of the barons by marrying William to Joan Muntchensy, coheiress of William Marshal. William's sister married the equally eligible John de Warenne, and William bought for his niece Alice a marriage with his friend and companion-in-arms Gilbert de Clare. In one of the tournaments in which they delighted, William and Gilbert were so beaten that they had to take a course of baths and fomentations (1253), and in his old age William became one of the overseers of tournaments for Edward I. William and his brother Aymer quarrelled with Archbishop Boniface of Savoy, thereby annoying the archbishop's niece, Queen Eleanor. William was disliked for lawlessness. Once, when thirsty out hunting, he broke into the manor of the Bishop of Ely, and, as there was only beer to drink, he forced the cellar door and made his huntsmen drunk on expensive wine and left the floor awash. He invaded Simon de Montfort's lands (1256) and Simon would have stabbed him, if Henry had not stepped between them. Yet even worse were his servants, especially his steward William de Bussey. A dog barked at a youth in a lane in Trumpington, so Bussey threw a stone at it which accidentally killed a poor woman's hen. Her complaint brought round the neighbours and she refused as compensation twice the value of the hen. Bussey cast the youth into prison and there he soon died of ill-treatment. His corpse rotted on a dunghill for some days, but the priest buried it. Bussey heard of this three days later and had it exhumed and hung rotting on a gibbet. Valence was, however, the most loyal supporter among the magnates of Henry III and a friend of his son, the Lord Edward. Simon de Montfort said (1258): 'You may rest assured that you will either give up the castles which you hold of the king, or you will undoubtedly lose your head'. The barons agreed with Simon, and the Poitevins knew that they would be starved, if they went to any of their castles, for the people would besiege them, even if the barons did not. They accordingly fled while dinner was being prepared, pretending that they wanted to dine, to hide their intentions of flight. As they fled they kept looking behind them, and made retainers climb high towers to see if the barons were in pursuit. Nor did they spare their horses' sides until they reached Winchester, where William's brother, the unpopular Aymer, was bishop elect. When William reached Boulogne, St. Louis, King of France, would not let him travel through to Poitou because his Queen disliked him on account of his quarrel with her sister the Queen of England. Meanwhile the baronial council 'froze' money deposited by the Poitevins in the New Temple and various monasteries in south-east England. They seized much money deposited by William in Waltham Abbey. They generously made an allowance for William's wife, and she loyally followed him with as much cash as she could smuggle out in wool-packs. William's brother Aymer died at Paris in 1260 and 'England praised God for his goodness'. Henry was eventually able to recall William (1264). William had learned a lesson in exile and replied 'very humbly' to the barons' demand that he should obey the Provisions of Oxford and answer charges against him. He became a more responsible person and his loyalty repaid Henry's favours. In 1264 he was one who advised arbitration between king and barons by Louis IX; and when Louis's verdict in the 'Mise of Amiens' was rejected, he was one of the first to join Prince Edward in arms. Edward and William quickly captured de Montfort's son, Simon, at Northampton, while the anti-royalist Londoners retaliated by plundering William's London property, including his deposits at the Temple. At the Battle of Lewes (1264) he was with Prince Edward in the headlong but tactically disastrous pursuit of the routed Londoners. After the defeat William retired to France for a year. The Earl of Gloucester quarrelled with de Montfort over the latter's growing friendship with Llywelyn, and thereat William landed in Pembroke with his brother-in-law, John de Warenne, and 120 men and rallied South Wales. William's help was decisive in winning the campaign that culminated in Prince Edward's victory, with his support, at Evesham (1265). His loyalty was rewarded. All chroniclers before 1258 hate William and none gives him the compliment of calling him Earl of Pembroke, but in the reign of Edward I he is often called Earl of Pembroke. He accompanied Edward as a crusader, and he served him as a diplomat in French and Scottish negotiations; but his great service was in Wales. In Edward's Welsh war of 1277 Edward's attack from Chester was made possible by William's attack from Pembroke. The Welsh killed William's son (1282) and this nerved his arm in crushing revolts in Cardiganshire (1282–3) and suppressing the last Welsh rising of 1294. In old age he was personally as grasping as he had been in youth, even ready to make his niece out to be a bastard in order to get her land; but William presents the interesting spectacle of a hated foreigner spending fifty years in England and becoming a loyal Englishman. He was regent in 1285, and though he died at Bayonne, he was buried in Westminster Abbey. Instead of an upstart seeking betterment by marriage he became father of a family sought in marriage. One of his daughters married Hugh de Baliol, another married John Comyn of Badenoch and a third married John de Hastings, a claimant to the Scottish throne and ancestor of the Hastings Earls of Pembroke. One of William's nine sons was the tall and pale Aymer, Earl of Pembroke (d. 1323), who was nicknamed 'Joseph the Jew' by Piers Gaveston and who is also buried in Westminster Abbey.

William de Valence
(Westminster Abbey)

F. R. Lewis on William of Valence, *Aberystwyth Studies*, vol. 13, 11–35, vol. 14, 69–92 (1934–5).

HUMPHREY DE BOHUN VII (d. 1298), third Earl of Hereford and second Earl of Essex, was an ally of Roger Bigod, Earl of Norfolk (d. 1306), in opposing Edward I. Bohun was great-grandson of the first Earl of Hereford (d. 1220), an enemy of King John; but the second earl had fought for Henry III against de Montfort. Humphrey served in Wales (1286) and, like Bigod, fought at Falkirk against the Scots (1298). With Bigod, he resisted Edward I's legal changes, refused to serve in Gascony (1297), and demanded reconfirmations of Magna Carta and a charter which limited royal forest rights (1297). He bore the proud title of Constable of England but this was taken from him in 1297. Edward I made Humphrey's son, the eighth Humphrey, marry his daughter Elizabeth (1302) and surrender the Bohun estates, on the understanding that those estates were to be granted back, but under conditions;

after Bohun's death, if there should ever be no direct descendants, then the estates should pass to the crown. The obverse of the Bohun seal (plate 12) shows the Bohun badge, a swan, above the coat of arms. Mary, the daughter of Humphrey de Bohun, the seventh and last earl, married Henry IV. This is why the Lancastrian royal house adopted the swan as one of its badges. This explains the significance of swans in the life of Henry V, as devices at his marriage feast and as an omen when the invasion fleet sailed for Normandy (see p. 220).

WILLIAM WALLACE (*c.* 1272–1305) was the son of a small landowner, Malcolm Wallace of Elderslie near Paisley, a free-tenant of the king's steward in Renfrew. He was bold, determined, of gigantic size, and became the hero of Scottish resistance to Edward I. In May 1297 in the name of King John Baliol he attacked the royal garrison in Lanark and killed Sir William Hezelrig, a royal sheriff. Only a year before, it had seemed that Edward I had conquered Scotland; but, though Wallace suffered a reverse at Irvine and had to withdraw into Selkirk forest, he drove the English out of Perth, Stirling and Lanark shires and besieged Dundee and Stirling castles. The same year he defeated the army of the Earl of Warenne at Stirling Bridge and proceeded to ravage Northumberland, Westmorland and Cumberland (1297). He was given the title of guardian of Scotland and leader of its armies. On 22nd July, 1298, Edward I defeated him at Falkirk, but he continued waging a guerrilla war until 1299 when he withdrew to France in quest of foreign aid. Although he failed to get help from Pope Boniface VIII or King Philip the Fair of France, he returned to Scotland in 1303 and resumed guerrilla fighting for two years. In 1303 he was excluded from a general pardon issued by Edward I. In 1305 he was betrayed at or near Glasgow. After a trial in Westminster Hall (23 August) he was dragged to the Tower. On 24 August he was hanged and quartered at Tyburn. His quarters were placed on gibbets at Perth, Stirling, Newcastle-on-Tyne and Berwick, and his head was impaled on London Bridge. Blind Harry or Henry the Minstrel (flourished 1470–92) created in a famous poem on Wallace a folk-hero who killed his first Englishmen with a fishing rod.

J. Ferguson, *William Wallace Guardian of Scotland*, 1938.
E. Linklater, 'William Wallace and Robert the Bruce', *History Today* 3 (1953).

JOHN COMYN THE RED (*d.* 1306) belonged to a family which had been of great importance in Scotland during the reigns of Alexander II (1198–1249) and Alexander III (1241–85). Its founder was William Cumin, a chancery clerk of Henry I of England who had become Chancellor of David I (1084–1153). John's father, John Comyn, 'the Black', was one of the three strongest claimants to the Scottish throne (1291) through descent from Hextilda, daughter of Donald Bane, the brother of Malcolm Canmore (d. 1093). The Black Comyn inherited Badenoch in 1258 and supported John Baliol as king (1292). He married Margaret Baliol and thus transmitted to Comyn the Red a twofold claim to the Scottish throne. Comyn the Black, like Alexander III, had been closely connected with the English court for thirty years. When Edward I invaded Scotland, Red Comyn was among those captured at Dunbar. By 1298 he had become the leader of Scottish resistance. His rival Robert Bruce, grandson of the old Robert Bruce who claimed the throne in 1291, hated him; and an English spy reported (1299) that they had a fierce quarrel. At a meeting of the Scottish leaders to discuss the disposal of the lands of William Wallace, Red Comyn seized Bruce by the throat. The nobles elected Comyn joint guardian of Scotland (1299), the year after he had fought at Falkirk, and in 1302 he expelled Edward I's officials. In 1303 he beat the English at Roslyn, near Edinburgh, but in 1304 he was among those who submitted to Edward at Strathorde (Perthshire). His end came on 10 February, 1306. He had arranged to meet Bruce in the Minorite church at Dumfries. They quarrelled again and Bruce struck him down. 'I doubt I have slain the Red Comyn', Bruce is reported to have said as he left the church. 'Doubt?', answered Sir Roger FitzPatrick, 'I'll make siccar'. Comyn had kept faith with Edward for two whole years and when Bruce was crowned at Scone (25 March, 1306) Bruce was, in Edward's opinion, a traitor and a murderer. Edward was carried in a litter to Westminster. There he knighted his son Edward and three hundred other young men. At the feast two swans were brought to the table and Edward I swore 'before God and the swans' to avenge the death of Comyn and the insult to the church.

J. H. Round, 'The Origin of the Comyns', *The Ancestor*, vol. 10, (July, 1904).

ROGER BIGOD (1245–1306) was the fifth Bigod to be Earl of Norfolk. The first earl, Hugh, had rebelled against Henry I, fought on alternate sides in the reign of Stephen and joined in rebellion (1173) against Henry II. The second earl, Hugh (d. 1225), joined the barons against John (1215). The third earl, Hugh (d. 1266), was Henry III's chief justiciar (1258–60). The fourth earl, Roger (d. 1270), became Earl Marshal (1246). He eventually transferred his support from Henry III to Simon de Montfort. The fifth earl, Roger (d. 1306), was a stubborn champion of baronial rights. He was Marshal of England but refused to serve in Gascony unless Edward I, who was then bound for Flanders, went there too (1296). The story is often told that Edward said 'You shall either go or hang', to which he replied 'By God, I shall neither go nor hang'. He explained that he would only do the military service which he was bound to do in the way that he was bound to do it. He was willing to go before the face of the King in battle. His action was not that of a mutineer; but the military service due from him did not include going abroad without the King, and he did not go. It was his duty, with the constable (Bohun), to enrol the names of those who would serve in Flanders, but they refused to do this (1297). They were not traitors, but they had as much regard for their rights as Edward had for his. They felt that he was ignoring Magna Carta and the Charter of the Forest, that his demands for men and money were unlawful, and that Scotland, not Flanders, needed attention. Wallace's victory at Stirling (11 Sept., 1297) led to a confirmation of the charters and other royal concessions (10 Oct.). Edward gave Bigod and Bohun the kiss of peace at York and they were in the van at the Battle of Falkirk (1298). They complained of the length of time they had to serve in the north and continued to show their distrust for Edward. In 1301 Bigod gave up his symbolic rod of office as Marshal. Edward I made him give up his lands and receive them back as a royal grant for himself and the heirs of his body. As Bigod had no children this meant that the land would go to Edward when he died. See plates 11 and 12.

S. Painter, *Studies in the History of the English Feudal Barony*, 1943.
N. Denholm-Young, *Seignorial Administration in England*, 1937.

EDWARD I (1239–1307), son of Henry III, was so called after his father's favourite saint Edward the Confessor. His godfather was Simon de Montfort, his uncle by marriage. He was a delicate child, but became governor of Gascony before he was thirteen and married Eleanor of Castile when fifteen. He could understand French, Latin and English, was good-looking, and, although he stammered, became a good speaker. He was known while Henry lived as the Lord Edward and as a youth his progresses, accompanied by 200 horsemen, were marked by incredible violence. They drove the monks out of Wallingford priory and beat their servants; and once he ordered his followers to cut off the ear of a harmless youth whom they happened to meet, and to pluck out one of his eyes. He began to learn responsibility as early as 1252–4 when his father granted him his outlying territories, the lands he claimed in France, all land held in Wales, the Earldom of Chester, Ireland and also certain English cities. Their revenue was to maintain his court, and their administration gave him useful experience in how to avoid his father's mistakes. Edward loyally fought Henry's enemies, capturing Simon de Montfort the younger at Northampton (1264). He hated the Londoners for insulting his mother, Eleanor, and pursued them fiercely at the battle of Lewes (1264). Meanwhile he learned political and tactical lessons from his foe and was thus able to beat Simon de Montfort the elder at Evesham (1265) and his supporters at Kenilworth (1266). When his father died (1272), Edward was on crusade and had recently been wounded by the poisoned dagger of the Emir of Jaffa who pretended to be attracted by Christianity (see p. 141). He returned home in 1274 but to the end of his life he looked forward to a further crusade. His return saw him risking his life in a rough tournament at Châlons, but thereafter he devoted himself to an intelligent and sustained effort to strengthen the monarchy. He avoided the errors of his father and grandfather. He sought the advice of the magnates, his natural friends, instead of unsuitable foreigners, though he was not prejudiced against foreigners and made much use of Italian financiers. Applying ideas learned from de Montfort, he gave more national and county business to the knights. With them he called burgesses from the towns to Parliament. He did this not from any democratic theory about the desirability of a parliament as such, but because he wanted to be able to check the power of the magnates. Like Henry II he brought laws and institutions up to date in accord with recent social changes. Edward had splendid advisers in his Chancellor, Robert Burnell, in Bishop Bek and in great judges like Hengham and Britton and in the famous Italian legal scholar, Francesco Accursi. His first parliament (1275) covered the whole field of law in what is called the Statute of Westminster I. He followed up an inquiry into the extent and nature of the private administration of justice by the barons in his Statute of Gloucester (1278). Under it royal commissioners went round to ask by what right (*quo warranto*) the lords exercised the authority which they did. It was in answer to the inquiry that the Earl of Warenne, Edward's uncle by marriage, was said to have made a reply which the *Dictionary of National Biography* has been blamed for repeating. The legend runs that he produced a rusty sword as his warrant, for William the Conqueror 'did not by himself subject the land; our ancestors were his partners'. Next year, 1279, Edward's Statute of Mortmain aimed at protecting the rights of all lords (and as king he was himself the greatest of lords), from loss of profits which were obtainable when those who held land were under age or married or died. As long as mortal tenants held land such profits were safe, but if a tenant gave land into the 'dead hand' of a corporation such as a monastery, loss followed.

Edward actively encouraged the growth of towns and displayed at Winchelsea and Berwick an active interest in town-planning. To later eyes Edward's measures make him appear to have been consciously creating a national community under his leadership, but he was a child of his age. The modern idea of nationhood did not exist and it would not have occurred to him to attack the barons any more than he would have willingly allowed them to usurp more than their due. He relentlessly pursued his legal rights, as he understood them, whether in Gascony, Ireland, Wales or Scotland, with an indifference to nationalist considerations which was complete for they did not yet exist.

In annexing Wales he ignored the sentiments of the Welsh; and as 'Hammer of the Scots' he both overtaxed England's strength and made the Scots hate England. In the beginning of his reign he collaborated with barons and bishops. His demands united them in opposition. He succeeded in getting the great estates of the earldoms of Norfolk, Hereford, Cornwall and Gloucester under the control of himself or his kin. He humiliated Bek, the proud Bishop of Durham, and exiled Winchelsey, the Archbishop of Canterbury, and was fortunate to end his reign with one of his Gascon subjects, Clement V, as Pope (1305). His strength in defence of his rights was obvious to barons and Pope, but he was neither anti-feudal nor anti-papal, for barons and Pope were among the chief characters in the world he knew. Changing historical fashion, with its love of revising accepted opinions, has seen Edward as a strong ruler, a national king, an inventor of a 'model parliament' (1290), an economist who understood the wool trade, an aspiring tyrant (especially in 1297) or a mere conventional lord. He was certainly 'a prince of chiefe renowne', a good swordsman with limbs which earned him his name 'Longshanks', an enthusiast for Arthurian romance who loved tournaments and hunting, and an adroit student of the foreign politics of his day. His military operations included such triumphs as the construction of castles in the latest style at key points in Wales, and the transfer by sea from Lynn of prefabricated wooden bridges to cross the Forth (1303). At sea it was an age when the invention of the first movable rudders and of bowsprits reflected technical progress, and Edward was the first king (about 1295) to confer the title of admiral on a single officer with a unified command. The failure to keep Scotland conquered was his great sorrow. His hair had become white on his lofty forehead but he remained vigorous long after his contemporaries. Failing health did not deflect his determination to crush Robert Bruce, and he died on his painful way northwards at Burgh-on-Sands. He had slain Llywelyn ab Gruffydd and his brother Davydd, champions of Wales. He had slain William Wallace, hero of Scotland. He had arrested all the Jews and goldsmiths in England (1278) and had banished all the Jews from England (1290), an act for which parliament and clergy were grateful. He obtained from Clement V absolution from his oath to keep the charters and he used this to cancel concessions he had made about the royal forests. He is, however, one who is to be judged as having profited by an enemy's advice in the 'Song of Lewes': 'if thou wouldst have a kingdom reverence the laws . . . they shine like a lamp. Therefore avoid and detest treachery; labour after truth, and hate falsehood.' He died at a time when the greatest Italian poet and artist, Dante (1265–1321) and Giotto (1266–1336), were in their prime in Italy. See plates 1 and 13.

T. F. Tout, *Edward the First*, 1920. See pedigrees, pp. 55 and 176.

F. M. Powicke, *King Henry III and the Lord Edward*, 1947.

ANTONY BEK (d. 1310), Bishop of Durham (1283) and titular Patriarch of Jersusalem (which was then held by the Saracens), was the son of Walter Bek, Baron of Eresby (Lincs.) and brother of Thomas Bek, Bishop of St. David's. He was one of a baronial family which produced in the next generation two brothers, also called Antony and Thomas, the Bishops of Norwich (1337–43) and Lincoln (1340–47), two of the only fourteen bishops in the reign of Edward III to be of aristocratic birth. Antony, Bishop of Durham, was an overbearing royal servant and landowner, with a household often numbering 140 knights. Such was his arrogance that he would not hesitate to give the benediction in the presence of cardinals and would continue toying with his hawks even in the presence of the Pope. He took an active part in many public events in Edward I's reign and his career can be followed in unusual detail. He was one of the three great councillors of Edward I and was called second only to the King. It was he who was appointed to arrange the marriage of the King's son and Margaret of Scotland (1290); he was an important adviser during Edward's negotiations with Baliol and it was he who held the Isle of Man for Edward (1298–1310). He played an important part in the Scottish expeditions of 1296 and 1298. He once besieged the monks of Durham in their own church for two months, and when supported by Edward he could assert himself against his ecclesiastical superiors. In 1297 even he joined the opposition to Edward, telling him that the rebellious lords were working for the profit and honour of the kingdom. Edward was angry and deprived him for a time of his temporal income as bishop. His humiliation was not permanent. He regained his income, thanks to the support of the Pope, and Edward II, when he became King, made him sovereign of the Isle of Man.

C. M. Fraser, *A History of Antony Bek, 1283–1311*, 1957.

PIERS GAVESTON (d. 1312) was a young Gascon for whom Edward II had an excessive and disastrous affection. When Edward became king he recalled Piers after a brief exile on his accession (1307), enriched him and made him Earl of Cornwall. 'Brother Peter' or 'Perrot' was a provocative deviser of nicknames for his betters, calling Warwick 'blac hounde of Arderne', Lancaster 'cherl', Gloucester 'Horesonne' and Lincoln 'Brost Bely' (burst belly) (though Lincoln had approved of his elevation to the Earldom of Cornwall). He was no mere churlish coward, as his enemies suggested, but he flaunted royal purple and played an invidiously prominent part at Edward II's coronation. He was extravagant and was an early owner of a fork. The lords insisted on repeated exile

(1308–9) and (1311–12) and Archbishop Winchelsey pronounced excommunication if he should return. On his third return the enraged Warwick said he was out to bite him as if he were a dog. Gaveston was executed in the presence of Thomas of Lancaster at Blacklow Heath.

Edward II, the Lords Ordainers and Piers Gaveston's Jewels and Horses (1312–13), Camden Misc. vol. 15, 1929 (in Latin).

ROBERT DE WINCHELSEY (d. 1313) was a learned and active priest, Chancellor of Oxford (1288), and a well-known man when he was elected Archbishop of Canterbury by the monks of Christ Church, Canterbury, with the full approval of Edward I in February 1293. The office of Pope remained vacant for some time so Winchelsey was not consecrated by the new Pope until September 1294. This delay abroad forced him to get into debt with Italian merchants. He was enthroned at Canterbury in October 1295 in the presence of Edward I, eight bishops and five earls. He had to resist arbitrary royal taxation and was successful in so doing. Though Edward I was reconciled to him, he never forgave Winchelsey. Winchelsey was sympathetic to Edward's need for money caused by an expedition to Gascony, a Welsh rebellion and a dangerous alliance of France and Scotland; but he was anxious to preserve the rights of his office. Pope Boniface VIII (1294–1303) repeated a rule of the Church that all royal taxation of the clergy required permission from the Pope. In his bull *Clericis Laicos* he pronounced dire penalties against all who ignored this; and Winchelsey published this bull (1297), for he took seriously his allegiance to the head of Christendom as well as to the King of England. In 1300 Winchelsey, who was often in conflict with Edward on particular points, reluctantly found himself bringing him an order from Pope Boniface to stop fighting in Scotland. He reminded Edward of the Psalm 'They who have trust in the Lord are as Mount Zion which cannot be moved . . .' and Edward retorted 'By God's Blood, for Zion's sake I will not be silent . . .', quoting Isaiah. Edward I came to regard Winchelsey as one of his chief enemies; and, especially after a parliament held at Lincoln in 1301, cooperation between them became as impossible as it had been between Henry II and Becket. This made it difficult for Winchelsey to enforce discipline, especially upon royal clerks. Winchelsey objected to Edward's banning the export of money for alien priories with land in England (1305). That year a subject of Edward, Bernard Got, became Pope Clement V. Edward's representative at the papal coronation was Walter Langton, his treasurer. As Bishop of Coventry and Lichfield Langton annoyed Winchelsey by trying to follow the example of the Bishop of Winchester in getting exemption for life from the jurisdiction of the Archbishop. Winchelsey had not only resisted this successfully, but had accused him, unsuccessfully, of trafficking in church offices for money, adultery, murder and intercourse with the devil. Now Langton had his revenge. He persuaded Clement V to suspend Winchelsey from office and summon him to Rome. Winchelsey sought protection in vain from Edward. Edward gave him permission to return, saying 'Merciless you have been to others, mercy to yourself we shall never show'. On the accession of Edward II most of Edward I's faithful servants were dismissed and in the general reversal of policy Winchelsey was recalled from exile (1307). In time, however, he found himself in opposition again and became one of Edward II's leading enemies, the Lords Ordainers (1310) (see p. 163). In 1312 it was he who excommunicated Edward's favourite, Gaveston. He suffered from weak health and died at Oxford. Miracles occurred at his tomb at Canterbury.

Rose Graham, 'The Metropolitan Visitation of the Diocese of Worcester by Archbishop Winchelsey in 1301', *Transactions Royal Historical Society*, 4th ser., 2 (1919); and her 'Archbishop Winchelsey from his Election to his Enthronement', *Church Quarterly Review*, vol. 148 (1949), 161–75.

JOHN DE BALIOL (1229–1315) was the son of a namesake (d. 1269) who had founded Balliol College in 1263. He was one of the three strongest candidates out of thirteen competitors for the Scottish throne after the death of Alexander III and the Maid of Norway. Through his mother, Devorguilla, Baliol represented the elder line of descent from David (d. 1214), the brother of William the Lyon. The line of William the Lyon was extinct, but Baliol was one generation further removed from the parent stem than his rival Robert Bruce. Edward I was asked to arbitrate, and he summoned the candidates to Norham (1291). After long discussions Baliol was the successful candidate and did homage to Edward I (1292). He was crowned at Scone on the ancient 'stone of destiny'. The Scots disliked him and nicknamed him 'the toom tabard' (meaning 'empty jacket'). Baliol's homage was understood by Edward to imply that he should answer in an English court a case brought against him by a Gascon wine-merchant of Alexander III. In 1293 Baliol attended the English Parliament. He then refused, unless advised by his council, to answer appeals made to Edward I, his overlord, by parties to lawsuits in Scottish courts. Baliol was, however, forced to yield (1294). In 1295 he made a treaty with France against England. Edward I thereupon 'conquered the realm of Scotland and searched it in twenty-one days and no more'. On 7 July, 1296, at Stralathro Baliol appeared before Edward I with a white rod in his hand. Stripped of all his royal ornaments, he surrendered his baton and staff of office and renounced the throne. The French treaty was renounced and Baliol was sent to Hertford in honourable confinement. Edward gave the Stone of Scone to Westminster Abbey, where it was later set in the coronation chair. Baliol was released (1299) and ended his life peacefully at Château Gaillard (Normandy).

Documents illustrative of the History of Scotland and Transactions between Scotland and England, Ed. F. Palgrave, Record Series, 1837. See p. 85 (pedigree) and plate 1 (coin).

GUY DE BEAUCHAMP, EARL OF WARWICK (d. 1315), was one of seven earls who attached their seals to a protest to the Pope rejecting papal authority in Scottish political affairs. He was nicknamed 'blac hounde of Arderne' by Piers Gaveston and he helped to get Gaveston banished in 1308. In 1309 he was alone in objecting to the return of Gaveston from exile. He was one of the magnates chosen a 'lord ordainer' to take over the government in 1310. As such he marched to London

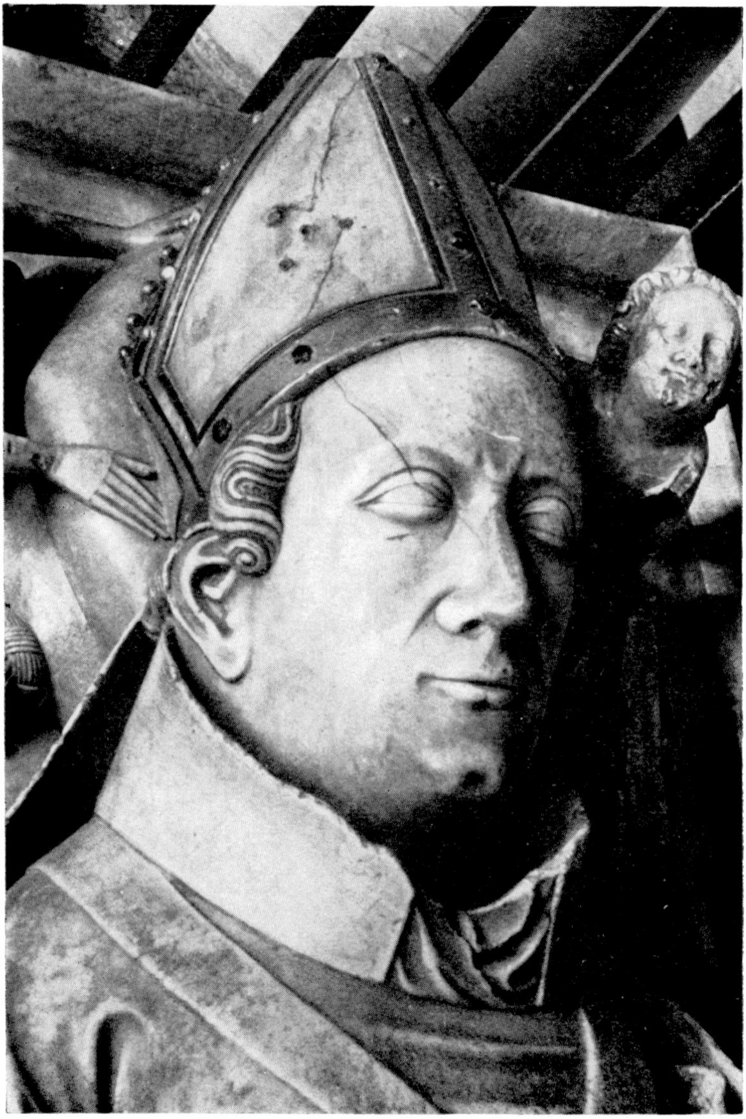

Plate 21

Archbishop Courtenay (alabaster, Canterbury)

Canterbury Pilgrims

Plate 22

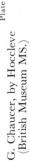

G. Chaucer, by Hoccleve
(British Museum MS.)

to concert measures against Gaveston and swore at St. Paul's to keep the Ordinances (1311). On 10 June, 1312, he seized Gaveston when asleep at Deddington (Oxon.) and took him off half-dressed and 'compelled him to go afoot' to Warwick Castle. Guy was not, however, responsible for Gaveston's murder, as that occurred on Thomas of Lancaster's land nine days later; and Guy had Gaveston's corpse removed from land under his own jurisdiction when it was carried into Warwick.

THOMAS, EARL OF LANCASTER (?1277–1322), also Earl of Leicester, Derby, Lincoln and Salisbury and Steward of England, was son of Edward I's crusading brother Edmund Crouchback, Earl of Lancaster and 'King of Sicily' (1255–63). Thomas hated Piers Gaveston and the Despensers, the friends of Edward II, and, as Edward would not regard them as traitors, he was Edward's enemy, despite various reconciliations and loyal phrases. He made Edward accept the rule of twenty-eight barons called 'Ordainers' (1310), and had Gaveston executed (1312); he obtained complete control of Edward after the disastrous Battle of Bannockburn (1314), and he forced Edward to banish the Despensers (1321). He knew that Edward had said 'I have not yet forgotten the wrong that was done my brother Piers Gaveston'. In 1322 Lancaster was captured at Boroughbridge, shut in a tower which he had just built in his own castle at Pontefract and beheaded there. The populace pelted him with snow as he rode to death, and some contemporaries said 'violent deeds bring their own punishment' and noted his private failings. His supporters said that the 'gentile erle' was shamefully killed 'with-outen cause and resoun'. Pilgrims put candles in St. Paul's in front of a tablet which commemorated his deeds, a child was brought to life and cripples were healed at his tomb; and the Earl of Kent asked the Pope to canonize Thomas. His enemies, Aymer de Valence, the Despensers, Arundel and Harclay, perished violently. He owed his very powerful position to being the richest landowner in England. He was violent and greedy, with no political foresight or real policy. Because he opposed the King he gained much popularity. See pedigree, p. 55.

W. E. Rhodes, 'Edmund Earl of Lancaster', *English Historical Review* (1895), 19–40, 209–37.

N. Denholm-Young, *The Life of Edward the Second by the so-called Monk of Malmesbury*, Nelson Medieval Texts, ed. by V. H. Galbraith and R. A. B. Mynors, 1957.

HUGH LE DESPENSER, the elder (1262–1326), Earl of Winchester, bore the same christian name as his father (d. 1265) and his son (d. 1326). His father was slain fighting for de Montfort at Evesham. Hugh gained the trust of Edward I, and, unlike most of Edward I's friends, he retained the friendship of Edward II. When the latter was in disgrace as a young prince, Hugh sent him a gift of raisins and wine. He was the sole supporter of Gaveston in 1308, and after Gaveston's murder (1312) he became leader of Edward II's court party. Unlike Gaveston he was a man of position and mature years and, as brother-in-law of the Earl of Warwick, was a member of the traditional ruling class. After the English defeat at Bannockburn (1314) Hugh's enemies had him excluded from the king's council; but he reasserted himself in strong support of Edward II, aided by his son, though his son, an ambitious young man, had been an opponent of Gaveston. In 1321 Thomas of Lancaster had both Hughs, father and son, exiled. Their manors were plundered. Edward II triumphed the following year, recalled both Despensers, and made the elder Hugh Earl of Winchester (1322). The Despensers were the only men whom Edward could trust. Queen Isabel hated them; and her ally, Mortimer, had local reasons for fearing their competition for local power on the Welsh border. Isabel and Mortimer invaded England in 1326, saying that they had come only to fight the Despensers. The Despensers fled from London with Edward II. The queen captured the elder Hugh at Bristol and executed him. The younger Hugh was executed at Hereford (1326). Despenser alienated his old allies because he had packed the court and departments of state. He was no mere court favourite. He was able, but greedy and unscrupulous. His desire to build up a great lordship on the Welsh border aroused opposition especially from Mortimer.

The Despensers have received much attention in recent learned articles. B. Wilkinson in *English Historical Review*, vol. 63 (1948); G. A. Holmes in *Speculum*, vol. 30 (1955) and *English Historical Review*, vol. 69 (1955); and E. B. Fryde in *Economic History Review*, 2nd ser., vol. 3 (1951).

EDWARD II (1284–1327) was son of Edward I who made him the first Prince of Wales and a pupil of the unlearned Walter Reynolds, who became Bishop of Worcester (1307) and Archbishop of Canterbury (1313). Edward became nominal regent at nine years old (1297–8) and was knighted on the eve of an expedition to punish Bruce for the murder of Comyn (1306). His marriage with Isabel, daughter of Philip the Fair of France (1308), was an unhappy one. Through it Edward became the first English king murdered since the Conquest and from it came that claim of Edward's descendants to the throne of France which caused the Hundred Years War with France. A roll containing hundreds of his letters gives more details about his early years than are available for any earlier ruler. He was fond of luxury, gambling, horse-breeding, dog-training, music, swimming, and even of "vulgar" pursuits like boating, thatching and ditching. As soon as he became king (1307) he dismissed his father's ministers and judges and made a foppish favourite, Gaveston, Earl of Cornwall. The outraged barons forced Edward to banish Gaveston (1308 and 1311) and eventually slew him (1312). The barons forced Edward to accept the governance of twenty-one Lords Ordainers (1310) and after his natural inability to hold down the Scots had culminated in Bruce's victory at Bannockburn (1314) he had to submit to Lancaster. In 1318 a parliament at York made reforms, wars in Scotland and Ireland improved and the harvest was good, but in spite of these encouraging facts hostile rumour was rife, an attempt to take Berwick failed (1319) and Edward had to banish his favourites, the Despensers (1321). The following year he asserted himself successfully, taking Leeds castle, recalling the Despensers and capturing his arch-enemy Lancaster at Boroughbridge and beheading him (1322). To preserve Aquitaine from French designs Edward let Isabel go on his behalf to pay homage for it and for Ponthieu. His fondness for the younger Despenser vexed her as much as his fondness for Gaveston had done and she met Mortimer, her lover, in Paris.

Mortimer was a baronial opponent of Edward and had recently escaped from custody in the Tower. This pair, aided

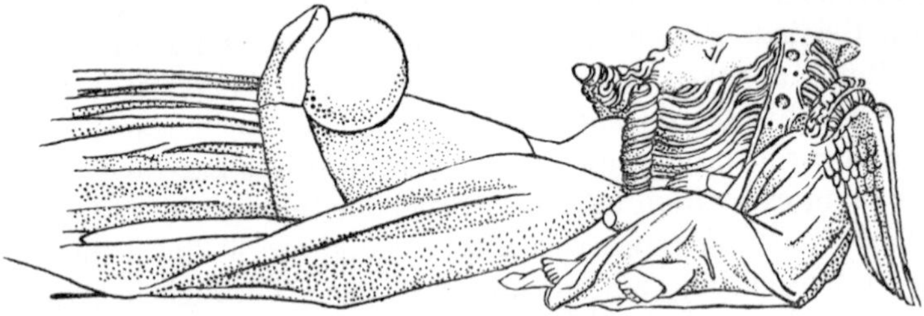

Edward II (Worcester Cathedral)

by the propaganda of Bishop Adam Orlton, forced Edward to abdicate on their return to England (1326). He fled westward from them, was captured at Neath, and was murdered at Berkeley Castle by having a red-hot spit thrust in his entrails.

If Edward II had been as efficient as his father, instead of utterly incompetent, English royal power might have become much stronger both in England and Scotland. In Edward's struggles with the barons Parliament grew in importance as it was called upon to legalize the victories of first one side and then the other. Thus the feebleness of Edward II, like that of Henry III, helped the growth of political liberty. See p. 55.

Hilda Johnstone, *Edward of Carnarvon, 1284–1307*, 1946.

T. F. Tout, *The Place of Edward II in English History*, 2nd ed. revised by Hilda Johnstone, 1937.

The Life of Edward II by the so-called Monk of Malmesbury, transl. with introduction and notes by N. Denholm-Young (an admirable contemporary memoir written soon after November, 1325).

ROBERT DE BRUCE VIII (1274–1329), the Liberator, Earl of Carrick, was son of the Lord of Annandale (1253–1304), warden of Carlisle Castle, who fought for Edward I against

John de Baliol (1295) and paid Edward homage not only for English lands but as King of Scotland (24 August, 1296). His grandfather, Robert de Bruce VI (1210–95) was a claimant to the Scottish throne who accepted Edward's arbitration (1291)—King William the Lyon's niece had married his father, Robert de Bruce V (d. 1245).

The Liberator became head of the family in 1304 and was confirmed in his father's estates for helping to subjugate Scotland although he had rebelled in 1298–9. He came to blows with his only rival, John Comyn of Badenoch, Baliol's heir, at the Grey Friars' in Dumfries (1306). His squires killed Comyn before the altar and Bruce seized Comyn's horse, drove the royal justices from Dumfries and was acclaimed King at Scone, though he had paid homage to Edward as King of Scotland (24 August, 1296). In 1297 he made a belt out of the skin of Hugh Cressingham, treasurer of Scotland. Aymer de Valence, Earl of Pembroke, scattered Bruce's army at Methuen (19 June, 1306). Bruce fled to the Highlands while Prince Edward cruelly ravaged the land. Old Edward I died struggling north to suppress Bruce (1307) and the quarrels of Edward II's reign let Bruce make steady progress until he took Roxburgh and Edinburgh and threatened Stirling (1314). Edward's attempted relief of Stirling ended disastrously at Bannockburn, the English never reconquered Scotland and the Scottish maidens taunted the English:

> 'Maydenes of Engelande, sare may ye mourne,
> For tynte ye have youre lemmans atte Bannokis bourne
>   With hevalowe.
> What wente ye Kyng of Engelande
> To have gete Scotlande
>   With rumbelowe'.

Bruce took Berwick (1318), ravaged Yorkshire (1322), won papal recognition as King of Scotland (1323) and made peace with Edward III (1328). He died of leprosy, aged fifty-four, and was buried at Dunfermline. His heart was buried at Melrose. Robert's son David II (1324–71) was defeated at Halidon Hill by Edward Baliol, whom Edward III supported as claimant

(1333). He thereupon spent seven years with the King of France at whose request he invaded England in 1346, where he spent eleven years in captivity. See plate 13 and p. 85.

A. M. Mackenzie, *Robert Bruce*, 1934.

JAMES DOUGLAS (?1286–1330), the Good, is one of Scotland's most famous heroes. His father, William Douglas the Hardy, of Douglas, had married (without the necessary royal permission) the widow of William Ferrers and had done homage with other Scots to Edward I (1296). In 1297 William was the first Scottish baron to revolt. His English lands were seized and he submitted. As he failed to produce hostages he was imprisoned in Berwick castle and was 'very savage and abusive'. He died in the Tower of London. James, then aged three or four, became a protégé of Wallace's friend William Lamberton, Bishop of St. Andrews. James thrice destroyed English garrisons in Douglas castle and twice burnt it. He often raided England, and was knighted at Bannockburn (1314). He defeated the Archbishop of York and the Bishop of Ely at Mitton (Yorks.) (1319) and defeated Edward III. He was killed when on a pilgrimage to the Holy Land, carrying with him the heart of his devoted friend Bruce, as that monarch had desired. His natural son, Sir Archibald Douglas, 3rd Earl of Douglas, the Grim or the Black, invaded England in 1389.

Sir. H. Maxwell, *History of the House of Douglas*, 2 vols., 1902.

ROGER DE MORTIMER (?1287–1330), eighth Baron of Wigmore and first Earl of March, was the most prominent member of a family which has been important politically for generations. The family's strength lay in its estates and castles on the Welsh border, and to understand the nature of such families is to understand an important aspect of the realities of English medieval history. The Mortimers first acquired confiscated lands on the Welsh border, including Wigmore, in 1074. The name was derived from Mortimer-en-Brai where the first Roger de Mortimer (flourished 1054–74), a relative of William I, had won a victory twelve years before the Norman conquest of England. Other ancestors had fortified Bridgnorth, Cleobury and Wigmore castles in the reign of Stephen, had opposed the accession of Henry II, had supported John, and had fought against the barons for Henry III. The eighth baron was descended through a daughter from Llywelyn the Great. Her son, Roger's grandfather, Roger the sixth baron (d. 1282), had been one of three notables who ruled England between Henry III's death (1272) and the return of Edward I to England.

Roger went to Ireland (1308). There he fought his relatives the Lacys and became justiciar (1319). In 1320 began the last decade of his life, during which he became at last the most powerful and hated man in England. That year he helped his uncle and namesake, the lord of Chirk, to resist the Despensers, courtiers of Edward II, who were threatening the independence of the Mortimers in the Welsh marches, the borderland where they had been powerful for nearly two and a half centuries. Edward's queen, Isabel, had her youngest child in July, 1321, and some time later Mortimer became her lover. In 1322 Edward recalled the Despensers from a temporary dismissal. He forced the Mortimers to submit and sent them to the Tower. Thence Roger escaped (1324) and fled to Paris. There he met Isabel and plotted revenge (1325), They landed at Orwell (1326) and Mortimer's tool, Adam of Orleton, the rebellious Bishop of Hereford, obtained Edward's deposition by Parliament (1327). Mortimer and Isabel ruled England together for the first four years after her fourteen-year-old son was crowned Edward III. Mortimer obtained various estates and dignities. He became Earl of March (1328), kept a retinue of 180 knights, and saw his daughters married to various magnates. This aroused jealousy, and he was thought to have been responsible for the horrible murder of Edward II and for the 'Shameful Peace' made at Northampton with Scotland (1328). He was suspected of making concessions to Scotland in order to have there a place of refuge should the wheel of Fortune turn. Henry of Lancaster, who had become Earl of Lancaster after his brother Thomas was executed by Edward II (1322), had opposed Edward II; but in 1329 he turned against Mortimer and Isabel. In 1330 they executed

Edward II's brother, Edmund, Earl of Kent, for plotting against them in the belief that Edward was really still alive. Finally Sir William Montacute and Sir Humphrey de Bohun (whose father and grandfather had made that name famous by opposing Edward I and II) incited young Edward III to assert himself against Mortimer. The conspirators entered Nottingham castle through a secret passage. They cut their way to the bedroom of Isabel's 'gentle Mortimer' and seized him. Mortimer was taken to Westminster and tried for ignoring the Council, confounding the kingdom, killing Kent, attacking Lancaster, murdering Edward II and embezzling public money. He was condemned unheard and executed as a traitor on 29 November 1330 at the Elms, Tyburn, near the modern Marble Arch, London.

RICHARD DE BURY (1281–1345), the greatest book-lover of medieval Europe, was son of Sir Richard Aungerville and was born near Bury St. Edmunds. He lost his parents while young. Like nine of Edward's other bishops, he worked as a clerk in the royal wardrobe, then an important government office. He became a diplomat, Lord Chancellor, Bishop of Durham and Lord High Treasurer (1337). Critics now doubt whether he was tutor of Edward III or author of the *Philobiblon*, a fascinating book about books, with which his name will ever be associated. He was a prime mover in the overthrow of Isabel and Mortimer. Training in his household was a valuable education, enjoyed by Thomas Bradwardine, Archbishop of Canterbury (1349), Thomas FitzRalph, Bishop of Armagh (d. 1345), Walter Burley, said to be tutor of the Black Prince, Robert Holcot, a Dominican theologian (d. 1349) and Walter Segrave, Bishop of Chichester. Bury had a beautifully clear handwriting, though the celebrated Italian poet, Petrarch, could not get him to answer his letters. Many of his letters (in Latin) have been printed. He had more books than all the bishops in England. In his bedroom books were stacked in piles on the floor.

Richard Aungervyle or Richard de Bury, *Philobiblon*, translated by A. Taylor, University of California Press, 1948.

N. Denholm-Young, *Collected Papers on Medieval Subjects*, 1946.
T.S.I.H., i, 151 (mishandling books).

WILLIAM OF OCKHAM (d. ?1349), called 'the invincible doctor', was born at Ockham, Surrey, and studied at Oxford and Paris. He was a great Franciscan writer on logic, philosophy and political theory. It is hard for people who are not students of philosophy to grasp his ideas. They caused many scholars to doubt the power of reason and the value of knowledge. He regarded abstract ideas as human inventions and he regarded the existence of God as a probability rather than a certainty. His philosophy is called nominalism. After teaching at Oxford (1318–24) he was accused of heresy and was summoned to the papal court, then at Avignon. His opinions spread and he propagated the theory held by the Franciscans about the desirability of 'evangelical poverty'. Of this Pope John XXII disapproved. He escaped from prison at Avignon (1328) and fled to the Pope's enemy, Lewis of Bavaria. For him he wrote 'Eight Inquiries on the Pope's Power', discussing the relationship between God and Caesar, Church and state. He championed Caesar and showed that Edward III might tax the clergy for just wars. He attacked Popes John XXII and Benedict XII for heresy and even tried to undermine papal power as such. He died, perhaps of the Black Death, at Munich, and was buried there. His greatest work, the 'Dialogue', is incomplete. It treats of the relation of Emperor and Pope.

William of Ockham, *Philosophical Writings, a Selection*, ed. and tr. by P. Boehner, 1957.

ISABEL OF FRANCE (*c.* 1292–1358), the 'She-wolf of France', was the daughter of Philip IV the Fair (k. 1285–1314) and sister of his three successors Louis X le Hutin (1314–6), Philip V le Long (1316–22) and Charles IV the Fair (1322–8). Her marriage with Edward II took place after the death of Edward I (1307) who had arranged it (1299); and through it her son Edward III derived a claim to the French Crown when it passed to her cousin Philip VI of Valois. Isabel landed in

February, 1308, six months after Edward II's accession, a fortnight after their marriage in Boulogne Cathedral and nine years after her betrothal. Isabel was sixteen and Edward twenty-three. Her father gave Edward jewels and rings for a wedding present, and she was hurt when her husband immediately gave them to his favourite, Gaveston. Edward's affection for Gaveston and his general unconventionality unsettled her, but the birth of the first of her five children after four years of marriage brought the pair together for a time. Edward's enemy, Thomas of Lancaster, had sympathized with her dislike of Gaveston and this common distaste may have helped her to mediate between Edward and the barons (1313, 1316 and 1321). The death of Eleanor of Castile, her mother-in-law, in 1318 released many manors for her, but that year a rumour that Edward was really a changeling, a carter's son, 'troubled the queen beyond measure'. Six years later the influence of the Despensers, Edward's new favourites, deprived Isabel of her estates (1324), but in 1325 Edward entrusted her with a diplomatic mission to her brother, Charles the Fair. Four years previously Isabel had been travelling on pilgrimage to the shrine of St. Thomas at Canterbury when she had been refused admission to Leeds Castle by Lady Badlesmere and six of her retinue had been slain by a volley of arrows from the walls. This had touched off a war between Edward and the barons and in it he had captured two important lords of the Welsh Marches, Roger Mortimer of Chirk and his nephew Roger Mortimer of Wigmore. Edward put them in the Tower and there the elder Mortimer died of starvation; but the younger Mortimer had made friends there with Isabel and then had managed to escape. When Isabel went to Paris for her husband she met Mortimer again, and together they plotted the downfall of the Despensers. They raised troops together and returned with Isabel's friend Sir John of Hainault, uncle of Philippa, the proposed bride for Isabel's son Edward. The invaders soon executed the Despensers and deposed Edward. They chased him across England and when they passed through Oxford Bishop Orlton of Hereford preached a treasonable sermon. A delicately illuminated manuscript of the Chronicle of the Counts of Flanders, made in the fifteenth century by an artist who worked for Mary of Burgundy, has a picture of the entry of Isabel into Oxford on this occasion (see plate 14). By January 1327 Edward was in prison and on the anniversary of her landing he was murdered in Berkeley Castle. For three years Isabel and Mortimer were supreme. Then her son, Edward III, asserted himself and almost maddened her by killing Mortimer. Her disgrace (1330) was brief and by 1337 her income was restored. Her last twenty-eight years were spent in retirement at Castle Rising (Norfolk). The accounts of the queen's exchequer record details of this period and of the previous twenty-two years; and an inventory lists her valuables, including a ring made by St. Dunstan, the equipment of her chapel and eight romances.

Hilda Johnstone, 'Isabella, the She-wolf of France', *History*, N.S. vol. 11 (1936), pp. 208–218.

PHILIPPA OF HAINAULT (1312–69) was the second cousin of her husband, Edward III; for her mother, like his, was a granddaughter of Philip III of France. Philippa's father was William the Good, Count of Holland and Hainault, and her mother was Countess Joan, sister of Philip VI of Valois, whose claim to the French throne Edward III disputed. When Isabel of France was plotting revenge on the Despensers and perhaps on her husband, Edward II, as well (1325–6) she won the support of Count William and arranged a marriage between Philippa and Edward, her son, both aged fifteen. Edward II did not wish this and the council were not consulted. Philippa's marriage portion was partly paid in the form of troops intended to fight the bridegroom's father under William's brother, John of Hainault. After Edward III became king (1327) the council sent Bishop Orlton to seek a princess from Hainault as his bride and he was told to choose 'her with the finest form'. He chose Philippa who was 'full feminine'. A papal dispensation was obtained (1328) and John of Hainault conducted her to England, accompanied by her squire Walter de Manny (d. 1372), destined to be one of the bravest of knights and founder of the Charterhouse in London. Edward III was then fighting the Scots and the marriage was celebrated at York Minster (1328). The birth of Edward, the Black Prince (1330), at Philippa's favourite palace of Woodstock encouraged Edward III to assert himself against his mother's regency. In 1338 Philippa accompanied Edward III as far as Herenstals when he went to visit the Emperor at Coblentz (Germany). She stayed in great splendour at Antwerp, where fortunes were spent upon her, and a son was born named Lionel, after the lion which formed the heraldic arms of Brabant. In 1340 the birth of another son occurred in Flanders, and he was called, after his birthplace, John of Gaunt (Ghent). An important result of her connection with the Low Countries was the encouragement which she gave to John Kempe and other Flemish weavers to migrate to her favourite city of Norwich. In 1346 she repelled a Scottish invasion, while her husband was busy in France, and she is said to have been present at the battle of Nevill's Cross, reviewing her troops on a white charger. There King David was captured. He was taken to London and led through the streets to the Tower on a tall horse. She then joined Edward III at Calais (1346) and there, on its surrender (1347), occurred the famous scene when she interceded with Edward for the lives of six burghers of Calais whom he had said he would execute. The same year she interceded with Edward for some carpenters who made some royal pavilions which collapsed beneath the royal party at a tournament in Cheapside. Another instance of her mercy had occurred in 1343 when she had persuaded Edward not to punish de Beche for neglecting his duty as castellan of the Tower. Froissart was received by Philippa when he came to England (1361) and she made him her secretary. He described her as 'tall and upright, wise, gay, humble, pious, liberal and courteous, decked and adorned in her time with all noble virtues, beloved of God and of mankind . . . and so long as she lived, the kingdom of England had favour, prosperity, honour and every sort of good fortune'. She had seven sons and five daughters. Through their many descendants almost every old noble and gentle family of England became connected by blood or marriage. She died of dropsy and after her death a terrible decline took place in the character of Edward III. Her bust is in Bristol Cathedral and her effigy is at the feet of Edward III in Westminster Abbey. It was not she, but her chaplain, John Eglesfield (d. 1349), who founded Queen's College, Oxford (1341). See descendants, p. 178.

B. C. Hardy, *Philippa of Hainault and her Time*, 1910.

SIR JOHN CHANDOS (d. 1370) was a gallant soldier whose merciful and statesmanlike character shines against the black background of the Hundred Years War. As constable of Guienne (1362) and Seneschal of Poitiers (1369) he showed that he was a statesman as well as a soldier, and he did his best to restrain the Black Prince. The victories of Crécy (1346) and Poitiers (1365) had crushed the French and they had ceded the whole of Aquitaine including Poitou to Edward III; if more English soldiers had been like Chandos perhaps the French would not have been goaded into renewed resistance. Froissart says of his appointment in 1362 to receive the faith, fidelity and homage of the counts, viscounts, bailiffs, and officers, towns and castles, 'most worthy was he also of this high distinction; for he was a sweet-tempered knight, courteous, benign, amiable, liberal, courageous, prudent, and loyal and valiant in all affairs; there was none more beloved and esteemed than he was by the knights and ladies of his time'. In 1346 Edward III had enraged the Norman population by ravaging the countryside most wantonly in the course of the march which culminated in his victory at Crécy. On that march Sir John Chandos was distinguished not only for his bravery but also for his humane treatment of the sufferers. Throughout the battle of Poitiers (1356) Chandos never left his post beside the Black Prince, and the vigilance of Chandos saved the life of Edward. Before the fight he had ridden near one of the French flanks and on his way back he met Lord John de Clermont who had been making a similar reconnoitre of an English flank. Both had the same armorial device on their surcoats. Each asked the other why he was using his arms (see the end-paper). Lord Clermont said that if there were not a truce he would have proved that Chandos had no right to wear them, and Chandos said that Clermont would find him on the morrow in the field ready to prove his right. During the so-called peace Chandos beat the French for the Duke of Brittany at the battle of Auray (1364) where the French hero Duguesclin was captured. There Chandos dealt such desperate blows with his battle-axe that all avoided him. Chandos fought in a battle at Navaretta (1367), when the Black Prince found occasion to fight the French over a disputed succession to the crown of Castile, and fell three years later fighting on the border of Aquitaine and Poitiers. He was wearing a long robe, blazoned with his arms. The ground was slippery after a hoar frost, and his robe tripped him. Just then a French squire thrust him with a lance under the eye. He fell twice, turned over in agony and never spoke again. The squire was mortally wounded too. After the French withdrew Sir John's servant gently disarmed him and he was carried, laid upon shields, to Mortemer. The Poitevin barons and knights mourned: 'O Sir John Chandos, flower of knighthood, cursed be the forging of the lance that wounded you'. He survived only one day and was buried at Mortemer where there are verses upon his tomb.

Sir John Froissart, *The Chronicle*, Tr. by Sir J. Bourchier, Lord Berners, 6 vols. (Tudor translations), 1901.

EDWARD OF WOODSTOCK (1330–76) (called the 'Black Prince' since 1569) was born heir apparent of Edward III (1330), became Earl of Chester (1333), first Duke of Cornwall (1337), and Prince of Wales (1343) and died of dysentery in 1376. The herald of his comrade Sir John Chandos called him 'fair to look upon' in a metrical biography, and his effigy remains in Canterbury Cathedral. Victor of Crécy (26 Aug., 1346), Poitiers (19 Sept., 1356) and Nájera (3 April, 1367) and generous host of his captive King John of France at Ely Place, Holborn (1357), Edward fulfilled the courtly ideal of Froissart and the patriotic Elizabethan ideal of Holinshed and Shakespeare. A founder of the Order of the Garter, in legendary black armour with bit and visor of his own invention and the costly ostrich plumes which he adopted, the Black Prince rides eternally in English historical pageantry. When Edward was seven years old Sir Walter Manny became his tutor, associated with the learned Walter Burley of Merton College. That year (1337) he received two cardinals as ambassadors and in 1338, 1340 and 1342 he was Keeper of the realm. He learnt to read and later wrote 'Humout, ich dene', his mottoes, on official documents. He loved to honour the Trinity, but unfortunately his home, though religious, taught him to gamble and to drink heavily. He lost as much as 106 shillings in one bout to his father. His cousin, Joan of Kent (aged thirty), made him her third husband (1361). Their son, Richard, resembled him, and it was to secure his succession that the Prince 'animated' the 'Good Parliament' (1376). His cruelty, extravagance and pride alienated Aquitaine (ceded to Edward III in 1360, made a Principality in 1362 and ruled by the Prince, 1363–71); and his raid from Bordeaux to Narbonne (1355) and his massacre at Limoges (1370) were utterly inhuman. Edward never visited Wales, and he visited Cornwall first in 1354. He generally dwelt at Berkhamstead, Kennington or Vauxhall.

J. Cammidge, *The Black Prince*, 1943.
P. Shaw, 'The Black Prince', *History*, New Series, vol. 24, 1939.
T.S.I.H., i, 151 (Crécy).

EDWARD III (1312–77) became king at the age of fifteen and married Philippa of Hainault the following year, but power still remained with his mother, Isabel, and her favourite, Mortimer. At the age of eighteen, when his eldest son, the Black Prince, was five months old, Edward asserted himself, hanged Mortimer at Tyburn and pensioned off his mother with £1,000 a year at Castle Rising (Norfolk). He had in this the powerful support in the north of the blind earl, Henry of Lancaster, who had only backed Isabel and Mortimer so as to recover the wide estates which Edward II had confiscated from Henry's brother Thomas.

Through Isabel Edward III would have been King of France, if the 'Salic Law' had not forbidden inheritance through a female. For a time he stopped using the lilies of France in his own arms, but not for long. He sheltered Robert of Artois,

THE INTERNATIONAL ANCESTRY OF THE PARENTS OF KING EDWARD III

John, King of England, d. 1216 (see p. 55) Isabel of Angoulême, dau. of Aymer of Angoulême, d. 1245	Henry III, King of England, d. 1272	Edward I, King of England, d. 1307	Edward II, King of England, d. 1327, father of Edward III (see pedigree of descendants, p. 178)
Raymond IV of Provence, d. 1245 Beatrice of Savoy, dau. of Thomas, Count of Savoy	Eleanor of Provence, d. 1291		
Alfonzo IX of Leon, d. 1230 Berengaria of Castile, dau. of Alfonzo	Ferdinand III, King of Castile, d. 1252	Eleanor of Castile, d. 1290	
Simon of Dammartin, Count of Aumâle Marie of Ponthieu	Joanna of Ponthieu, d. 1279		
Louis IX, King of France, d. 1270 Margaret of Provence, dau. of Raymond IV	Philip III, King of France, d. 1285	Philip IV, King of France, d. 1314	Isabel the She-wolf of France, mother of Edward III
James I, King of Aragon, d. 1276 Yolande of Hungary, dau. of Andrew II, King of Hungary	Isabella of Aragon, d. 1271		
Theobald I, King of Navarre, d. 1253, son of Theobald III of Champagne Margaret of Foix, dau. of Count of Foix	Henry I, King of Navarre, d. 1274	Joanna of Navarre, d. 1305	
Robert, Count of Artois, d. 1250, son of Louis VIII, King of France Matilda of Brabant, dau. of Henry II of Brabant	Blanche of Artois, d. 1270		

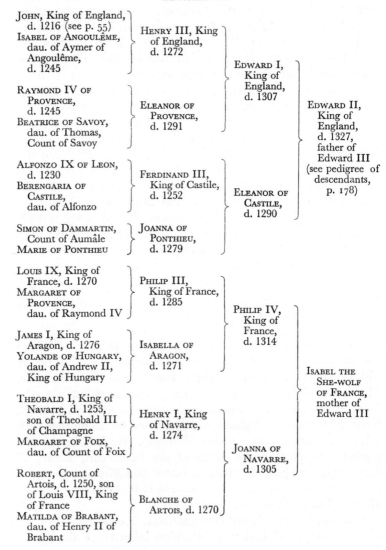

Plate 23

Henry IV (National Portrait Gallery), autograph (British Museum MS. Vespasian F. iii, ff. 5 and 6).

Plate 24

Joan of Navarre and Henry IV (Canterbury)

the enemy and brother-in-law of his rival Philip VI of Valois, King of France. Robert had made waxen images of Philip's queen and eldest son to kill them by black magic (1332) and he had had to flee to England disguised as a merchant. There he egged on Edward III to attack France. Froissart tells a picturesque tale of the Vow of the Heron typical of the world of unstatesmanlike chivalry in which Edward lived. Robert caught a heron, when out hawking with John of Hainault, a friend of Isabel who fought the Scots for England but who was at the French king's side at Crécy. Robert gave the heron to Edward, as 'the most timid bird for the most timid king, who had let slip his claim to France'. Edward was nettled and swore by God and the heron that within a year he would give the French crown to his queen even if the English fought one to six. He said he took this oath on the heron in allusion to the 'Oath of the Peacock', described in a popular romance. This romance had fostered a fourteenth-century custom to swear on some bird to which a symbolic meaning was attached. There was a Vow of the Sparrow Hawk and Edward I swore a Vow of the Swan (1306).

Such romantic trifles contributed to the Hundred Years War with France. 'Gracious Edward' was tall and handsome like his feeble father, but he had the audacity of his mother and retained her energy until he reached an old age, embittered by discontent and dishonoured by his submission to the influence of his mistress Alice Perrers.

His biography is the story of mid-fourteenth-century English, and indeed European, history, with its luxuriance of pointless military achievement and diplomatic intrigue and its drive to secure taxes to pay for the luxury of strife. It is a tale of glorious aggression in Scotland, France and Spain bringing ruin on a world with the aid of plague; and if Dante had lived later he would doubtless have portrayed the Napoleonic Edward III with Alexander the Great in the Blood Bath reserved for their like. Edward III regarded both Scotland and France as his by right and he allowed the world and himself no respite in his struggle to gain them both, though to have attained either of them alone would have been a hard task.

DESCENDANTS OF EDWARD III

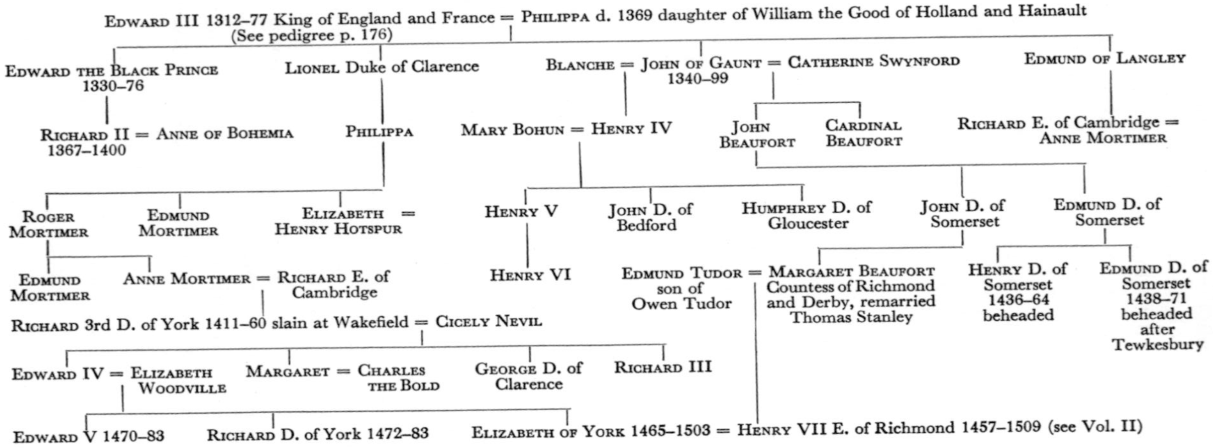

He beat the French at Sluys (1340) because he realized that ships should be manoeuvred and not treated as floating castles. The first known picture of a cannon was painted for him in a book on the Instruction of Princes (1326–7), and at Cambrai (1339) he was the first to employ cannons in battle; but was not a really skilled general. His use of the long-bow plied by yeomen wrought havoc among the French knights. Forty years of hard labour brought him famous victories like Crécy (1346) and Poitiers (1356). The vast suffering caused was not justifiable as a means to any reasonable end, and the protests of poor peasants began to be heard in the poem Piers Plowman, but fourteenth-century chroniclers loved the polish of romantic chivalry, and twentieth-century sentiment remembers that Edward founded the Order of the Garter and built St. George's Chapel, Windsor. Selfish, extravagant, unscrupulous, ambitious and ostentatious, Edward must be judged by his own standards, and the idea of the pursuit of material happiness for the greatest number of individuals was not the idea of his age; and even by such modern standards it must be remembered that he encouraged the wool trade and faced the unpopularity of introducing Flemish craftsmen (1332). During Edward's reign occurred the Black Death (1348–9). Prices and wages rose and his Statute of Labourers (1350) tried to keep down wages and a statute of 1372 ordered labourers who left home for higher wages to be branded on the forehead with a letter F (for 'False'); but feudal England was changing into the England of Chaucer, Wycliff and Wat Tyler and the events of the reign were more important than the king. Although Edward was essentially a knight of chivalry he was the first English king who could write. Under him there was domestic peace.

Conan Doyle, *White Company* describes a company of hired soldiers such as Edward used in France.

R. L. Stevenson, *Black Arrow* shows the disorder which they brought back into England. See plates and 16–18.

SIMON OF SUDBURY (d. 1381), so called from his birthplace in Suffolk, studied law at Paris. He became chaplain of Pope Innocent VI (1352–62), Chancellor of Salisbury, and

Bishop of London. As Archbishop of Canterbury (1375) he crowned Richard II (1377); and, though much more tolerant than his successors with their policy of having Lollard heretics burnt, he enjoined silence on Wyclif (1378) and imprisoned John Ball. Sudbury's predecessors, Simon Islip and Simon Langham, had failed to silence Ball with excommunications, and when imprisoned Ball had prophesied that he would soon be set free from the archbishop's prison at Maidstone by twenty thousand men. Sudbury's writ (dated 26 April, 1381) said that Ball had not sought absolution but had 'slunk back to our diocese, like a fox that evaded the hunter, and feared not to preach and argue both in the churches and church-yards (without the leave or against the will of the parochial authorities) and also in markets and other profane places, there beguiling the ears of the laity by his invectives and putting about such scandals concerning our person and those of other prelates and clergy and—what is worse—using, concerning the holy father himself, language such as shamed the ears of good Christians'. Wat Tyler's followers released John Ball, received a welcome from the people of Canterbury, and burnt all documents found in Sudbury's palace. Wat Tyler interrupted Mass in the Cathedral saying that Sudbury would die as a traitor and that a successor should be elected as archbishop. Sudbury withdrew to the Tower with Richard II and the court, and on 14 June, 1381, early in the morning he tried to escape by boat, but a woman raised the alarm. That day Richard and his mother and advisers went out to meet the rebels at Mile End. They left Sudbury and Robert Hales, the Treasurer, who was hated as 'Hob the Robber', responsible for the Poll Tax. These two, when left in the Tower, began to prepare for death in the chapel. The King sacrificed his archbishop as a scapegoat and told the rebels at Mile End 'that they might take those who were traitors against him and slay them wheresoever they might be found'. Sudbury made a long and bold dying speech saying that if he were killed England should be under an interdict; but this was greeted with mocking laughter for the rebels said they did not fear the Pope or his interdict. He was then executed with Robert Hales, and Richard's confessor, on the traditional place for the block on Tower Hill. The heads were paraded round the streets and put on London Bridge in the usual way. At least the executioners did not draw and quarter the victims.

WAT TYLER (d. 1381) 'of Kent' or 'of Essex' was chosen leader of the peasants in revolt at Maidstone, and was murdered nine days later. He shook the world. A story that he, or rather John Tyler, was an artisan of Dartford whose daughter was insulted by a poll-tax collector first appears in the works of John Stow, an Elizabethan student of London antiquities. Tyler probably came from Colchester, the home of John Ball. In his own generation he is described as a highwayman, or a discharged soldier, a 'crafty fellow of an excellent wit but lacking grace' with an 'intelligence great, but applied to evil'. He did not hesitate to suppress looting by death and he kept his followers in good order, marshalling them by towns and villages; but he had no qualms about carrying out their intentions of executing 'traitors' responsible for the poll tax and for the French disasters, if he could catch them, and he regarded the total destruction of John of Gaunt's new palace of the Savoy in the Strand as a duty. The rebellion aimed at the abolition of manorial burdens and therefore the rebels destroyed manorial records when possible, but the immediate cause was the poll-tax levied on all people above fifteen years old in 1377, 1379 and 1380. From Maidstone he went via Canterbury and Rochester, where he was welcomed, to London. On Wednesday, 12 June, 1381, he camped at Blackheath. On Thursday, 13 June, London fell without a blow. He thus formulated his demands:

1. All should be free from bondage. There should be no serfs.
2. All insurrections, treasons, felonies, transgressions and extortions should be pardoned.
3. All should be free to buy and sell in every county, city, borough, town, fair, market, etc.
4. No acre held in bondage or service should be held for

more than 4d. an acre. If it had ever been less it should not be increased.

On Friday, 14 June, Tyler's host received young Richard II and his terrified advisers at Mile End. Richard said that Tyler might execute traitors, and he ordered thirty clerks then and there to draw up charters granting the peasants' petitions. He handed his royal banner to Tyler to show that he was acting on his behalf. At this point the soldiers in the Tower admitted the peasants, and Archbishop Sudbury, Treasurer Hales and a few other scapegoats were executed on Tower Hill. On the evening of Saturday, 15 June, there was a final meeting at Smithfield. Accounts are coloured and vary. Froissart tells a famous story of Richard's heroism which seems less correct than what follows. He apparently wished to flatter the King. Tyler came alone except for an attendant with a banner. He knelt to Richard and shook his hand saying 'Brother, be of good cheer and joyful, for you will soon have the fifteenth (a money grant) pledged by the Commons, more than you had before, and we shall be good comrades'. Richard asked why the peasants had not gone home. Tyler read out his demands: 'Let no law but the Law of Winchester prevail, and let no man be made outlaw by the decree of judges and lawyers. No lord shall exercise lordship over the Commons; and since we are oppressed by so vast a horde of bishops and clerks, let there be but one bishop in England. The property and goods of the holy church should be taken and divided according to the needs of the people in each parish, after making provision for the existing clergy and monks, and finally let there be no more villeins in England, but all to be free and of one condition'. Richard II replied 'All that you have asked for I promise readily if only it be consistent with the regality of my crown. And now let the Commons return home, since their requests have been granted'. There was a hush. Tyler asked for a drink. He rinsed his mouth and spat some water on the ground; then he drank a great draught of ale. Before he could ride away a page called out that he knew Tyler as the greatest thief in Kent. Tyler demanded that his accuser should stand forth, and, according to the *Anonimale Chronicle*, 'at last the lords made him go out to him, to see what he would do before the king'. The page said that he was speaking the truth and apologized for arguing in Richard's presence. Tyler drew his dagger. Then the Lord Mayor of London, William Walworth, said he would arrest anyone who drew in Richard's presence, and wounded Tyler in the head and neck. Tyler fell back on his horse and Ralph Standish and John Cavendish there attacked him. Tyler spurred his horse towards his followers but soon fell. The peasants were alarmed and in their uncertainty about what was happening might have attacked. Richard advanced and said 'Tyler has been knighted. Your demands have been granted'. Tyler would join them in St. John's Meadow (Clerkenwell, between the present St. John Street and Goswell Road). Meanwhile Tyler had been laid in the Master's room in St. Bartholomew's Hospital nearby. Walworth dragged him out, decapitated him and rode with his head on a lance to Richard. The meeting at Mile End had been graced by the presence of Richard's mother, but not the meeting at Smithfield. When Richard rejoined her she said 'Ah, fair son, what pain and anguish have I had for you this day'. Richard replied 'Certes, madam, I know it well. But now rejoice and praise God, for today I have recovered my heritage that was lost, and the realm of England also'.

R. H. Hilton and H. Fagan, *The English Rising of 1381*, 1950 (from the rebel standpoint).
T.S.I.H., i, 168 (from the City standpoint).

JOHN BALL, (d. 1381), 'the mad priest of Kent', preached sedition, taking as text:

> 'Whan Adam dalf, and Eve span,
> Wo was thanne a gentilman?'

He had been in trouble as early as 1366, was often reprimanded and had been imprisoned for his preaching at Colchester, and also (in the archibishop's prison) at Maidstone. From there he was rescued by his followers. Froissart says he used to collect a crowd in the market-place and say: 'My friends, things won't go well in England until everything is held in common, without serfs or lords, when lords are no more masters than we are. What ill treatment! Why do they keep us in chains? Are not we all children of Adam and Eve? What right have they to be on top? They wear velvet and rich stuffs, with ermine and other fur; we must dress cheaply. They have wines, spices and good bread; we have rye and husks and only water. Fine manor houses for them, but wind and rain for us toiling in the fields. They call us slaves and thrash us if we slack, and we have no king to complain to or willing to listen. Let's go and protest to him. He's young, and we might get a kind answer. If not, we must raise our own standard of life.' That is how he harangued people in his own village every Sunday after mass. He did the same again when he came out from two or three months in the archbishop's prison.

Such was the propaganda which preceded Wat Tyler's rebellion. Froissart adds that after the trouble John Ball and Jack Straw were found in an old ruin waiting for things to blow over. Their own men betrayed them. The king and barons were delighted, and had their heads, and that of Wat Tyler, fixed on London Bridge, instead of the heads of those the rebels had slain. The judge who condemned him was Sir Robert Tresilian, who met a similar end seven years later.

William Morris, *Dream of John Ball*, an imaginary picture by a socialist poet.
G. M. Trevelyan, *England in the Age of Wycliffe*, 1909.
C. E. Petit-Dutaillis, *Studies Supplementary to Stubbs's Constitutional History*, vol. 2, 1914.
P. Lindsay and R. Groves, *The Peasants' Revolt, 1381* (1950).
T.S.I.H., i, 166 (from Froissart).

JOHN WYCLIF (c. 1329–84), Master of Balliol College, Oxford (1361), was a philosopher, a theologian and a teacher of heretical doctrines. He was responsible for the Bible being translated into English (1378–pre-1400). He is probably the subject of more biographies than any other medieval Englishman, but they are largely based on guesses and written without an understanding of the medieval background. He was born near Wyclif, the place from which his surname is derived, at Hipswell and it is remarkable that the family of Wyclif remained true to the old faith after the Reformation. John Wyclif himself has been called the Morning Star of the Reformation and he is a father of English nonconformity; but, though scholars may suggest that Wyclif should no longer be described as inspiring the Reformation, he put the authority of the Bible before that of the Church and he gave logical form to anti-clerical feelings which many felt in his own time and which were given effect by Henry VIII. This he did with authority as even his enemies admitted his eminence as a thinker, and as an original thinker he influenced John Hus in Bohemia who in turn influenced Luther in Germany.

Nothing is known about the circumstances of his childhood and though he wrote forty large volumes they reveal nothing about his personality save that 'their author was learned, subtle, ingenious, opinionated, tirelessly argumentative and rather humourless'. Wyclif is not to be confused with a namesake at Queen's College or another at Merton College, both at Oxford. The clue for his connexion with Balliol College may lie in the fact that it was founded by John Baliol, Lord of Barnard's Castle, which stands across the River Tees from Wyclif. Wyclif was undoubtedly one of the outstanding figures of his age, and his followers were important enough to threaten the throne of Henry V, who followed his family tradition of persecuting them. Those who wish to belittle his memory may call him a 'negligent pluralist', enjoying the incomes of more livings than he served properly, whether or not his attack on the church's abuses was embittered by 'disappointed ambition'. If he had died ten years earlier his name would have been remembered about as much as that of any other scholar; what matters about him is his attempt to spread his views among common men, unused to such an approach. This meant that many who did not understand him revered him, and many who did understand him hated him. Wyclif was sent to Bruges (1374) as ambassador to treat with Pope Gregory XI's delegates about the non-observance of the Statute of Provisors, limiting papal rights in England. There Wyclif objected to the worldliness of the clergy; and his high opinion of the rights of lay lords pleased John of Gaunt who asked him to preach in London (1376). The St. Albans chronicler said that Wyclif had long been 'running about from church to church' and 'barking against the church'. Those who supported William of Wykeham prevailed upon Archbishop Simon Sudbury to prosecute Wyclif for heresy (1377). His philosophical opinions and his theory of 'Dominion by Grace' led to opinions which undermined the authority of priests. He demanded the disendowment of the clergy so that they could return to the simple poverty of the apostles. He believed the king should be supreme and ought to reform the church. He criticized the Pope and denied the truth of transubstantiation. The Peasants' Revolt and the murder of Sudbury (1381), though not his doing, strengthened orthodox conservative opinion. A Council at Blackfriars (1382) condemned Wyclif for ten heresies and fourteen errors. He was excluded from the Oxford schools, but his ideas were influential even as far away as Bohemia. Latterly he was a very sick man, and he died of a stroke on Holy Innocents' Day while hearing Mass, aged fifty-five. It was not his first stroke. His last years, spent in retirement at his living of Lutterworth, were not disturbed. The Bishop of Lincoln burnt what were thought to be his bones and cast the ashes into the River Swift at Lutterworth (1428).

H. B. Workman. *John Wyclif*, 1926.
K. B. McFarlane, *John Wycliffe and the Beginnings of English Nonconformity* (Teach Yourself History), 1952.
T.S.I.H., i, 186 (Lollards at Leicester).

WILLIAM WALWORTH (d. 1385) was apprenticed to John Lovekin, a saltfish-merchant who had been Member of Parliament for London twice and Mayor four times (1347–66) at a time when London fishmongers had come to rival vintners in civic importance and had not yet been in turn rivalled by the mercers. On Lovekin's death Walworth succeeded to his business and to his post of alderman of Bridge Ward (1368) and his name is famous outside the annals of the city because he happened to be Mayor in the year of the peasants' revolt (1381). As the rebels of Kent approached London Bridge they burned some houses at Walworth and Southwark which belonged to Walworth and were let to some disreputable Flemish tenants. A few aldermen decided to open the gates, and all Walworth could do was to get Tyler to agree to pay for anything taken and to avoid doing damage. Walworth was with the party which returned with Richard II to the Tower and advised a night attack on the 'shoe-less ruffians'. A policy of parley was, however, preferred. At the second parley, at Smithfield, Walworth found occasion to strike Tyler. He later dragged his wounded body from St. Bartholomew's Hospital and decapitated it. The city and the Fishmongers' Company were proud of his act and came to fancy, wrongly, that the sword in the corner of the city arms was his sword which they cherished as a relic. Actually the sword in the city arms represents that of St. Paul. A few months after the rebellion Walworth's enemy John of Northampton became mayor, a keen-witted and stout-hearted champion of the small craftsmen against the monopolies of the victuallers, and especially of the fishmongers. Northampton gained the support of John of Gaunt, who cherished an 'ancient hatred' against the liberties of London and the power of its financiers. Walworth was one of these financiers.

Ruth Bird, *The Turbulent London of Richard II*, Longmans, 1949. This contains an accurate sketch-map of London in 1381 by Marjorie B. Honeybourne which can be compared with her similar map of Norman London in the Historical Association leaflet on *Norman London*. These are rare examples of utter simplicity and clarity based on an exhaustive study of the numerous available documents of the time. Lanes, monasteries and all the one-hundred-and-nine city parish churches are marked.

SIR ROBERT TRESILIAN (d. 1388), Chief Justice of the King's Bench, began his career, as a good Westcountryman, at Exeter College, Oxford. There he was a Fellow about 1354. He accompanied Richard II to St. Albans after the Peasants'

Revolt and, as justiciar, tried and hanged John Ball (1381). Thomas Walsingham, the St. Albans historian, describes how he produced a list of ringleaders and forced an unwilling jury to indict them. He had some of them hanged and drawn for riot and imprisoned the leading townsmen. In 1386 Thomas of Woodstock, Duke of Gloucester, forced his nephew, Richard II, to accept a commission of discontented magnates, the Lords Appellant, to purge his household and the kingdom of those whom they disliked, but who were in fact his best friends. Richard could not raise armed support, but he obtained the formal opinion of Chief Justice Tresilian and the other judges. The judges considered that the commission was unlawful and infringed the royal prerogative (1387). When Gloucester heard this, he prepared for war; and he and his supporters charged Richard's advisers, including Tresilian, with treason. The boldest adviser, Robert de Vere, Duke of Ireland and Earl of Oxford, raised troops, but they were dispersed at Radcot Bridge (20 Dec., 1387). Froissart says de Vere had sent his cousin Tresilian to observe events in London. He rode on a wretched hackney from Bristol to London disguised as a poor tradesman. He lodged at an inn where he was unknown and collected all the public gossip. He heard the dukes and council were to meet at Westminster, so he took a room overlooking Palace-yard in a tavern opposite to watch. He waited so long that at last a squire of the Duke of Gloucester recognized him, though he withdrew from the window. He went in and asked the landlady who it was drinking upstairs. She said she did not know, but that he had been there a long time. The squire went up and did not show that he knew he was right, but said 'God preserve you, master, I hope you will not mind my intrusion, but I thought you were one of my farmers from Essex.' 'No', said Sir Robert, 'I'm tenant of Sir John Holland from Kent, and want to complain to the council about the encroachments of the Archbishop of Canterbury's tenants.' 'If you come into the hall, I'll introduce you.' 'Thanks, not now; but I won't refuse help.' The squire ordered a quart of ale and left. He hurried to the council chamber and asked the usher to let him see Gloucester at once. He said he had great news and would tell it aloud as it touched all present. He had seen Tresilian dressed as a peasant, in an alehouse by the gate. Gloucester said he would like him to dine and give news about his master, de Vere. The squire took four bailiffs, telling them to stay behind and come and seize Tresilian when given a sign. He went upstairs. 'Tresilian, you're up to no good here. My lord of Gloucester wants you.' 'I'm a tenant of Sir John Holland. I am not Tresilian.' 'Your body is his, but not your clothes.' He signalled and the bailiffs arrested him. Gloucester questioned him closely about de Vere's plans. 'How is it you come as a spy, not dressed as an honest man? If you wanted news you should have come looking like a knight or someone respectable . . . Tresilian, Tresilian, you are unfair and dishonest and you're a fool to come here. You and your party have damaged me and my brother (John of Gaunt). But now you'll pay. I shall not eat or drink while you're alive.' Sir Robert was terrified and made grovelling excuses. The hangman took him to Tyburn. There he was beheaded and hung by the arms to a gibbet. His enemies, the Lords Appellant, began their rule by strengthening the Statute of Labourers, and their 'Merciless Parliament' made further executions; but the other judges who had joined Tresilian in supporting Richard II were only banished to Ireland.

MICHAEL DE LA POLE (*c.* 1330–89) was son of Sir William de la Pole of Hull, the greatest merchant of England and the first to found a noble family (d. 1366). Michael married Catherine de Wingfield, a Suffolk heiress. He loyally served Edward III and the Black Prince abroad and defended the court in Parliament (1376). He went to Bohemia to arrange Richard II's marriage and became his worthiest adviser. He built fine houses in Hull, London and Wingfield and became Lord Chancellor (1383–6) and Earl of Suffolk (1385). He was unpopular and Thomas Arundel called him covetous and William Courtenay called him false. Parliament fined and imprisoned him (1386) and the Lords Appellant (see p. 202) condemned him to hang (1388). He fled disguised as a Flemish poulterer, but was caught at Calais. He finally escaped to

Paris, where he died (5 Sept., 1389), the butt of political poets and chroniclers.

N. B. Lewin, 'Article VII of the impeachment of Michael de la Pole', *English Historical Review*, vol. 42 (1927).

Catherine and Michael De La Pole, Earl of Suffolk (Wingfield Church)

THOMAS BRINTON (after 1320–1389) was a member of an unimportant Norfolk family. He studied at Gloucester College, the chief Benedictine foundation at Oxford, and from being a monk and a scholar became, as Bishop of Rochester (1373–89), a statesman and vivid preacher who was a friend of the poor, but who earned the respect of Edward III and the Pope. Before 1373 he had been serving for a time at the papal court, then at Avignon. Brinton was zealous for the reform of the church, but from within, and he was perhaps the only member of the church party who always had the courage of his convictions. In 1381 he was on the commission to try Wat Tyler's Kentish supporters and in 1382 he assented to the condemnation of Wyclif's doctrines at Blackfriars (London). Old age and infirmity made him spend his last six years in retirement.

Sister Mary Aquinas Devlin, *The Sermons of Thomas Brinton, Bishop of Rochester (1373–1389)*, Camden Society Publications, Third Series, vols. 85–6, 1954.

ANNE OF BOHEMIA (1366–1394) was born at Prague and was sister of King Wenceslaus of Bohemia. Her parents were Charles IV, the Holy Roman Emperor (1347–78), and a niece of Queen Philippa. Her marriage to Richard II was arranged by his favourite half-brother, Thomas Holland, Earl of Kent (1379), but her arrival was delayed by Wat Tyler's rebellion (1381). On the way she stayed at Brussels with her aunt, the heiress of Hainault and Duchess of Saxony. The Channel crossing was in December and it was so rough that after she had disembarked at Dover she saw the vessel break up. The king's uncle, Thomas Duke of Gloucester, conducted her with pomp to Canterbury and the Goldsmiths welcomed her in London with showers of florins and gold-leaf. She was married quietly in St. Stephen's Chapel, Westminster (14 Jan., 1382), and she waited at Windsor until the regalia of Aquitaine had been pawned to pay for her coronation in Westminster Abbey, where is the funeral monument of the affectionate royal pair holding hands. Anne earned the name of 'Good Queen Anne' because she saved the lives of many condemned rebels whose names were excepted from a general pardon; but the cost of her journeys and her household with its Bohemian retinue, and her lack of a marriage portion, contributed to Richard II's troubles with Parliament. She began the fashion for ladies to wear caps with tall, wide horns supporting large veils, introduced pins for dresses, and started the use of side-saddles for ladies. Her badge was an ostrich with iron in its beak, a medieval symbol of endurance derived from the ability of an ostrich to swallow hard objects. She was a supporter of Wyclif. She hoped to arrange a marriage between Richard's friend, Robert de Vere, ninth Earl of Oxford and Duke of Ireland, and one of her German ladies, although he was already married. When the Merciless Parliament (1388) condemned Sir Simon Burley, Richard's former tutor, she pleaded for his life, because it was he who had escorted her to

England and she liked him. He was executed with Tresilian and she was advised 'Pray for yourself and your husband, for the request is useless'. Richard quarrelled with the Londoners about a loan which they had refused and a Lombard banker whom they had killed (1392); he cancelled their privileges and fined them 3,000 marks and £100,000. Anne interceded with him for the Londoners, just as Queen Philippa had interceded with Edward III on behalf of the citizens of Calais, and he restored their privileges and remitted the demand for £100,000 at her request. The day of reconciliation was marked by outstanding pageantry. Richard rode in procession from Sheen Palace (Richmond), while Anne followed in a second procession on her palfrey followed by a red wagon full of her ladies. She put on her crown at Southwark to cross London Bridge and there one of the wagons was upset by pressure of the onlookers and the ladies were only saved by their horned headdresses. At the Cheapside Conduit mechanical angels bore gold circlets for Richard and Anne. They drank 'Peace to the City' in gold cups of the red wine which was flowing from the conduit. The mayor gave her a white pony, and at the Temple she was given gold tablets showing the life of St. Anne. There the mayor reminded her that she had promised to intercede with Richard, which she did on her knees when she found Richard seated on the king's bench in Westminster Hall. Thereat Richard bade Anne sit beside him and he gave back to the mayor the key and sword of London in token of restoration to his favour. Anne died of plague at Sheen on Whit-Sunday, 1394, and her funeral delayed Richard's departure for Ireland. In frenzied grief he cursed the place where she died and levelled the rooms to the ground. To her Chaucer dedicated his 'Legend of Good Women'. Without her calm and loving influence Richard deteriorated. In rage he struck Arundel to the ground for disrespect at the funeral. See plate 20.

JOHN BARBOUR (?1316–95), the earliest great Scottish poet, was perhaps an Aberdonian and studied at Oxford and Paris. He wrote an epic, the *Brus* (1375), a long *Legends of the Saints* (in 33,533 lines) and a lost genealogical poem on

Catherine of Valois, Death Mask

Henry V
(P.R.O.,
E.28/34)

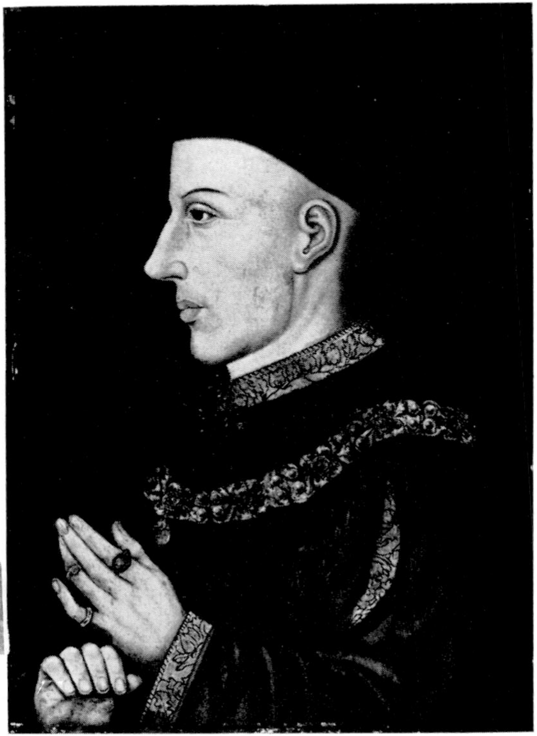

Plate 25

Henry V (National Portrait Gallery)

Plate 26

John, Duke of Bedford (British Museum MS. Add. 18850)

the Stuarts which traced the descent of the Scottish kings back to 'Dardane, Lord de Frygya'. The *Brus* is inspired by a belief in national and personal independence and in the interest and importance of historical facts. It may be largely derived from eye-witnesses, but it confuses Robert Bruce the liberator of Scotland with his grandfather, the competitor against Baliol for the Scottish crown. Barbour's writings did much to fix his Northumbrian 'Inglis' in the form called 'broad Scotch'.

The Bruce, ed. W. W. Skeat, 2 vols. Scottish Text Society, vols. 19 and 20, 1893–94.

THOMAS DE LA MARE (1309–96) entered St. Albans Abbey (1326), became Prior of its dependent house of Tynemouth (1340), and was Abbot of St. Albans for forty-seven years (1349–96). The stirring events of the Peasants' Revolt (1381) occupy one-tenth of Thomas Walsingham's history, and as he was one of De la Mare's monks he has much to say of the abbot's troubles with the tenants and townsmen led by William Gryndecobbe. Many great abbeys had periodical troubles with riotous neighbours and subordinates, and Walsingham's account shows a clear insight into such events and the hopes and fears they inspired. The head of a great abbey would have to resist any encroachments by popes or kings; and De la Mare had further the need to resist a royal mistress, Alice Perrers. De la Mare spent liberally on his abbey and also cared for the maintenance of scholars at Oxford. In the wider world he was a councillor of Edward III. Much real history is however local and the counties of England were dominated not only by the local barons, but also by the heads of monasteries. St. Albans is fortunate in having its affairs well recorded by its monastic historians; and we are fortunate that one of the best surviving brasses of a fourteenth-century prelate is that of the man who weathered the Peasants' Revolt at St. Albans. He defeated the trouble largely by the royal method of issuing privileges which he cancelled when it was safe to do so. This would not have been at all dishonourable according to his lights, for his intellectual and moral background would be full of tales in which the hero defeats Satan through deceit. Thomas Walsingham says that De la Mare's handwriting was bad but rapid and that many people, even magnates, used to treasure specimens of it. See plate 19.

D. Knowles, *Religious Orders in England*, i, 39–48.
T.S.I.H., i, 171–8 (Gryndecobbe).

WILLIAM COURTENAY (1342–96) was a champion of the church in a difficult period, when the livelihood of its priests might have been taken away from them and given to the courtiers. He was born near Exeter. His parents were the Earl of Devon and Margaret, daughter of Humphrey de Bohun, Earl of Hereford. In 1370 he became Bishop of Hereford, and in 1375 Bishop of London. He supported the Black Prince and William of Wykeham against the anti-clerical party of John of Gaunt. In 1377 he summoned Wyclif on a charge of heresy. John of Gaunt and his retainers accompanied Wyclif to the hearing and a quarrel followed between Gaunt and Courtenay. Gaunt alleged that Courtenay relied on family connections, but that they would be no protection. The Londoners hated Gaunt and would have burnt his palace of the Savoy in the Strand, if Courtenay had not restrained them. Four years later Wat Tyler's men murdered Archbishop Sudbury, the Chancellor (1381), and Courtenay succeeded him both as Chancellor and as Archbishop. He resigned the chancellorship, because Richard II's government broke faith by declaring invalid the charters of freedom given to the rebels (1382). Courtenay managed to get Lollard doctrines condemned at a meeting at Blackfriars (London). The proceedings were disturbed by an earthquake, which Courtenay interpreted as being the living God rousing those present to bestir themselves in the Church's cause. 'By a mighty effort the earth is purging itself of noxious vapours, foreshowing that this realm must purge itself of heresy, though it will not be without a struggle and commotion'. Courtenay was a bold man. He succeeded in making the University of Oxford withdraw the protection which it gave to the Lollards. He once reproved Richard II for the extravagance of the court and provoked him so sorely that the king would have struck him but for the restraining interference of his uncle, Thomas of Woodstock. Courtenay visited the Lollard stronghold of Leicester and persuaded the chief citizens to support his efforts against heresy. In 1390 and 1393 he struggled against Parliament's desire to limit the power of the Pope. He died on 31 July, 1396, at Maidstone. In the presence of Richard II he was buried at the feet of the Black Prince at Canterbury. The Courtenay family, with their seat at Powderham (Devon), remain a family of importance. For Courtenay's arms see the end-paper. See plate 21.

JOHN OF GAUNT (1340–99) was the fourth son of Edward III and was born when his mother, Philippa of Hainault, was at Ghent ('Gaunt'). At two years old he became Earl of Richmond. He married Blanche of Lancaster. Blanche's father was nephew of Thomas of Lancaster (1277–1322) and had been the first Duke of Lancaster. By this marriage John became Duke of Lancaster himself and acquired the vast Lancaster estates (1362). John served with his elder brother, the Black Prince, in France and Spain and was with him at the Battle of Nájera (1367) and the recapture of Limoges (1370). After a second marriage, with Constance, daughter of Pedro the Cruel of Castile, John assumed the title of King of Castile (1372) and liked to call himself 'Monseigneur d'Espagne'. He attempted to enforce his claim, but resigned it for 600,000 gold francs (1387) in favour of his daughter Catherine, when she married John of Castile, grandchild of Henry of Trastamara, Pedro's rival and illegitimate brother. At home John opposed rich churchmen who occupied powerful positions of state, like Wykeham, and he therefore supported Wyclif and the Lollards. The clergy blackened him as a coward who urged his men on, but never led them in person, as an unfaithful husband, an unscrupulous politician, a changeling, and a would-be usurper of the crown. The Good Parliament (1376) attacked his followers, and the Londoners (except for the party of John of Northampton) detested him, although they were largely anti-clerical. On Richard II's accession (1377) John of Gaunt was of great importance as one of the young king's uncles, and he played leading parts in many diverse fields throughout the reign. When Richard asserted himself (1389) he took John of Gaunt, despite differences in the past, as his trusted counsellor; but Shakespeare's portrait of him as a noble patriot is historically false. In 1396 John married his third wife, his mistress, Catherine Swynford. She was the daughter of Sir Payne Roelt, a follower of Philippa of Hainault, and she was the widow (since 1372) of one of John's retinue. Her sister perhaps married Chaucer. John gave to her children the name Beaufort, and had them made legitimate (see pedigree on p. 178). In 1407 the Act which legitimized the Beauforts was re-enacted with a clause excluding the right of possible succession to the Crown. From Catherine, however, not only was Henry VII descended, but also almost every other European royal family. On John's death Richard confiscated the Lancaster estates; and this led to the return of John's son, Henry of Lancaster, to regain his inheritance and to gain Richard's kingdom as Henry IV. He was the first King of the House of Lancaster. In 1381 Tyler's rebels sacked John of Gaunt's palace, the Savoy, one of the aristocratic mansions which lined the Strand between London and Westminster. The site is marked not only by the Savoy Hotel but also by the office of the Duchy of Lancaster.

R. T. Bodey, '*Time Honour'd Lancaster*', 1926, has not superseded J. Armitage-Smith, *John of Gaunt*, 1904.
T.S.I.H., i, 189 (Gaunt and the Lollards). See pedigree, p. 178.

GEOFFREY CHAUCER (*c.* 1340–1400) was born in London, the son of a prosperous wine-merchant. The date of his birth is approximate, as is that of most of his poems, but though nothing is definitely known of him before 1357, it is clear that he had a good education, though almost certainly not at Oxford or Cambridge. He was, much more than most poets, a man of the world, at one time or another soldier, courtier, official in the public service, and diplomatist, and well acquainted with fortune's ups-and-downs. Legend of course was often busy with his name, but a good many stories, such as that of his beating a friar in Fleet Street, and other less attractive exploits, have been uprooted by the patient researches of such scholars as Tyrwhitt, Skeat, and Furnivall. After two years as page to the Duke of

Clarence, Chaucer saw military service in France where he was taken prisoner. That he was ransomed by Edward III for £16 shows him to have been a not unimportant young man. In 1367 he was granted a pension 'for good service' by the king, who also appointed him a 'valettus', a post always filled by one of gentle birth, though bed-making was one of its duties. At about this time he married; nothing is known for certain about his wife's identity or character, except that internal evidence from his poems seems to show that she did not make Chaucer happy. He had one son, Lewis, who died young. His prosperous period was from 1372 to 1386, during which he filled various civil service posts, went on several diplomatic missions, and became an M.P. But after 1386 he lost most of his posts, possibly for political reasons, but more likely because he was no great man of business. He was writing poetry during these years, and discharged his duties largely by deputy. He was soon in debt, depending for the most part on pensions and loans, and was no doubt a cheerful spender. In 1394 an annual grant of £20 from Richard II made little apparent difference to his poverty, but when Henry IV, the son of his old patron, John of Gaunt, came to the throne, Chaucer's pension was at once doubled. With characteristic resilience he thereupon took a house on a 53-year lease; but a year later he died, and was buried in Westminster Abbey.

No English poet has ever been regarded with more almost personal affection than Chaucer, founded mainly of course on the many sidelights on himself scattered throughout his poetry. Here, we feel, is a man to make a friend of, humorous, good-tempered, and understanding. Even if he does see our weaknesses every bit as clearly as our merits, that is a small price to pay for the rich enjoyment of his company and talk—a perpetual fountain of good sense, as Dryden called him. That is Chaucer the man, known to all who in spirit have ridden with him down the road to Canterbury in 1388. But he was a voluminous poet apart from the *Canterbury Tales* and it was not of them alone that Spenser was thinking when he called him 'Well of English undefiled', or Tennyson 'the Morning Star of Song'. His poetic works had three well-marked periods when in turn he was under French, Italian, and English influences. In the first period came the 'Boke of the Duchess', in memory of John of Gaunt's first wife. There is not much else, as, though he translated the famous French poem, the *Roman de la Rose*, the version printed among his works, like a good many other poems and translations originally ascribed to him, is held to be very dubiously his. On his visit to Italy in 1372, it is probable that he met Petrarch and Boccaccio, to whom more than one of his poems owe much. The story of his his greatest poem before the *Canterbury Tales*, *Troilus and Cressida*, is taken from Boccaccio's *Filostrato*, and a third of it is an actual translation. As has been said of this poem, it shows what a dramatist Chaucer would have been in one later age, and what a novelist in another. There is much fine poetry in its 8,239 lines, especially at the beginning and the end. At about the same time came his *House of Fame* and the *Legend of Good Women*. Like many other of Chaucer's, both poems are unfinished. The most probable reason seems to be that he was tired of translating and adapting ancient legends, and wished to get closer to the life and people of his own day. This he emphatically did in his third, his English period, in the *Canterbury Tales*.

The plan of the *Canterbury Tales* was ideally suited to the story-teller's free and easy genius—a series of tales told by pilgrims on the way to Canterbury. There is a prologue to each tale, and a general Prologue in which, with masterly skill and clarity, the pilgrims are introduced. We see and hear how they looked and spoke, and share Chaucer's benign and never contemptuous enjoyment of their various foibles and follies. Their characters range from the gentle Knight to the flamboyant Wife of Bath, their tales from the Prioress's exquisite and moving tale of the little clergy-boy murdered to the coarse horse-play of the Miller's. From the very beginning 'Aprille with his shoures soote' sheds a spring freshness over the whole scene, and one's heart is warmed by the poet's frank enjoyment of the world as he found it and the men and women in it. No summing-up of Chaucer's great achievement is better than Dryden's brief, 'Here is God's plenty'.

The best portrait of Chaucer is said to be that which Occleve (*fl.* 1420) painted from memory—a kindly, white-bearded face with downcast eyes, the expression wise and tranquil with a tinge of ironic humour (plate 22).

There have been many editions of Chaucer's works since Caxton's in 1475. The most complete is Skeat's in six volumes, 1894–97, and there are many cheap ones. Many have written about him, none perhaps more interestingly to a modern reader than J. R. Lowell in *My Study Windows* and G. K. Chesterton in his *Chaucer*. G. W. L.

WILLIAM LANGLAND or LANGLEY (?1332–?1400). Most of the little that is known for certain about the author of *Piers Plowman* is based on the internal evidence in his poem and does not amount to much. But it seems fairly well established that his christian name was William, and that his roots were in the Midlands as is presumably shown by the scene of Piers Plowman's vision being in the Malvern Hills; scholars too are agreed that the poem's dialect is west midland. Nothing is known of his education, but somehow he acquired a good deal of learning; he took what were called minor orders, and when at about the age of thirty he lived, as he says, 'in and on London' he earned a bare livelihood as a singer of masses, and by various odd jobs in the Church. The first version of *The Vision of William concerning Piers the Plowman* appeared in 1362–63. This is known as the A text. The poem was greatly enlarged, and the end of it altered in the B text (1377), and this in its turn was to a lesser extent rearranged and added to soon after 1392 (C text). The authorship of B and C has long been disputed. Some critics maintain that internal evidence of style and standpoint points to one author of all three texts; others aver that it shows precisely the opposite. Nearly 600 years later the question is not of great interest or importance. Langland certainly wrote A, admittedly the most forceful and coherent of the texts. The poem is an allegory or series of allegories, the dramatis personae are abstractions, the versification is unrhymed and alliterative. Such ingredients might seem to guarantee a dreary insipidity, but the characters

—Reason, Conscience, Hunger, the Seven Deadly Sins, etc.—are given such vitality, and Langland's picture of the times, in all their harshness and cruelty and widespread unrest, is so powerfully drawn that it is easy to see why he is commonly placed second to Chaucer alone among our early poets. Though his fierce temper is at the opposite pole from Chaucer's, several of his targets are the same. Friars, pardoners, idle clergy, lawyers, etc., are all condemned by Langland's lofty standard; and though he had immense sympathy with the 'underdog,' and compassion for his sufferings, there was no sentimentality in his scornful invective against the idle or thriftless labourer. These qualities of Langland's have always been recognized, and the popularity of *Piers Plowman* until the end of the sixteenth century is attested by the existence of nearly 50 MSS. and frequent allusions to it. There were also a good many imitations, so much in the manner of *Piers Plowman* that some scholars have ascribed them to Langland. This popularity would probably not have particularly pleased the grim, sincere man, either as poet or preacher; for his style of versification was soon to die out, and the fifteenth century paid as little attention to his exposure of human crime and folly as all other centuries have paid to anyone else's. G. W. L.

HENRY YEVELE (*c.* 1320/30–*c.* 1400) was a craftsman who migrated to London after the Black Death (1348–9) and became England's greatest architect, perfecting the perpendicular style under the patronage of Edward III and Richard II. As master mason he earned 12d. a day. By 1358 he was working for the Black Prince at Kennington Manor (Surrey). He built Westminster Palace clock tower (1365) and was warden of London Bridge. His work is recorded at the Tower, Rochester, Leeds, Cowling, Portchester, Canterbury and Baynard's castles, Westminster Abbey, John of Gaunt's palace of the Savoy in the Strand which Wat Tyler's men burnt, Canterbury Cathedral where he designed the West gate, Old St. Paul's, New College, Oxford, Rochester Bridge, and the royal palaces of Eltham (Kent, still standing), Westminster, and Sheen (Surrey). At Westminster he made the vault of the north porch (1399–1400) and 2,000 painted tiles for the bathroom at Sheen were bought from Yevele's second wife-to-be. He made tombs for John of Gaunt and Richard II and probably those of Edward III at Westminster and the Black Prince at Canterbury. On 25 March, 1389, he dined with Hugh Herland at the high table of New College, Oxford, and on 27 September, 1389, Geoffrey Chaucer, as clerk of the works, paid him the arrears of his salary (£18.5.0 and a winter robe yearly). Between 29 April and 3 July, 1393, he was entertained nine times by William of Wykeham at the Bishop of Winchester's palace in Southwark.

John Harvey, *Henry Yevele, c. 1320–1400*, 1944.
T.S.I.H., i, 210 (baths).

RICHARD II (1367–1400) was born at Bordeaux on 6 January, the feast of Epiphany. The three kings to whom Christ was revealed on that day were therefore the patrons of Richard II and he adopted three crowns as his arms. He venerated as his patrons St. Edmund the King and St. Edward the Confessor and he tried to get Edward II canonized. He admired Henry III, believed the laws to be in the royal mouth and breast, and wished to reign absolved from all the rules of government. His reign suggests a comparison with that of Charles I (d. 1649), for like Edward II and Charles I, Richard II died in his enemies' power. At ten years old Richard inherited a country demoralized by the wars of Edward III and which no longer enjoyed even the consolations of victories (1377). Within four years came Wat Tyler's rebellion, and this was only defeated because the rebellious peasants shared Richard's faith in the divinity of kingship. Froissart, who dedicated poetry to Richard, has distorted history by a dramatic but untruthful propagandist picture of the heroic youth saving the situation when Tyler was murdered by calling to his partisans 'I shall be your leader'. Actually Richard was a frightened lad who merely carried out the clever instructions of his council or his mother, deceiving with insincere promises rough but simple peasants who trusted him (1381). He was, during the remaining four years of his mother's life, much influenced by her. During his minority (1377–81) his three uncles and other greedy magnates ruled. Then came a struggle for power (1381–6). Richard II made Michael de la Pole (d. 1389) Chancellor without consulting Parliament (1383) and created his uncles Edmund and Thomas Dukes of York and Gloucester to help play them off against John of Gaunt, Duke of Lancaster, the eldest of the three uncles. Gloucester overthrew Richard's attempted 'tyranny' and forced him to accept the rule of eleven 'Appellants'. Richard's friend De Vere, Duke of Ireland, resisted in vain when accused of treason (1387); and in 1388 in the 'Merciless Parliament' they took vengeance on Judge Tresilian and his other supporters. Richard managed to rule with the advice of those who slew his friends and they allowed him the royal pomp for which he craved (1389–92). Finally (1397–9) Richard achieved his aim of real monarchy in its literal sense of the rule of one man. He formed a standing army, manipulated Parliament, short-circuited chancery by using his private seal instead of the Great Seal, which the Chancellor controlled, and employed officials of the royal household. He thus emerged, as the sympathetic Kirkstall chronicle remarks, like the sun from the clouds. The sunburst was adopted as one of Richard's badges, in much the same way as Louis XIV declared that he was the State in France three centuries later and was called *Le roi soleil.* Success brought ruin, for Richard's summary treatment of the Dukes of Norfolk and Hereford (see p. 211) led to his imprisonment in Pontefract Castle (1399) and the usurpation of the crown by Hereford as Henry IV, the first king of the House of Lancaster with its apparent respect for parliamentary, not monarchical, principles. There was in Richard's character a feminine streak, as there was in the kings whom he admired. He was a dilettante connoisseur, tall but unmilitary, abrupt and stammering in speech, unstable of purpose and mood. One of his coats cost 30,000 marks, and his love of pageantry appeared on his marriage to the Emperor's daughter, Anne of Bohemia (1382). His temper may have been less passionate than is supposed, for one alleged hysterical outburst has been disproved by modern critical research; but after his beloved

Anne's death (1394) he degenerated, would sit in silent state through long evenings and was said to indulge in all-night drinking bouts, and 'whenever his gaze fell upon anyone, no matter of what rank, that man had to bend the knee'. An unpopular second marriage (1394) with the little Queen Isabel, eight-year old daughter of King Charles VI of France, was a formality. Richard's face is consistently portrayed in two manuscripts, a portrait at Westminster and the Wilton diptych. The diptych shows him as if still a youth presented to the Virgin by the patron saints who inspired him. Around are angels, wearing Richard's livery of the White Hart, a sort of royal ikon to remind royalists of a royal martyr for the Divine Right of Kings. See plate 20 and pedigree, p. 178.

A. B. Steel, *Richard II*, 1941 (from the political angle).

WILLIAM OF WYKEHAM (1323–1404) was born at Wickham (Hants.). He became clerk of the king's works at Henley and Easthamstead and surveyor at Windsor Castle in 1356, and in the following year was rewarded with the first of various livings, a rectory in Norfolk, for such services as the restoration of Dover Castle (1359) and the negotiation with France of the Treaty of Bretigny (1360). A recurrence of plague (1361)—for plagues were frequent and the Black Death was not just confined to 1348–9—gave him a chance to fill ten more church vacancies, though he was only ordained as an acolyte that December. Wykeham became Keeper of the Privy Seal (1364) and Froissart said that 'by him everything was done and without him they did nothing'. In 1367 he became Chancellor (1368–71 and 1389–91) and Bishop of Winchester (1367–1404). An anti-clerical agitation supported by John of Gaunt forced him to resign from being Chancellor in 1371 and he retaliated by joining in an attack made in 1373 by the Good Parliament on John of Gaunt and Edward III's mistress, Alice Perrers. In 1376 John of Gaunt and Alice Perrers returned to power. They deprived Wykeham of sources of income and forbade him to come within twenty miles of court and 'they hunted the seyd bishop from place to place both by letters and by writtes, so that no man could succour him throughout his diocese, neither could he nor durst he rest in any place'. He bought the favour of Alice shortly before Edward III died, and on the accession of Richard II (1377) he was restored to power and came to an understanding with John of Gaunt. In 1378 and 1380 he began to found Winchester College and New College, the richest of such foundations in England and planned on novel principles. His crozier is preserved in New College Chapel, Oxford. His effigy in Winchester Cathedral is extraordinarily lifelike.

G. H. Moberly, *Life of William of Wykeham*, 2nd ed., 1893.
G. C. Haseltine, *William of Wykeham*, 1932.

RICHARD SCROPE (*c.* 1350–1405), perhaps the most famous Archbishop of York (1398–1405), was son of the warlike Lord Scrope of Masham, a Yorkshire notable who fought at Halidon Hill (1333), and Sluys (1340) and Calais (1347). The family produced many prominent public figures in the fourteenth and fifteenth centuries and they were among the chief benefactors of York Minster. This explains why the Scrope arms, a blue shield with a golden 'bend' crossing it diagonally, occur in the cathedral. Richard became Bishop of Coventry and Lichfield (1386) and Archbishop of York (1398). In 1378 he had become Chancellor of Cambridge University. He helped to put Henry IV on the throne but voiced discontent against him and even took up arms at York in support of the rebellion of the Earl of Northumberland. At Shipton Moor the Earl of Westmorland (a rival of Northumberland) induced him to disband his men. He was condemned to death, though Chief Justice Gascoign refused to try him. He was executed on the Feast of St. William of York and asked the executioner, a criminal from York prison, to strike five times 'For His love that suffred five woundes for alle mankynde'. Many pilgrims visited his tomb, and the good repute of the martyred archbishop was attested by reports of miracles. The government had to put a barricade round the tomb to keep off the crowds. Later it forbade any offerings to be made at the shrine. The offerings were then diverted to the shrine of St. William. They brought in so much money that they helped to pay for the rebuilding of the choir. Henry IV was excommunicated for the murder, but he soon managed to make his peace with the Pope. Scrope's reputation never reached the height attained by Thomas Becket, and an attempt to canonize him failed in 1462. Nevertheless people often referred to him as St. Richard Scrope. In 1660 another Scrope, Adrian, was executed, because he was one of those who signed the death-warrant of Charles I. In 1829 Richard's tomb was opened and his decapitated head was found under his arm.

J. Solloway, *Archbishop Scrope* (York Minister Historical Tracts, 15), 1927.

HUGH HERLAND (*c.* 1330–*c.* 1405), son of a family of carpenters, was a royal master carpenter, paid 8d. a day (1364) and later 1s. (1379). He designed the tester of Edward III's tomb, which is the highest point attained in the design of decorative woodwork, and built the immense roof of Westminster Hall, the finest creation of its kind anywhere. The roof cost £2,000 (1394–1400). Herland worked at the Tower, Rochester, Canterbury and Leeds castles, Kingston Bridge and Great Yarmouth harbour and was employed by William of Wykeham at New College, Oxford, Winchester College and Highclere (Hants.). His vault in Winchester College Chapel is a landmark in the development of fan-vaulting. One of his sons, William, was an original scholar of Winchester (1394) and went to New College, but died in 1398. In 1366 Herland was granted an annual pension of 10 marks (£6.13.4), increased in 1397 to £18.5.0. He had a house in the outer ward of Westminster Palace for his tools and moulds. His portrait is that named 'Carpentarius' in the stained glass of Winchester College Chapel, an accurate redrawing from a mutilated original. His name is not in the *Dictionary of National Biography*, but the researches of John Harvey have recovered from scattered references the story of a man to whom England is deeply indebted for works of lasting beauty which contrast strangely with the selfishness of contemporary ruling circles.

J. Harvey, *English Mediaeval Architects, a Biographical Dictionary down to 1550*, 1954, pp. 127–32.

HENRY LE DESPENSER (or SPENCER) (d. 1406) was grandson of Hugh Despenser the younger (d. 1326) and was denounced by Wyclif as a fighting bishop. As Bishop of Norwich (1370–1406) he was active against riotous peasants (1381) and in the 'Flemish Crusade' (1383), when Philip Van Arteveld, regent of Ghent, asked for help against the Count of Flanders and the King of France. The French regarded Clement VII as Pope but there was a rival Pope, Urban VI. Urban authorized a 'crusade' against the French king. As leader of this, Despenser sailed in April, 1383. Van Arteveld had already been defeated and slain at the battle of Roosebeke and only Ghent was holding out. This unsuccessful and immoral 'crusade' lasted until September and was marked by terrible atrocities. Despenser called himself the 'Conqueror of West Flanders'. Wyclif and Lancaster opposed the 'crusade' and its failure led to Despenser's losing his temporal property through inefficiency. Richard II liked him and he was temporarily imprisoned on the accession of Henry IV for his loyalty to Richard.

HENRY PERCY (1342–1408), first Earl of Northumberland, was one of a line of Percys, traditionally christened Henry, who ruled like kings on the Scottish border. The first Baron Percy, Sir William, had come from Perci in La Marche (Normandy) and had obtained much land in Yorkshire and Lincolnshire (1067). The seventh baron, Sir Henry (?1228–1272), was the father of a Sir Henry who took an important part in the Scottish wars of Edward I, became first Baron Percy of Alnwick, and shared in the defeat of Bannockburn (1314). The next Sir Henrys, the second and third Barons of Alnwick, were Wardens of the Scottish Marches. Our Henry was son of the third baron, served in France and was also Warden of the Scottish Marches. At twenty-four he became knight of the Garter (1366). In 1377, the year in which he joined John of Gaunt in championing Wyclif, he was made marshal of England and first Earl of Northumberland. He quarrelled with Gaunt over a Scottish truce, and for a time he supported the personal rule of Richard II; but when Henry Bolingbroke invaded

England Percy helped him to become King Henry IV. Percy was then fifty-eight. His countess was a daughter of Ralph Nevil of Raby; but their marriage did not destroy a bitter rivalry between Nevils and Percys and the Percys disliked Henry IV's growing confidence in Ralph Nevil, Earl of Westmorland. Northumberland's son, 'Harry Hotspur', was thirty-five and famous for his exploits before being captured by the Scots at Otterburn, in what Froissart called 'the best fought and severest of all battles' (1388). Hotspur married a daughter of Edmund Mortimer, Earl of March, thus becoming brother-in-law of that Sir Edmund whom Henry IV much distrusted and uncle of one who would have succeeded Richard II but for Henry IV's usurpation. Though the Percys helped Henry IV to the throne, they felt he ought to pay them more than he did (or could) for their services on the Scottish and Welsh borders. In 1401 Hotspur quarrelled with Henry IV over the recompense for his services in north Wales. In 1402 the Percys beat the Scots at Humbledon Hill and captured many magnates for whom big ransoms were expected. Hotspur refused to send the chief prisoner, Douglas, to London and asked why Henry IV would not let Mortimer be ransomed from his captivity with Owen Glendower. Henry tried to appease Hotspur by granting (1403) most of the English conquests in southern Scotland to Northumberland, but Hotspur became Henry's foe. The Scots actively resisted Northumberland's attempts to establish himself in their country. Northumberland begged Henry IV for money and protested his loyalty. But when Henry marched north, as requested, the Percys openly revolted. Hotspur issued a proclamation saying that he realized his mistake in having made Henry of Lancaster king. Henry had broken his promise not to harm Richard, to avoid oppressive taxes, and to keep the laws. Now Hotspur would make amends by giving the crown to Edmund Mortimer, Earl of March. The northerners, except for the Earl of Westmorland, rallied to Northumberland and marched south to help Hotspur. On 21 July, 1403, there was a battle at Shrewsbury (Salop.) for 'three long hourse'. The rebels cried 'Esperance Percie' and 'Harry Percy King'. The loyalists cried 'St. George, St. George Victorie!' and 'Harry

Percy Dead!' Over 1,600 dead were cast into a common grave. Over this Henry IV later built a church in the district north of Shrewsbury still called Battlefield. Henry wept when he saw Hotspur's body. He let Lord Furnival bury it, but then had it dug up and taken in a cart to Shrewsbury. There it was salted and put between two millstones near the pillory before being beheaded and quartered. Hotspur's head was sent to York and displayed over the northern gate and the quarters were sent to London, Bristol, Chester and Newcastle. Newcastle-upon-Tyne refused to annoy Henry IV by admitting Northumberland's rebel army, so Northumberland withdrew to his castle at Warkworth. He submitted to Henry IV at York, under the North Gate, the grimmest place for a father that could have been chosen. Parliament decided only to punish Northumberland by a fine and even that Henry remitted. Northumberland swore to keep faith with Henry, but he rebelled again (1405). Archbishop Scrope joined him, but he was arrested through the 'subtilty' of Westmorland and was executed at York. Henry's 'gonnes' battered the walls of Warkworth and Berwick castles. Alnwick fell 'without assault'. Northumberland fled to Scotland. Henry was willing to exchange him for his prisoner, Douglas, and Northumberland fled to Owen Glendower. With Glendower and Mortimer he proposed to divide Henry's realm. Thence he fled to France and thence back to Scotland. In 1408 he was ready for a new rebellion and was killed in the snow at the battle of Bramham Moor (19 Feb., 1408). The quarters of his body, parboiled in a pickle of cloves, cumin and anice, were sent to Berwick, Lincoln, Newcastle-upon-Tyne and York. His grandson, Henry, son of Harry Hotspur, was restored to his titles and estates by Henry V (1416) as the second earl; and the name of Percy is still great in Northumberland.

G. E. C., *Complete Peerage*, 1910—(in progress).

JOHN GOWER (?1325–1408) shared with Lydgate the surprising honour of being regarded as Chaucer's equal as a poet. Ignoring legend, it seems to be established that he was of gentle birth, probably a man of Kent, and of good education,

Humphrey, Duke of Gloucester, Arras Manuscript

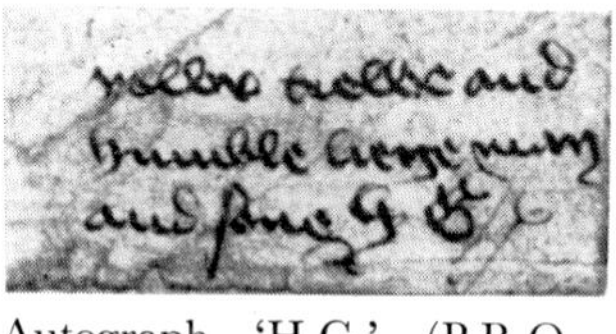

Autograph 'H.G.' (P.R.O., S.C. 1/43/191)

Henry VI, National Portrait Gallery

Plate 28

'R. H. nous avouns graunte c marcs' (autograph, P.R.O., E.28/58)

probably not an Oxonian or a clergyman. In his maturity he was connected with the court, at first eulogizing but afterwards hostile to Richard II, and subsequently a loyal supporter of Henry IV. He lived to a great age for those times, and was blind for many years before his death. At one time he was on good terms with Chaucer, whose label 'the moral Gower' has reverberated rather forbiddingly down the centuries. In Gower's *Confessio Amantis* he represents Venus calling Chaucer 'my disciple and my poet', but later this passage was omitted. The theory is that Gower was offended, taking Chaucer's line 'of all such cursed stories I say fy' in the introduction to his *Man of Lawes' Tale* to refer to an ancient indecorous story retold by Gower, the totally humourless man not suspecting that the author of the Miller's tale (and others) scolding the moral Gower might be merely a bit of fun. Gower's three chief poems were *Speculum Amantis*, probably his earliest, written in French, *Vox Clamantis* (1381) in Latin elegiacs, and *Confessio Amantis* (1383) in English. The first two are described by Andrew Lang as 'unmitigated sermonizing'. *Confessio Amantis* was his only English poem, probably written after he noticed Chaucer's extraordinary popularity in that language, but according to Gower, because King Richard had charged him that 'some newe thing I shulde boke'. This consisted of 33,000 rhyming octosyllabics, containing over 100 stories mostly from Latin literature, all illustrating some aspect of love. Each book is devoted to one of that indispensable fraternity in our early literature, the Seven Deadly Sins. Genius, the priest of the goddess Venus, instructs and rebukes the Lover (Gower) who admits his faults and professes contrition. Gower's verses run smoothly and he has some narrative skill, but he had little or nothing of the other qualities which keep Chaucer alive. His prolix attacks on human failings, though allegorical, are invariably frontal; he has little variety and is as incapable of fun as of fatigue. But Sidney and Spenser admired him, and Shakespeare—if he was the author—puts in his mouth the prologue to each act of 'Pericles'. The modern reader can choose between the verdict of Fuller who in 1662 called him 'the prince of poets', and that of J. R. Lowell who wrote in 1871 that 'his style has the hateful gloss and seemingly unnatural length of a coffin'.

Gower was buried in Southwark, where his effigy lies, his head resting on three volumes with the titles of his three long poems. His works were edited in 1899 by G. C. Macaulay who, in that year, discovered in the Cambridge University Library the MS. of his 'Speculum Meditantis' which for centuries had been supposed lost. G. W. L.

HENRY IV (1366–1413), **BOLINGBROKE,** was son of John of Gaunt by Blanche, heiress of Henry Duke of Lancaster; and was called Bolingbroke after his father's castle (in Lincolnshire, dismantled by the Cromwellians in the Civil War). His old grandfather, Edward III, made him a Knight of the Garter, and the same year (1377) Henry, aged eleven, bore the ceremonial sword 'Curtana' at the coronation of his cousin, Richard II. Henry Bolingbroke or Henry of Lancaster was also known as the Earl of Derby. He became Earl of Hereford through marrying (1380) Mary Bohun (d. 1394), coheiress of the Earl of Hereford, the tenth and last representative of a great family to be called Humphrey. Mary was only aged eleven, so she remained in the care of her widowed mother, the daughter of Richard FitzAlan, third Earl of Arundel. Ancestors of both Bohun and FitzAlan had fought against King John. Mary Bohun's sister Eleanor, the Countess of Gloucester, was already married to Henry's paternal uncle, Thomas of Woodstock. These aristocratic relationships are important because they explain a bond which links three of the characters in the drama of Richard II; for Henry joined Thomas and Richard FitzAlan, the fourth Earl of Arundel, in leading a violent opposition to the favourites of Richard II. This Richard FitzAlan was the uncle of Mary and Eleanor Bohun; and these representatives of families that had been prominent since the Conquest as servants of the crown resented, as such men often resent, the promotion of new men. Henry won a skirmish at Radcot Bridge (Oxon., 1387) and was welcomed as a hero by the Londoners. He had a town house in Bishopsgate Street, and after Radcot he showed

Richard crowds of Londoners surging round the Tower. There Richard had to submit to the directions of five Lords Appellant, Thomas, Henry, Richard, and two associates of the same class, Thomas Beauchamp, Earl of Warwick, and Thomas Mowbray, Earl of Nottingham and later Duke of Norfolk. These two were also descended from foes of John, and Mowbray was son-in-law of FitzAlan. Like all the Lancastrians Henry was devout and the accounts of his treasurer record his expenses

Joan of Navarre and Henry IV (Canterbury)

on crusades in Lithuania (1390) and Prussia (1392) and on pilgrimage to Jerusalem (1392–3). In 1397 he supported Richard II against three of the Appellants, Gloucester, Arundel and Warwick; and Richard gave him the sword and cap of honour as Duke of Hereford (1397). Henry denounced the fifth Appellant, Mowbray, for treason, and a trial by combat was arranged between them before a vast crowd at Coventry. Richard II prevented this duel at the last moment and banished Henry for ten years (1398). Richard then confiscated his estates and said the banishment should be lifelong. The reason why Henry had denounced Mowbray was that Mowbray had said that he feared that Richard's vengeance on the other Appellants might extend to themselves. Richard seemed to be confirming Mowbray's words. Henry went to Paris, Richard confiscated Henry's estates, and Henry plotted revenge. In 1399 Henry landed at Ravenspur to claim his inheritance, and the countryside welcomed him. Richard submitted to Henry at Flint, for his army had deserted. Richard abdicated and Henry claimed the throne by descent, as if his ancestor Edmund of Lancaster had been the elder, instead of the younger, brother of Edward I. He also claimed the throne by reason of Richard's misgovernment, but he disclaimed any right by conquest. Parliament then chose Henry to reign 'not so much by title of blood as by popular election'. On 11 October, 1399, Henry made forty new knights and from that date is reckoned the foundation of the Order of the Bath. On 13 October he was anointed with oil which the Virgin had given to St. Thomas and which Edward III had imported. Henry's time was unquiet. France regarded him as a traitor. Scotland was hostile. Owen Glendower led the Welsh in revolt. The popularity of a leader of opposition evaporated when he gained the responsibility of government. On 8 September, 1401, he found in his bed an 'iron with three branches so sharp that wherever the king had turned him it should slay him'. Revolts by Henry Hotspur (1403) and by Archbishop Scrope of York and Mowbray (1405) were suppressed. Hotspur was slain; but it was the execution of Scrope and Mowbray which did more than anything else to turn men against Henry. Reports of miracles performed by the martyred archbishop were the natural and embarrassing consequence. Rebellion might be crushed but financial difficulties grew. Henry became 'a leper', smitten, it was believed, on the very day of Scrope's execution; though when his tomb was opened in 1832 the condition of the face proved that chroniclers had exaggerated his plight. Henry's last years were darkened by the ambitions of his step-brothers the Beauforts. Henry lost the power of walking, and at last had a fit while praying before St. Edward's shrine at Westminster. He was removed to the abbot's house in agony and died in the Jerusalem chamber (20 March, 1413). He had four sons and two daughters by Mary Bohun. His second wife was Joan of Navarre (1403), daughter of Charles the Mad and widow of John IV, Duke of Brittany. Henry was a handsome knight 'well proportioned and compact', though short. His russet beard was thickly matted. He had good teeth. He liked discussing moral problems and could follow long Latin sermons. He was patron of the poets Chaucer and Gower. His portrait is at Windsor and his effigy at Canterbury. The statement that he was born while his father was winning the Battle of Nájera (1367) is probably inaccurate and his exact age at death is unknown. A seventeenth-century astrologer, anxious to find exact dates, believed he was forty-six. A desire for efficient government made Henry welcome; but he had, when in opposition, made many self-destructive promises to gain support from different interests and these prevented him from being a competent ruler.

Henry IV's portraits are discussed in *Notes and Queries*, Ser. 12, vol. 11, pp. 503 and 523. See plates 1 and 23–4 and pedigree, p. 178.

T.S.I.H., i, 183 (coronation described by Froissart).

THOMAS ARUNDEL (1353–1414) was Archbishop of York (1388) and of Canterbury (1396) and often served as Chancellor (between 1386–1412). In 1397 he was banished for the part he played in the opposition by the nobility to Richard II; and before he departed he severely criticized the luxury of the court. Two years later he landed at Ravenspur with his nephew, the Earl of Arundel, heir of the Archbishop's brother, the Earl who had been executed by Richard II. They helped Henry Bolingbroke to supplant Richard, and Arundel crowned Bolingbroke as Henry IV. Arundel used his influence to defend the Church against Lollard attacks. He encouraged the clergy (1401) to ask for action against heresy. The clergy, assembled in Convocation, summoned William Sawtre for refusing to deny a heretical view about the nature of bread in the Mass. Henry had Sawtre burnt to death at Smithfield (2 March, 1401). Before Parliament dissolved on 10 March it passed the Statute *De Haeretico Comburendo*. This enacted that obstinate or relapsed heretics should be given to the secular authorities by the clergy to be burnt in order to frighten others. If the burning of a few bodies in this world would prevent the burning of many deceived souls for ever in Hell, a humane man could wish for heretical teachers to be burnt. The execution of Scrope, a fellow archbishop, shocked Arundel so much that he became ill (1405). During his last seven years he was troubled by the increasing power of his rivals, the Beauforts, half-brothers of Henry IV. Arundel believed in more censorship of the expression of thought than was welcome at Oxford and he wanted Wyclif's body to be burnt and cast on a dunghill; but the Lollards were disappointed in hoping that the growing opposition to Arundel implied any sympathy with their own opinions. On 23 September, 1413, Sir John Oldcastle was brought as a prisoner before Arundel. Arundel tried conscientiously to persuade him to recant before excommunicating him and handing him over, in accordance with the Statute *De Haeretico Comburendo*, to the secular arm for punishment (see p. 215).

OWEN GLENDOWER (between 1349 and 1359–?1416), last independent Prince of Wales, has a name famous wherever Shakespeare's plays are known, but the Welsh call him Owain Glyn Dŵr. He is a uniquely attractive figure in a period of political selfishness and is rightly regarded as a Welsh national hero. After a placid early life he was driven to revolt. From being a raider he became a ruler and as 'Prince of Wales' took for his arms the four lions rampant of Gwynedd (see front end-paper). Early English writers, with the honourable exception of Shakespeare, despised him as a type or symbol of unsuccessful ambition and vanity, as Hall's *Chronicle* says reaping 'a finall reward mete and prepared by Goddes providence'; but many Welshmen loved him as a symbol of resistance to alien tyranny. Owen studied law at Westminster perhaps for seven years, then a common training for the upper classes. He then 'fought with distinction as a worthy squire' for Henry of Lancaster, and Welsh bards celebrated his exploits in Scotland. At Berwick (1385) he wore a scarlet flamingo feather in his helmet as with a broken lance he drove the Scots headlong like wild goats. He lived at Sycarth on the banks of the Cynllaith with his wife and children 'a good nestful of young princes'.

There he had a moated timber-built manor house with tiled roof and a lordly gatehouse. In 1400 Owen quarrelled with Reginald de Grey, third Baron Grey of Ruthin (?1362–1440), a friend and councillor of Henry IV. This quarrel developed into a revolt. The rebels burnt Ruthin but were dispersed. From this date Owen reckoned himself as Prince of Wales, but the English struck back, and Owen wandered as an outlaw into South Wales. In 1401 he threatened Caernarvon and in April, 1402, captured Reginald de Grey. In June he captured Edmund Mortimer, the ten-year-old heir of the house of Mortimer, in an English disaster which seemed to fulfil the portentous story that at Edmund's birth the horses in the stables at Ludlow Castle were found bathed in blood up to the fetlocks. On this occasion Henry IV's tent was blown down and only his armour saved his life. Rumour spread that Owen was a wizard. Owen's policy was to avoid major battles and elude capture. Acts of Parliament were passed in vain against the Welsh. Grey was ransomed but Owen managed to win over Mortimer and Mortimer's brother-in-law, Henry Hotspur, by promising to support Mortimer's claim to the throne which Henry IV had usurped. In 1404 Owen's triumphs allowed him to hold a Welsh parliament and he made an alliance with France. When Henry V became king a reconciliation was attempted in vain. Owen's end is unknown. Evidently he was dead by 1417 when his son received a royal pardon. His brief re-establishment of independence was economically disastrous and hindered the fusion of Welsh and English, but Welshmen believed that he would rise again in wrath when Wales was in sorest need.

J. E. Lloyd, *Owen Glendower, Owen Glyn Dŵr*, 1931.
J. D. G. Davies, *Owen Glyn Dŵr*, 1934.

JOHN OLDCASTLE (d. 1417), married Joan, Lady Cobham (1409), and was called by courtesy Lord Cobham.

He came of a Herefordshire family and served Henry IV on the Welsh Marches and no doubt knew the king's son, Prince Henry. He was a man of local importance, representing Herefordshire in parliament (1404) and serving as sheriff (1406–

7). The clergy accused him of supporting heretics in London, Rochester and Herefordshire (1413). Whether or not he had tried to convert Henry when prince, Henry V certainly tried to convert him; but he insisted on denouncing the Pope as anti-Christ. His views on the Eucharist and on confession were heretical, so Archbishop Arundel and the bishops handed him over to the secular arm for punishment. He managed to escape from the Tower and hid in London while his Lollard supporters rose in revolt. He was outlawed (1414) and lay hidden near Malvern (1415). There he may have incited the Scots to attack England. He was captured at Cae'r Barwn near Welshpool (1417). He was hanged 'and burnt hanging' in St. Giles's Field (London). At his execution he foretold his resurrection to John Duke of Bedford. His misguided followers damaged their eyes by anointing them with his ashes. His cause was silenced and fifteenth-century writers hated his memory. In the sixteenth century, protestant writers regarded him as a martyr and his tale is retold in Foxe's *Book of Martyrs*. He was never a wild, boon companion of Prince Henry, like Shakespeare's immortal, but unhistorical character, Falstaff, originally called Oldcastle (see p. 237). Shakespeare explains in the epilogue of *Henry V* that 'Oldcastle died a martyr, and this is not the man'. In Oldcastle's lifetime verses were written which express disapproval of a man in such a prominent position holding the opinions he did:

> 'Hit is unkindly for a knight
> That shuld a Kynges castel kepe,
> To bable the Bible day and night
> In restyng time when he shuld slepe.'

W. T. Waugh, 'Sir John Oldcastle', *English Historical Review*, vol. 20 (1905), pp. 435–56 and 637–58.

SIR WILLIAM GASCOIGN (?1350–1419) was a lawyer who became Chief Justice of the King's Bench (1400). In 1405, as Chief Justice, he is said to have refused to try Archbishop Scrope, because he was a leader of the Church and a peer. A famous legend that Henry V, when prince, was arrested at

Coventry by Chief Justice Gascoign for contempt of court first appeared in 1531 in Sir Thomas Elyot's *Boke named The Governour*. Fifteen years later Hall, the chronicler, vol. 2, gave the story circulation and Shakespeare (*Henry IV*, Pt. II, act i, sc. 2) has made it familiar to the civilized world. Lord Campbell and Agnes Strickland have made this untrue story appear authoritative to readers of *Lives of the Chief-Justices* and *Lives of the Queens of England*. Elyot's account runs as follows: 'The moste renomed prince, Kynge Henry the fifte, late kynge of Englande, during the life of his father was noted to be fierie and of wanton courage. It hapned that one of his servantes whom he well favoured, for felony by hym committed, was arrayned at the kynges benche; whereof he being advertised, and incensed by light persones, aboute hym, in furious rage came hastily to the barre, where his servant stode as a prisoner, and commaunded him to be ungyved and sette at libertie, where at alle men were abasshed, reserved the chief justice, who humbly exhorted the prince to be contented that his servant might be ordred accordyng to the auncient lawes of this realme; or, if he wolde have him saved from the rigour of the lawes he sholde obtain, if he myghte, from the kynge his father his gracious pardon, whereby no law or justice should be derogate. With which answere the prince nothynge appeased, but rather more inflamed, endevoured hym self to take away his servant. The juge consideringe the perilous example and inconvenience that might thereby ensue, with a valiant spirit and courage commaunded the prince upon his alegeance to leve the prisoner and depart his way. With which commandment the prince, being set in all fury, all chafed and in a terrible maner, came up to the place of jugment, men thinkyng that he wolde have slayne the juge, or have done hym some damage. But the juge, sitting styll, without moving, declaryng the majestie of the kynges places of jugement, and with an assured and bolde countenance, hadde to the prince these words folowyng: Sir, remembre yourself: I kepe here the place of the king, your soveraigne lorde and father, to whom you owe double obedience .... And now for your contempt and disobedience, go you to the prisone of the kynges benche, where unto I commit you.

. . . With which wordes being abasshed, and also wondering at the marvailous gravitie of the worshipful Justice, the noble prince, laying his weapon aparte, doing reverence, departed and went to the kynges benche as he was commanded.' This story has been ingeniously and completely disproved by F. Solly-Flood. It is, however, a fact that on Henry V's accession Gascoign ceased to be Chief Justice.

F. Solly-Flood, 'The story of Prince Henry of Monmouth and Chief-Justice Gascoign', *Royal Historical Society Transactions*, New Series 3 (1886), 47–152.

ANDREW WYNTOUN (?1350–?1422) wrote a versified Chronicle of Scotland in 1406. It was called 'The Oryginale' because it began with the Creation. He was a canon of St. Andrews and was elected Prior of St. Serf's Inch in Loch Leven. He called the language which he used 'Ynglis Sawe' but we would call it vernacular Scots.

Andrew Wyntoun, *Original Chronicle*, Scottish Text Society, 1903.

HENRY V (1387–1422) was born at Monmouth, the son of Henry of Bolingbroke (later Henry IV) by Mary de Bohun, coheiress of a line of Earls of Hereford which began in 1199. Enemies made Henry IV 'suspect that he wolde usurpe the Crowne, he being alive'. James Butler (1392–1452), Earl of Ormonde, whom Henry V knighted on the road to victory at Agincourt (1415), tells a strange tale of how as prince 'He disguised himself in a gowne of blewe satten or damaske made of iletts or holes, and at everie ilet the needle wherewith it was made hanginge there by the thridde of silke, and about his arme he wore a doggs collar sett full of S.S. of goulde'. He went to his father thus strangely dressed at Westminster and 'the kinge caused himselfe to be borne in his chaire (because he was diseased and might not goe) into a secret chamber [private room].' There the prince said that he understood that he was under suspicion, 'and therefore most redoubted lorde and father I desyre you in your honnor of God, for the easing of your harte heere tofore your knees to slaye me with this dagger.' He handed the king a dagger and reconciliation followed.

Henry is said to have been educated by Henry Beaufort at Queen's College; and there at New Year's day he would have known that threaded needles were symbols of thrift, *aiguilles* in allusion to the name of Eglesfield, the founder, distributed to diners at New Year's day with an injunction to 'Take this and be thrifty'. Henry's fanciful dress with needles was an answer to the charge that he was thriftless. On Henry IV's death Henry V promised a hermit at Westminster to abandon a thriftless life. This thriftlessness became legendary. During his lifetime Walsingham wrote: 'As soon as he was made king (1413) he was changed suddenly into another man zealous for honesty, modesty and gravity, there being no sort of virtue that he was not anxious to display'. It is not until the sixteenth century that chroniclers wrote that 'he strake the Chief Justice (see p. 217) with his fist in the face.' As a hero of the struggle in Wales against Glendower (1400, 1405–7) the prince was apprentice to Mars as well as Venus, and cannot have been wholly dissolute even if there were good grounds for such tales as his supposed robbery of his own rent-collectors. Like his father and his son he religiously suppressed the Lollards (1414), against whom he had petitioned as prince (1406). None the less a fifteenth-century chronicle says 'bishops and men of the spirituality doubted that he would have had the temporalities (worldly properties) out of their hands: wherefore they encouraged the king to challenge Normandy, so that he should not seek occasions to enter into such matters'. This is the historical truth behind Shakespeare's picture of Archbishop Chichele advising war, though in fact Chichele only became archbishop later in the year. Henry V demanded the provinces which had been ceded to Edward III at Brétigny (1360) as a condition of a marriage between himself and Catherine of Valois, for thus he would 'busy restless minds in foreign quarrels'. Ormonde told the tale of the tennis balls: the French king said that because Henry was young they would send him little balls to play with. Henry replied, 'If God so wills and my life lasts, I will within a few months play such a game of ball in the Frenchman's streets, that they shall lose their jest and gain but grief for their game'. Just as the Oath of the Heron of Edward III was taken in allusion to an oath of the Peacock, so this insult before the second act of the Hundred Years War alluded to the mocking dispatch of a handball by Darius to the Greek King in the same romance. A ball was a symbol of folly made familiar in illuminated psalters in the initial of the Psalm 'Insipiens' ('The fool hath said in his heart there is no God'), for that psalm was often illustrated by a fool about to strike a ball.

Henry told London that war would profit everybody and preparations were made. Swans had played a great part in the symbolic devices at Henry's coronation feast; and it is a picturesque detail of the expedition to France (1415) that 'as we left the shores of the Isle of Wight, swans came swimming amongst our ships'. Henry landed unopposed and, unlike Edward III, forbade harm to non-combatants. His guns, 'London', 'Messagere' and 'Kynges Doughter', reduced Harfleur, 'Among the houses the balles ren, And mad many a French men lame'. Henry's army was thinned by dysentery as he started a march for Calais much like the march of Edward III which had culminated in the victory of Crécy. The bridge over the Somme was broken, so 'we turned our steps along the river, thinking that we must march full sixty miles into the heart of France, till, when our eight days store of food was spent, our little band, grown weak and weary with long marches and short rations, should fall a prey to the great host of the enemy.' Then came the victory of Agincourt on 25th October, 1415.

A song of triumph written at the time, called the Agincourt song, is in the Bodleian Library and has been reproduced on a picture postcard. News reached London on 29th October, and bells rang from every steeple. On 23rd November, citizens in particoloured hoods of red and white rode to meet Henry at Eltham. 'To London brigge thanne rood oure King.' On the gate was a figure of a giant 'to teche the Frensshmen curtesye' and at the drawbridge St. George. Boys in white with angelic wings sang an anthem. Tapestries showing heroic deeds hung from the houses. Trumpets sounded. There were many allegorical pageants. Through crowded streets Henry passed to give thanks in St. Paul's Cathedral and in Westminster

Abbey. On 1st August 1417 Henry returned to France to conquer Normandy.

Henry was the patron of Lydgate and Hoccleve and liked books of romance and history and hunting; and it is an indication of such tastes that when he took Caen in September he only kept for himself out of the spoil 'a goodly French book of what history I have not heard'. Towns fell readily and Lisieux was found deserted save for two old people, for Henry was dreaded for his mercilessness to all who resisted. When Louviers fell (1418) he had eight gunners hanged, because a cannon-ball struck his tent. On 29th July, 1418, he besieged Rouen. A long poem tells how he refused to allow swarms of non-combatants out through his lines and let them starve in the moat; while in the town 'They ete doggys, they ete cattys, They ete mysse, horse and rattys'. Rouen surrendered on 19 January 1419, and there was dancing and more processions in London. By the Treaty of Troyes (1420) Henry was declared heir of Charles VI, Regent of France and Lord of Normandy, and he married Catherine of Valois: but fighting continued and Henry could now hang prisoners as rebels, which he did at Sens. Ormonde tells how at the siege of Melun (1420) English and French dug mines and countermines. To stop quarrelling between two lords about who should first enter the mine, Henry (who had led the assault of Caen) went in first. There he met the first French defender to go down, Barbazan. 'So that they fought together right mightely. And after a longe battaile betwixt them, and that either of them had demaunded other's name, at the first Barbazan knowledged his name to the Kinge uppon condicion that the kinge shoulde in like manner disclose his name unto him, and said unto the kinge: "I ame Barazon, the Captain of the Towne and castell." Then the Kinge, as he hadd promised said: "And I ame Henrie *par la grace de dieu*".' He died on 1st September, 1422, at Bois de Vincennes going to help his ally the Duke of Burgundy. His body was taken in procession across France and buried at Westminster. There a chantry was endowed in his honour. His last words were 'Good Lord! Thou knowest that mine interest hath been, and yet is, if I might live, to re-edify the wall of Jerusalem'.

The words were sincere for Henry yearned to unite Christendom in a crusade; for he was a real Christian hero by his own medieval standards, steeped in the tradition of King Arthur. Even Frenchmen joined in the general admiration of Henry as a just and almost ideal ruler. Distrust of military skill and of diplomacy patiently designed to supplement war may blind modern writers to Henry's virtues. Henry was aggressive, but only in seeking what he held to be his due. Later reverses in France do not lessen his achievement and he was a good man.

Several portraits survive to show his oval face, straight nose, ruddy complexion, dark smooth hair, and bright eyes, mild as a dove's when unprovoked, but lionlike in wrath (plate 25).

Shakespeare, like men who saw Henry, has celebrated his victorious acts. Within two years Henry had stilled all rebellion at home, 'rending every man throughout the realm who had money' to achieve his triumphs.

E. F. Jacob, *Henry V and the Invasion of France*, 1947.
T.S.I.H., i, 190 (menu of coronation feast) and 191 (French soldier's account of Agincourt). For the swan badge see plate 12. See pedigree, p. 178.

RICHARD WHITTINGTON (c. 1368–1423), thrice Mayor of London (1397–8, 1406–7 and 1419–20), is the London citizen who is remembered with most universal honour. Some call the fifteenth century a decadent period, and from the point of view of what the nobility stood for they are perhaps right; but it was a period when the merchants were full of enterprise and that enterprise is remembered in the tale of the boy who made a fortune by overseas trade.

The story of Whittington's cat, sold abroad for a fortune, is repeated in many pantomimes and first occurs in a ballad of 1605, though in other forms the same story occurs in the legends of both northern and southern Europe. Lysons believed that the story had a basis of truth and that as a vermin-killer a cat could be a highly prized treasure. Those who believed the story was older than 1605 said that a picture used to be at Mercers' Hall dated 1536 showing Dick and his cat; there was a statue of a man with a cat at his feet at Newgate, which

Whittington rebuilt; and in 1862 a figure of a boy with a cat, apparently made in the fifteenth century, was found in a house at Gloucester which the Whittingtons had occupied until 1460.

Various traditions have associated Whittington with Shropshire, Herefordshire and Lancashire; but on July 10th, 1860, the Rev. Samuel Lysons, an enthusiast for London history, paid a visit to Pauntley, Gloucestershire, which convinced him that there was the home of Whittington's family. Lysons observed in Pauntley church stained glass painted with the arms of Whittington 'gules a fesse componé or and azure', in the technical language of heraldry. Heralds record marriages by 'impaling' or dividing a shield between the arms of a man and his wife; and at Pauntley the arms of Whittington are impaled with those of Fitzwaryn. The marriage of Whittington to his master's daughter, Alice Fitzwaryn, is famous, so this glass makes it seem probable that Dick Whittington was one of the Whittingtons of Pauntley. Dick's father was a knight, Sir William, and his mother came of a gentle family from Devon. He was therefore not a friendless pauper of obscure origin. Sir William died an outlaw in 1360, but the family inherited the estate and kept it for two centuries.

Dick came to London about 1371 to be apprenticed to Sir Ivo Fitzwaryn, mercer and Merchant Adventurer, a younger son of a famous family from North Devon related to Dick's mother. A stone on Highgate Hill marks the spot where Dick is supposed to have heard the sound of Bow Bells in Cheapside hailing him as thrice Mayor of London. The mercers were the richest of the 'companies' of the City of London, and they received a charter in 1393. Whittington was Master of the Mercers in 1398, 1407 and 1420.

Dick's name first occurs in the city records in 1379 (two years before Wat Tyler's rebellion). He then contributed 5 marks to a city loan. This shows that he was among those assessed at the lowest rate. He was then about twenty-one. Ten years later he was one of the richest citizens, and he lent vast sums to Richard II, Henry IV and Henry V and was a liberal benefactor of the city. In Riley's *Memorials* is printed an account of his second election as mayor. Dick founded Whittington

College (suppressed, 1548) to maintain priests to pray not only for Henry IV but for Henry's enemy, Richard II. Reginald Pecock was first master of this college (see p. 238).

He supplied wedding dresses for two daughters of Henry IV and he was Member of Parliament for London in 1416. When entertaining Henry V and Queen Catherine, according to legend, he fed his fire not only with costly cedar wood but with bonds worth £60,000. He died a childless widower. Whittington gave a library to the Grey Friars, later incorporated into Christ's Hospital. The Great Fire (1666) destroyed a splendid tomb which he had built for himself in the church of St. Michael Paternoster Royal, another object of his charity.

Sir W. Besant and J. Rice, *Sir Richard Whittington, Lord Mayor of London*, 1881.

JOHN OF LANCASTER, DUKE OF BEDFORD (1389–1435), third son of Henry IV, was made duke in 1414, and governed England when his brother, Henry V, was fighting the Agincourt campaign in France (1415) and again in 1421. It was Bedford who repelled the 'Foul Raid' of the Scots (1417); and it was he, true to the Lancastrian tradition of repressing the Lollards by burning, who burnt and hanged at the same time the Lollard leader, Sir John Oldcastle. When Henry V fell ill, it was Bedford who took command in France (1422), and it was Bedford who bought Joan of Arc from her captors to burn her as a witch (1431). None the less he was undoubtedly one of the few notables of his age who really inspire respect. Like his royal brother, Bedford was a disciplinarian who knew how to control his soldiers. He prevented pillaging, suppressed brigandage and managed to pay his men with some regularity. He favoured the Treaty of Troyes (1420) and an alliance with the Duke of Burgundy. He respected the traditions of Normandy. During his regency Caen University was founded. He revived the Norman exchequer and office of seneschal and he held more than twenty meetings of the duchy estates to vote taxes and ventilate grievances as a parliament (1421–35). In 1423 he cemented an anti-French alliance by marrying Anne, daughter of the Duke of Burgundy, but ten years later

Plate 29

Alice Chaucer, Duchess of Suffolk, Effigy at Ewelme

Plate 30

Edward IV, National Portrait Gallery

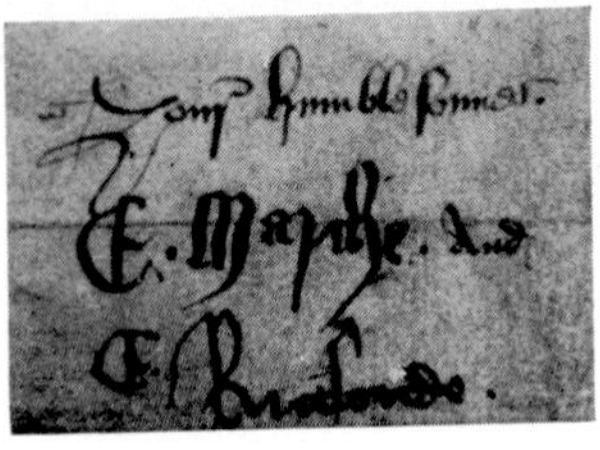

Autographs: Edward IV and Edmund Earl of Rutland (British Museum Vespasian F. iii, f. 16)

he offended Burgundy by marrying Jacqueline of Luxemburg. On 17 August, 1424, at Verneuil, he beat an ill-led French army in the biggest battle since Agincourt (1415); Jehan Wavrin, who took part in this campaign, has left a description of it. In 1431 he had Henry VI crowned King of France at

John, Duke of Bedford (Bodleian MS.)

Notre Dame, but his administration in France was severely criticized by Humphrey, Duke of Gloucester, his brother. Bedford died in 1435 aged forty-six. His widow caused scandal by marrying Sir Richard Woodville (d. 1469). Her enemies accused her, as Bedford's sister-in-law, Eleanor Cobham, had been accused, of witchcraft. See plate 26 and pedigree, p. 178.

T.S.I.H., i, 213 (Duchess of Bedford accused of witchcraft).

JAMES I (1394–1437), one of the ablest Kings of Scotland, composer of a famous poem, 'The Kingis Quair', and founder of St. Andrews, the oldest Scottish University, was the third son of Robert III (d. 1406), son of Robert II (1316–1390), son of the steward of Scotland by a daughter of Robert Bruce. Some English sailors from Cley (Norfolk) captured James on Palm Sunday, 1406, off Flamborough Head on his way to France. Thither he was being sent, as heir to the throne, to be educated away from the dangers of turbulent Scottish life. Some say that Robert III died on the very same day. Robert's brother, Albany, became regent. He was glad to have James out of the way; and Henry IV accepted Parliament's request not to surrender lightly the Scottish prisoners. James I was well educated at the English court and stayed in England eighteen years. Meanwhile the lowland Scottish defeated at Harlaw (1411) the over-mighty ruler of most of the Celtic part of Scotland, the Lord of the Isles. Throughout Henry V's reign relations between England and Scotland were only disturbed by pressure from the Scots to recover castles taken from them in 1355 and by the service of Scottish soldiers in defence of France. In 1420 Henry V took James to France and brought him to the siege of Melun. There he killed twenty Scottish prisoners as if, in fighting for the French, they were rebels against James. It was James's Scottish subjects who defeated the Duke of Clarence at Beaugé (1421). At the siege of Dreux (1421) Henry V put James in nominal command, jointly with Humphrey, Duke of Gloucester, to embarrass the Scottish soldiers of France. In 1423 negotiations for James's release led to the Scots agreeing (1424) to pay £40,000 for James's expenses. James was to marry the lady of his choice, Joan, niece of Cardinal Beaufort (see pedigree, p. 85). There was to be a truce for seven years. The first Parliament of James I (1424) passed twenty-seven reforming Acts and from it the Scottish Statute book dates. Private law was prohibited, royal power strengthened, titles to land registered, heretics punished and weights and measures regulated. Albany was executed for misgovernment (1425), a central law-court was established (1425–6) and the Highlands were reduced to order (1427). In spite of his alliance with the House of Lancaster, James I betrothed his infant daughter, Margaret, to a French prince (1428). As a dowry he sent six thousand Scottish soldiers. As Joan of Arc led the French triumphantly against the English in France, James became bolder. In 1436 he attacked Roxburgh. A few months later he was murdered by rebellious Highlanders at Perth and was buried there in the Carthusian convent. His heir, James II, was six years old in 1437. See p. 238.

RICHARD DE BEAUCHAMP (1382–1439), Earl of Warwick, was son of that Earl Thomas (d. 1401) who was imprisoned for opposing Richard II in the place still called the Beauchamp Tower in the Tower of London. In 1418 Richard was one of Henry V's chief generals in Normandy. There he reduced Domfront, in the south-east, after three months' siege.

Beauchamp and Henry VI (Rous Roll)

After further service in France Warwick became Henry VI's tutor in 1428 until the king reached the age of sixteen. The picture showing him carrying his little charge is taken from a famous roll about the Beauchamp family. When Warwick ceased to be tutor he returned to France (1437). There he died two years later aged fifty-seven.

'The Estates and Finances of Richard Beauchamp, Earl of Warwick', *Dugdale Society Occasional Papers*, No. 12.

HENRY CHICHELE (?1362–1443), Archbishop of Canterbury, was son of Thomas Chichele, the leading burgess of Higham Ferrers, Northants. His brothers were prominent grocers who had become sufficiently important by 1395 to be supplying Henry Bolingbroke (later Henry IV) with medicine. Henry himself was patronized by William of Wykeham and obtained his education at Winchester (1373) and Wykeham's new foundation of New College (1387). In 1391 he received the first of a series of appointments in the Church. He went as an envoy to Pope Innocent VII (1405), to Pope Gregory XII (1407), to a great church council at Pisa (1409) and to France (1410 and 1413) and became Bishop of St. David's (1408) and finally Archbishop of Canterbury (1414). Chichele approved of Henry V's intention of invading France and was leader of a deputation to the Guildhall to seek a loan for the Agincourt campaign (1415). He appointed a special thanksgiving for the victory of Agincourt. He was himself important as a financier and lent more money to Henry V than any other churchman, continuing until death to support Henry VI with loans. Like the other great men of his generation he was an active enemy of the Lollards (1416–22); and he strove for the repeal of laws which limited the power in England of the popes (1427–8). The register of his official activities as archbishop has been edited by Professor E. F. Jacob and it shows the efficient performance of his duties. As archbishop he protested against the gift by Pope Martin V of a cardinal's hat to Beaufort, for he could not approve of the elevation of that royally-connected Bishop of Winchester to a position in the Church in England which would overshadow the authority of Canterbury. For all his importance in church and state, Chichele was fundamentally a scholar. In 1424 he founded a college at Higham Ferrers and in April 1443 he granted statutes for his foundation of All Souls College, Oxford. This was to be not only a centre for the study of the arts and law but was to be a chantry where prayers were to be made for the faithful departed, especially for Henry V. It was a kind of Lancastrian War Memorial. It was not, as many writers incorrectly repeat, intended to calm a conscience disturbed by the deaths of many, English and French, in France; for Chichele did not incite Henry to go to war, as Shakespeare suggests, and he need never have doubted the justice of the war for it was Henry's duty to assert what seemed his rights.

Professor E. F. Jacob, *Henry Chichele and the Ecclesiastical Politics of his Age* (Creighton Lectures in History), 1952.

ELEANOR COBHAM (d. ?1446) was beautiful, charming and brave, and she came of a family which had risen in the service of Edward III, but her honour was besmirched. Her father was Reginald Cobham of Sterborough (Kent), commonly called Lord Cobham, and she became a lady-in-waiting to Jacqueline of Hainault, wife of Humphrey, Duke of Gloucester.

Eleanor accompanied Jacqueline to Hainault and on their return (1425) Eleanor became the mistress of Jacqueline's illustrious husband, and came to England with him.

The pair were friends of Humphrey's stepmother, Joanna of Navarre, who had survived her husband Henry IV for twenty-four years. Joanna had been accused of witchcraft and had been arrested by Humphrey's brother, the Duke of Bedford (1419). Eleanor too was suspected of witchcraft, and gossip attributed her power over Humphrey to potions provided by one Margery Jourdemain, called the Witch of Eye.

Eleanor bore Humphrey two children, and when a papal decree freed Humphrey from his marriage to Jacqueline they married (1428). Thence 'arose shame and more disgrace and inconvenience to the whole kingdom than can be expressed', and even the duke's admirer, Lydgate, condemned in verse the 'Cyroness' (Syren) who made Humphrey 'foule forsworne unto that godely faythfull truwe pryncesse', Jacqueline. Eleanor was publicly recognized as Duchess and provided with the robes of the Garter to wear at St. George's feast at Windsor (1436).

In 1441 she went to witness the spectacle of the Marching Watch which carried torches on every midsummer through the streets of London to celebrate, not just the longest day, but also the Feast of St. John the Baptist, that 'burning shining light'. John Stow, the Elizabethan writer on old London, has described this Marching Watch. Eleanor, as the highest lady in the land after Margaret of Anjou, went to see it from the 'Crown Seld in Cheap'. This had been built by Edward III for 'the Kings of England and other great Estates, therein to behold the shows of the city'. There she sat having supper on June 25th, 1441, when she was arrested. Two priests had been imprisoned for trying to kill Henry VI, as Randolph had tried to kill Henry V for Joanna, by black magic. One, with all his instruments, had abjured his arts on a platform in front of St. Paul's churchyard (July 16th). One said he had done it for the Duchess. The accused said that Eleanor 'had asked him to divine to what estate in life she should come', and a woman who asked the devil if she would be queen would not hesitate to use the devil's aid to remove any living obstacle. Eleanor fled for sanctuary to Westminster, but sanctuary could not shield heretics or witches, and she tried in vain to escape by water. After various trials before the bishops she was condemned. She had to do public penance, on three different days, in London. Eleanor landed from her barge at Temple Stairs one November Monday and walked 'openly barehede with a kevershef on her hede' via Temple Bar to St. Paul's 'with a meke and a demure countenance, carrying a 2 lb. candle to offer at the High Altar. On Wednesday Eleanor landed at Swan Stairs (Upper Thames St.) and went thus via Bridge St., Gracechurch St., and Leadenhall St., to Holy Trinity Priory, Aldgate. On Friday she came from Queenhithe through Cheapside (by the Crown Seld) to St. Michael, Cornhill. Each day the mayor and sheriffs escorted her. Eleanor was luckier than Joan of Arc and the witch of Eye who were burnt, one at Rouen (1431), the other at Smithfield. One of the priests was hanged, beheaded and quartered; the other died in prison. Eleanor was imprisoned at Chester and Kenilworth until her death about five years later. One of her custodians was Sir Thomas Stanley, King of the Isle of Man, who later assisted at Bury when Humphrey in turn was arrested. 'The Lament of the Duchess of Gloucester' and other verses dwell on the pride which preceded Eleanor's fall. Her fall weakened Humphrey much. As Shakespeare says (*2 Henry VI*, act ii, sc. 9), 'See! how the giddy multitude do point, And nod their heads, and turn their eyes on thee'.

HUMPHREY, DUKE OF GLOUCESTER (1391–1447) is called 'the Good Duke Humphrey', because he was a patron of writers, although he was neither good as a husband nor as a statesman. He became Duke in 1414, commanded a division at Agincourt (1415) and served at Lisieux (1417), Cherbourg

(1418), Rouen (1419) and Melun (1420). On Henry V's death he hoped to be regent but he had to serve under his brother, the Duke of Bedford (1422). His marriage with Jacqueline of Hainault brought him into conflict with England's ally, Philip, Duke of Burgundy, but after six years (1428) he had his marriage annulled and married his mistress, Eleanor Cobham. In 1441 he was unable to save her from prosecution for witchcraft. For a quarter of a century politics in England largely turned upon the jealous rivalry between Humphrey and his uncle, Cardinal Beaufort (see pedigree p. 178). In 1447 Humphrey was arrested on suspicion of designs on the life of Henry VI. He died in custody and foul play was suspected, without real reason. His enemy, Beaufort, died the same year. Polydore Vergil, who wrote a history of England for Henry VII, pointed out that the title of Gloucester seemed unlucky, for it was held by King John, Thomas of Woodstock and Richard III, as well as by Humphrey.

Humphrey cared for the writers of Greece and Rome before other Englishmen had acquired such tastes. His repute as a patron of learning was international. Titus Livius of Forli, Leonardo Aretino, Lydgate, Capgrave and practically everyone of the day who wrote in English enjoyed his patronage. Capgrave was an Augustinian canon of Lynn, who wrote a *Chronicle of England* which was one of the first chronicles to be written by a monk in English and is an important source for studying the period. Lydgate praised Humphrey's piety, declaring 'in this londe no lolard dar abide'. Humphrey befriended St. Albans Abbey; yet his importance lies in his encouragement not of medieval, but of the new learning based on ancient pagan civilization and expressed in modern languages. The University of Oxford said that Humphrey's future fame would be immortal, not for his military and political glories, but for his constant liberality to its members. He was its 'great protector'. In 1438 he gave 129 books to it and in 1444, 134 more, though the statement of the Oxford antiquary, Anthony Wood, that he gave 539 is an exaggeration. The University told Humphrey 'We wish you could see the students bending over your books in their greediness and thirst for knowledge'. It asked if he would approve of the library's being called after his name. 'Duke Humphrey's Library' in the Bodleian at Oxford is a room still full of scholars, but his books were scattered in the sixteenth century. The atmosphere at Humphrey's table can be recaptured from John Russell's *Boke of Nurture*, for Russell says he was servant to Humphrey 'with whom Uschere in chamber was I, and Marshall also in Halle'. A manuscript at Arras contains a portrait, probably taken by Jacques le Boucq, a sixteenth-century herald, from a lost contemporary picture. The long, clean-shaven face (plate 27) contrasts with the bearded personage copied at the head-piece of the old catalogue of Bodleian manuscripts (1697) from glass in Greenwich church, destroyed in 1710.

Ruth Putnam, *A Medieval Princess. Jacqueline, Countess of Holland*, 1904.
K. H. Vickers, *Humphrey, Duke of Gloucester*, 1907.
T.S.I.H., i, 205 (*Boke of Nurture*).

HENRY BEAUFORT (1374 or 1375–1447) was son of John of Gaunt and Catherine Swynford. He was born at Beaufort Castle in Anjou and was made legitimate in 1397. While in his early twenties he became Bishop of the vast diocese of Lincoln, but the usurpation of his half-brother, Henry IV, made him even more important than he had been under his first master, Richard II, and for nearly half a century he was one of the chief figures in English politics. Beaufort was educated at Aachen as a lawyer, but also studied at Peterhouse, Cambridge (1388–9), and Queen's College, Oxford (1390–1). He was Chancellor to the three Lancastrian kings (1403–11, 1413–17 and 1424), in 1404 he succeeded Wykeham as Bishop of Winchester and in December, 1417, Henry V was forced to put a tactful check on the arrogance of 'his oldest uncle and closest councillor' for becoming a cardinal and papal legate without royal leave. Beaufort was England's 'greatest merchant of wools' and recent detailed study has revealed his shady financial transactions with the Crown and shown that the Tudor chroniclers were right in calling him a usurer. Until his death loans from 'the Rich Cardinal' supported Henry VI. The

Tudor chronicler Hall called him 'more noble in blood than notable in learning . . . and rich above measure of all men, and to few liberal', but Beaufort did patronize the celebrated scholar, Poggio Bracciolini, and helped build the chapter library at Canterbury. He was, however, not to be compared with Humphrey, Duke of Gloucester, a real patron of learning, and his chief benefactions were directed rather modestly to the Hospital of St. Cross at Winchester, the foundation of Henry of Blois, an earlier royal bishop of Winchester. The Duke of Gloucester opposed Beaufort's desire to be sole regent (1422), and attacked him in the 'Parliament of Bats' (1426), to which members came armed with cudgels, as weapons were forbidden. Shakespeare represents him as calling Beaufort a 'scarlet hypocrite' and his bitter opposition reached a climax in 1439–41.

Other enemies of Beaufort were Archbishop Arundel, who had him dismissed from the Council (1411), and Archbishop Chichele, who protested against his appointment as *legate a latere* (1418) to represent the Pope in England over the head of the Archbishop of Canterbury. Unlike his father, Beaufort opposed the Lollards and collaborated with Arundel at Oldcastle's trial (1413) for heresy. He fought the Hussite heretics in Germany (1420) and enlisted soldiers against them (1428). Latterly his policy was one of peace with France. On May 30th, 1431, Beaufort sat in his cardinal's robes in Rouen market place and watched Joan of Arc burn; and ten years later he was associated with Cardinal Kemp in condemning Eleanor Cobham for witchcraft. It was he who crowned Henry VI as King of France in Paris (1430). He died in retirement on Palm Sunday, 1447, at Wolvesey Palace, Winchester. Shakespeare represents him as in 'black despair', full of remorse for the alleged murder of Humphrey, Duke of Gloucester, and unable to give Henry VI even a dumb sign of hope of forgiveness (*2 Henry VI*, act iii, sc. 2). The Chronicle of Croyland preserves an eyewitness account of a happier scene. In the evening Beaufort read his will to his household and added a last codicil to it. The next day the Prior of St. Swithun's celebrated Mass for him. His will was read to him. He confirmed it and said good-bye in an audible voice before dying. His effigy is in Winchester Cathedral. See pedigree, p. 178.

L. B. Radford, *Henry Beaufort, Bishop, Chancellor, Cardinal*, 1908.

JACK CADE (d. 1450) posed as a doctor called Aylmer and led a revolt of national importance under the name of John Mortimer. The government regarded him as a violent Irishman. In 1449 'the sonne in his risyng and goyng doune apperid as reed as blood as meny a man saw', prices were high, the government was unpopular and England was on the verge of civil war. On June 10th or 11th, 1450, Cade, gaily dressed in scarlet, led a well-ordered host of Kentish rebels to Blackheath and fortified a camp.

The first ten paragraphs of Cade's manifesto are against evil royal councillors. Cade wanted the recall of the Duke of York to court, the removal of 'the fals progeny and affynyte' of the Duke of Suffolk and revenge for the death of Humphrey, Duke of Gloucester. The only social or economic demand was the repeal of the Statute of Labourers.

Cade demanded of all foreign merchants in London '12 harnesses, 24 brigandines, 12 battle axes, 12 glaves, 6 horses completely harnessed and 1000 marks ready money'. On June 18th a royal force attacked the rebels and was beaten. The remaining royal forces mutinied and the king retreated to Kenilworth although the Londoners begged Henry VI that 'he wolde tarye in the cite and wolde lyve and dye with them, and pay for his costes of household an halff yere'. Revolts occurred in various counties and in Wiltshire the Bishop of Salisbury, a 'wonder convetous man,'' was torn to pieces and his goods plundered. On July 3rd Cade cut the ropes of the drawbridge of London Bridge and forced his way into the city with the 'favour of some of the men of London, especially the poor'. Now he rode in blue velvet, his shield studded with gold nails, with golden spurs, and a naked sword in his hand, preceded by Robert Poynings Esq. of Southwark with a sword of State.

The keys were handed to him. Cade struck London Stone crying, 'Now is Mortymer Lord of this City.' On June 4th

Cade's men executed Lord Say, the Treasurer, in Cheap. They also executed Say's son-in-law, Crowmer, the sheriff of Kent. Some citizens obtained the help of the garrison of the Tower and attacked the rebels in Southwark. The drawbridge caught fire and separated the combatants. On July 6th the royal council accepted the rebels' demands and pardoned them. On July 8th the rebels went away to Rochester. On July 10th Cade attacked Queenborough Castle in Sheppey and that day he was publicly cried a traitor. On July 12th he was captured in a garden near Lewes and was mortally wounded. He was drawn naked on a hurdle towards London and he died on the way. The hostess of the White Hart in Southwark identified Cade's body and it was beheaded and quartered.

Cade's rebellion heralded the Wars of the Roses.

George Kriehn, *The English Rising in 1450* (a dissertation presented to Strasbourg University), 1892.

J. Clayton, *The True Story of Jack Cade*, 1909.

THOMAS HOCCLEVE or OCCLEVE (?1370–?1450) was a poet who worked in the privy seal office for twenty-four years. He complained of poverty and delays in the receipt of his salary, but used to eat and drink too much, belonged to a dining club in the Temple, and frequented taverns and cook-shops at Westminster. His *De Regimine Principum* comprises 5,488 lines of poor English verse. A manuscript of it in the British Museum contains the best portrait of Chaucer (see plate 22), his admired acquaintance.

Hoccleve, *Works*, Early English Text Society extra series, vols. 61 and 73, 1892–99.

WILLIAM DE LA POLE (1396–1450), grandson of Michael, first Earl of Suffolk (d. 1389), served for seventeen years in France and once had to yield to Joan of Arc (1429). Suffolk favoured peace and arranged Henry VI's marriage with Margaret of Anjou (1445). The deaths of Gloucester and Beaufort (1447) left him supreme and he became Duke of Suffolk (1448), but he was unpopular and was banished from the king's realms of England and France in 1450. A ship called

'The Nicholas of the Tower' intercepted him and 'one of the lewdest men on board' beheaded him with six strokes of a rusty sword. Henry had his body removed from Dover beach for burial at Wingfield (Suffolk). There his effigy remains. Political poets pilloried his memory.

JOHN LYDGATE (?1370–?1451), often called 'the monk of Bury', was perhaps the chief of the immediate followers of Chaucer, whom he greatly admired and probably knew, and with whom he was in his own day frequently and inexplicably classed. Even as late as the eighteenth century Gray expressed a high opinion of his poetry. Modern readers are more likely to agree with the bibliographer Ritson's description of him as 'a prosaic and drivelling monk', and 'a most prolix and voluminous poetaster'. 'Drivelling' may be a little severe, but there is not much amiss with the other adjectives. Lydgate's *Falls of Princes* is over 36,000 lines long, *Troy Book* 30,000, and *The Pilgrimage of Man* over 20,000. Besides these he wrote a great number of other poems of every conceivable kind in octosyllabics, heroic couplets, or 'Rhyme Royal' (7-line stanzas). Life would hardly be long enough to read all Lydgate's works, even if they were easier to come by than they are, but a brief perusal is enough to show that their quality does not vary much; there are very few plums indeed in a vast quantity of dough. For Lydgate had three major defects—inexhaustible facility, little or no imagination, and a very imperfect ear. Many of his lines are impossible to scan; they hobble implacably and woodenly along, and at the end leave nothing in the reader's mind but amazement at his great and undoubted popularity even in those unsophisticated times. Critics generally seem to regard the *Falls of Princes* as his best poem, but to us by far his most readable poem is a comparatively short one called 'London Lickpenny', describing a countryman's visit to London. In this he shows himself a genial fellow with some satirical humour, and a love of country scenes and pursuits. Lydgate, as often used to happen, took his surname from the Suffolk village where he was born, and became a monk of St. Edmunds, Bury. He was for a time at

Oxford (Gloucester Hall now Worcester College), and lived mainly in London where he soon found powerful patronage. His *Troy Book* was written at the request of Prince Henry, afterwards Henry V. Another patron, Humphrey, Duke of Gloucester, Lydgate repaid for his generosity with the portentous *Falls of Princes*. In fact for some time he was really the court poet, and wrote several poems in connection with Henry VI's Coronation. But he continued none-the-less in his monastic calling (frequently complaining of his poverty) and celebrated in verse the life and miracles of St. Alban at the same time and with the same facility as he pored over poems to royalty and the nobility. In 1423 he became Prior of Hatfield Regis, and in 1434 returned to Bury where he lived for his remaining years.

'The fifteenth century adored him because he combined all its worst faults, and the sixteenth seems to have accepted him because it had no apparatus for criticism.'—*Saintsbury*. G.W.L.

FASTOLF, SIR JOHN (1378–1459) was born at Caister, Norfolk, where he later used the profits of war to build a castle of which the tower still rose ninety feet high within living memory. He was one of the most famous English captains, a veteran of Agincourt (1415), Verneuil (1424) and 'the Battle of the Herrings' (1429); and now 'Falstaff' is the most famous character in Shakespeare, although he is a mere caricature of the original. Indeed Shakespeare originally called his Falstaff by another name, Sir John Oldcastle, and only altered the name in deference to Lord Cobham who claimed descent from Oldcastle; and Fastolf was no spendthrift old debauchee or boon companion of Henry V when prince.

In 1429 he suffered a reverse at Patay when Joan of Arc's reputation demoralized the English, and this incident led to his losing the Order of the Garter.

The Duke of Bedford restored it, when he learnt the circumstances, but Shakespeare immortalized the disgrace in Henry VI, part I where he fuses the brave Fastolf with the disreputable Falstaff (his exact opposite).

Fastolf's association with the unsuccessful French war made

him unpopular and in Cade's rebellion he was denounced as the greatest traitor in England or France who was to blame for the loss of the king's French inheritance. Fastolf had a house in Southwark and this he fortified when Cade rebelled. On Cade's approach he withdrew over London Bridge into the Tower. He was an early benefactor of Magdalen College, Oxford, the foundation of his friend Bishop Waynflete. As an irritable old friend and neighbour and a grasping man of business in farming matters, he lives in the Paston letters. He died speechless and childless, aged seventy-seven.

K. B. McFarlane, 'Investment of Sir John Fastolf's Profits of War', *Transactions of the Royal Historical Society*, 5th series, 7, pp. 91–116.

JAMES II (1430–60), succeeded his father, James I, as King of Scotland (1437) at the age of six. The quarrels between the Scottish nobles meant that there was peace with England for a decade. The Scottish throne was endangered by the power of the family of Douglas; and James II personally murdered its head at Stirling (1452). Douglas's heir was defeated at Arkinholme (1455) and fled to England. James pacified the Highlands and reformed the administration of justice and the coinage. In 1455, and again in 1456, he was encouraged by the weakness of Henry VI to incite Charles VII of France to attack Calais while he attacked Berwick. Margaret of Anjou was ready to gain James's support for her husband, Henry VI, against the Yorkists by sacrificing important English interests. As her ally, James II sheltered her after the battle of Northampton (1460). That year he was killed by the explosion of a cannon, while besieging the English in Roxburgh. See p. 85.

A Short Chronicle of James II, King of Scots, ed. T. Thomson, 1819.

REGINALD PECOCK (?1395–?1461) was a Welshman who came to Oriel College, Oxford (1409) and became author of a monument of fifteenth-century English prose, *The Repressor of Over Much Blaming of the Clergy*. He preached an unpopular sermon at Paul's Cross (1447) against church reform; and tried to combat the Lollards by reason; because they claimed the right to understand the scriptures by faith and rejected the authority of experts. He is important as the first to write in English the kind of discussion hitherto confined to Latin. He was charged with 'presuming of mine own natural wit and preferring the judgment of natural reason, the "doom of reason", before the New and Old Testament and the authority and determination of our mother Holy Church'. Archbishop Bourchier offered him the choice of recanting and burning his books or of being burnt himself. He recanted on December 4th, 1457, and within a fortnight his books were burnt at Carfax in Oxford. He made an appeal to Rome and the Pope ordered restitution; but as the Pope died soon afterwards, the order was ineffective and Pecock died in confinement at Thorney Abbey. People who have ignored Pecock's medieval background have seen in him a rationalist born before his time.

One of the last acts of the first Duke of Suffolk, the unpopular Lancastrian, was to make Pecock (1450) Bishop of Chichester. Pecock accordingly fell as an unpopular Lancastrian unable to survive the rise to power of the Yorkists. Pecock considered that a belief in Christ's descent into Hell, a popular theme of medieval art and literature, was unnecessary to salvation. He also denied that the Apostles' Creed was authentic. This he argued in a work called 'The Provoker', of which no single copy has survived.

V. H. H. Green, *Bishop Reginald Pecock*, 1945.
Professor E. F. Jacob, *Reynold Pecock, Bishop of Chichester* (The Raleigh Lecture of the British Academy, 1951).
T.S.I.H., i, 209 (Pecock's recantation).

JAMES KENNEDY (?1406–1465) was the greatest figure in mid-fifteenth century Scotland. He was a nephew of James I of Scotland and became Bishop of Dunkeld (1438–41) and of St. Andrews (1441–65). He considered the power of the Douglases a danger to the throne. Their ally, the Earl of Crawford, and other enemies raided his diocese (1445). He retaliated by cutting them and theirs off from the community of Christians with sentences of excommunication and interdict; and exactly a year later, as if by some divine judgment,

Crawford was mortally wounded. As one of the regents, Kennedy ruled Scotland with great success during the first five years of the minority of James III (1460–5). The Scottish historians mention his foundation of St. Salvator's College at St. Andrew's, the building of a mighty ship called 'the Bishop's Barge' and the erection of a great tomb for himself. Kennedy died in July, 1465.

Anne I. Dunlop, *The Life and Times of James Kennedy, Bishop of St. Andrew's*, 1950.

JOHN PASTON (1421–66) was the son of William Paston (1378–1444), a judge, who founded the fortunes of the family. His papers are an important source for fifteenth-century history, though largely concerned with Norfolk business. His wife, Margaret (d. 1484), was a cousin of Sir John Fastolf. For him Paston supervised the building of Caister Castle and after Fastolf died he claimed to inherit his estates. He kept most of these in spite of the opposition of the Dukes of Norfolk and Suffolk.

Paston Letters 1422–1509, ed. J. Gairdner, 1900.

JOHN TIPTOFT (?1427–1470) was called the 'butcher of England' because of his great cruelty when Constable of England (1462–7, 1470), but he was also the most important aristocratic scholar of his day. He was descended from a Baron Tiptoft who had gone crusading with Edward I, and was son of a Baron Tiptoft (?1375–1443), a soldier, courtier and diplomat who had been elected Speaker of the House of Commons (1406) and had written a well-informed chronicle of fifteenth-century events. The surname occurs in the Battle Abbey Roll of William the Conqueror's knights and a branch of the family were still living in Normandy in the fifteenth century. The name 'Tiptofts' survives as that of a fourteenth-century farmhouse at Wimbish (Essex). Wimbish was one of the manors which belonged to the Tiptofts and Wimbish church contains fourteenth-century armorial glass of the Tiptofts and of families related to them. The arms 'argent, a saltire engrailed gules' (see the end-paper) occur on Tiptoft's effigy at Ely. They also occur twice in a famous illuminated manuscript made in

Edward V (Canterbury glass)

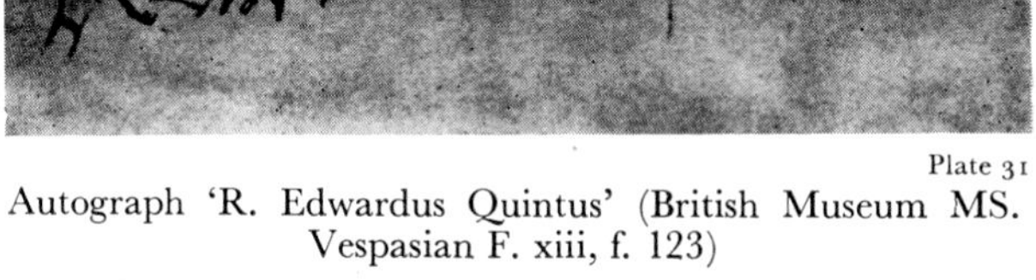

Plate 31

Autograph 'R. Edwardus Quintus' (British Museum MS. Vespasian F. xiii, f. 123)

Plate 32

Richard III
(National Portrait
Gallery)
Autograph
(British Museum,
Vespasian F. xiii,
f. 124)

East Anglia in the early fourteenth century for one of the Tiptofts. This is called the Gorleston Psalter. In the nineteenth century it was one of the treasures of William Morris, the poet, and it is now in the Pierpont Morgan Library (New York). John Tiptoft studied at Balliol College, Oxford, where he was a friend of the learned John Free. Like him he was a pupil of Guarini at Ferrara. In 1458–61 he went on a pilgrimage to Jerusalem. He was a scholarly young nobleman with protruding eyes. He studied Roman law for nearly two years at Padua and heard John Argyropoulos lecture on Greek at Florence, when the study of Greek was something novel and exciting. His own writings include a translation from an Italian dialogue showing that the new 'humanist' ideal man is better than the old medieval ideal. Tiptoft's admirer, Caxton, the first English printer, printed this rendering of Buonaccorso's *Declaration of Nobleness* as early as 1460. He also printed a translation by Tiptoft of Cicero, *On Friendship*. Tiptoft was made Earl of Worcester in 1449, and, as a Yorkist, held various high state offices for Edward IV. In 1467 he went, as he had gone ten years before, as Deputy to Ireland. He took some of his books with him, but there he was guilty of murdering two little FitzGerald boys after executing their father, the Earl of Desmond, in order to please Queen Elizabeth Woodville. His other cruelties included the execution of John, Earl of Oxford (1462), Sir Ralph Gray and various Lancastrians (1464) and twenty of Clarence's party, captured at sea (1470). The latter he hanged and impaled, for Tiptoft introduced the Turkish practice of impaling condemned people on stakes. When Edward IV had to flee for a time (1470) Tiptoft was executed. He asked the headsman to take three strokes in honour of the Trinity. The contents of his library have been reconstructed. This library was typical of a scholar deeply interested in the revival of the classical learning of the ancient world, and included writings by Lucretius, Suetonius, Tacitus and Sallust. Tiptoft had more in common than other Englishmen with the cruel but cultured princes of the Italian Renaissance.

R. J. Mitchell, *John Tiptoft*, 1938.

SIR THOMAS MALORY (*fl.* 1470). Almost nothing is known of Malory. Bishop Bale, who wrote a history of English writers, says he was a Welshman, but the statement has no confirmation. A certain Thomas Malorie of Newbold Revell, who was a soldier, and, according to Bale, engaged in affairs of State, seems to have possessed the least shadowy claim, but more than that cannot be said. The author in his work calls himself Maleor or Mallore, but as little weight can be put on fifteenth-century spelling of names as on the emphatic professions of religious piety through which the knightly author has led some to assume that he was in holy orders.

Malory's *Morte d'Arthur* was translated from 'certain books of French' in 1469–70. It was printed by Caxton in 1485, and by him broken up into chapters. It is a compilation, without much order or cohesion, of legends about King Arthur and his Knights, mainly taken from the French, but with occasional interpolations from English legends, or even of Malory's own. But there is no effect of disharmony in the telling of the tales. In these there is, as in the 'Iliad', a certain monotony, for fighting was the main occupation of medieval knights, however lofty the aims and impulses which Malory imputes to the heroes of chivalry, the Lancelots and Gawaines and Tristrams. It is essentially a world of fairyland; passions rise and are acted upon with childlike promptitude and causelessness. The characters are commonly drawn in black and white; knights are simple and brave or treacherous, their ladies are simple and fair, or frail; neither are selfconscious or subtle. But many of the episodes, especially those connected with the search for the Holy Grail, are related with real depth of feeling and considerable beauty, largely arising from the clarity and simplicity of the language, and the gentle rise and fall of its rhythms. In spite of its French origin Anglo-Saxon words and phrases predominate over Latin. Sentences proceed straightforwardly full of monosyllables, and linked more often than not by a simple 'And so' or 'Then', but there is no denying the extraordinary charm of Malory's limpid style.

Most modern readers will know the story of King Arthur and his Round Table, if they know it at all, from Tennyson's twelve

Idylls of the King, which nearly a century ago were very popular. But even then there were many who found their Victorian atmosphere the very opposite of medieval, and the versification, as Ruskin said, showing '. . . too much art and finish', though others delighted in the numberless felicities, and the rich music and colour of Tennyson's imagery. Andrew Lang says: 'Next to Chaucer's poems, Malory's romance is the greatest thing in English literature from "Beowulf" to Spenser'.

G.W.L.

HENRY VI (1421–71) was born on St. Nicholas Day, 6th December, 1421, and when his father, Henry V, died (1st September, 1422), he became king when nine months old. His maternal grandfather, Charles VI of France, died on 21st October and Henry was proclaimed King of France too. On 21st February, 1423, Alice Butler was appointed his attendant with power 'to chastise us reasonably from time to time'. The nature of his upbringing, or of his early reputation for saintliness, may be learnt from a story written as early as 1430. It says that in 1423–4, when Henry was less than three years old, he kicked and screamed when they tried to make him travel on a Sunday. In 1425 the Council decided that all nobles in royal wardship should be brought up at Court, each with his own master. The Court thus became a sort of school for the aristocracy, such as Henry later founded at Eton, just over the river from Windsor. Before Henry was four years old he had to appear at public functions and at Whitsun, 1428, his little 'gracious hands' dubbed a number of knights. In summer he lived at Wallingford and Hertford castles and in winter at Windsor and Berkhamstead. Richard Beauchamp, fifth Earl of Warwick, son of the former Governor of Richard II and father-in-law of Warwick 'the Kingmaker', was appointed Henry's governor 'to chasten him when he doth amiss' (1428). His childhood was marked in France by a decline of English power and in England by a struggle for power between his uncle, Humphrey, Duke of Gloucester, and his great-uncle, Bishop Henry Beaufort. Henry was crowned in London and Paris in 1430; and Warwick declared that Henry was grown in years and person 'and also in conceit and knowledge of his royal estate, the which cause him to grudge with chastising'. The council accordingly admonished Henry to obey Warwick. There were swords 'some greater and some smaller, for to learn the king to play in his tender age', and 'little harness that the Earl of Warwick made for the king . . . garnished with gold'. In 1437 Warwick went to France as regent and Henry was not only free of a tutor but began to show such independence in the Council that he was able to impair the royal revenue by imprudently generous grants. In 1442 Henry came of age, and the policies of old Cardinal Beaufort and of William de la Pole, Earl (later Duke) of Suffolk, began to prevail over those of Humphrey, Duke of Gloucester. A truce was made with France (1443) and a marriage with Margaret of Anjou was arranged (1445). Henry's first years of marriage saw France free from fighting and England free from faction. At this time Henry completed his new educational foundations, Eton and King's College, Cambridge. Despite frequent royal progresses throughout the country, discontent grew. In 1450 Kent rose under Jack Cade. Henry fled and the suppression of the rising was effected for him by Archbishop Kemp and Bishop Waynflete. After order was restored Henry personally sat giving severe judgments and reaping a great 'harvest of heads'. English power in France continued to decline and royal finances in England became worse. A struggle between the Dukes of York and Somerset became more bitter despite the efforts of Henry. Then 'a sudden and thoughtless fright' turned Henry VI into a speechless idiot (1453–4). Meanwhile Queen Margaret bore Henry an heir; and a Great Council, headed by the Duke of York, ruled, and Somerset was sent to the Tower. At last Henry became well enough to recognize his son. Some said that Henry declared that the child must be the son of the Holy Ghost. Somerset was released and York returned to Sandal Castle (Yorks.). In 1455 open civil war, 'the Wars of the Roses', began. York killed Somerset at St. Albans (1455) and brought Henry back to London. Henry wore dark, unfanciful clothes, a gown like a burgess's and wide shoes like a countryman.

He hated swearing. He loved improving literature. Ladies

with low-necked dresses made him cry 'Fie, fie for shame! For sooth ye are to blame!' Queen Margaret was the mainspring of the Lancastrian side, full of zeal for her feeble husband and for the rights of her little son; but when the French landed at Sandwich (1457), the national disgrace encouraged seditious rumours and men said that Prince Edward was the son of one of her favourites, Somerset or the Earl of Wiltshire. In flight after the battle of Hexham (May 15th, 1465) Henry left his 'cap of estate' behind at Bywell Castle. In July he was captured in Lancashire with a few attendants. Warwick led him through London with his feet tied in the stirrups with leather thongs. Henry was put in the Tower but was treated well and was allowed to see any visitors who wanted to come. On May 21st, 1471, Prince Edward was killed at Tewkesbury. The Yorkist leader, Edward IV, entered London in triumph leading Queen Margaret captive. That night Henry VI died. No Lancastrian could doubt that he was murdered, though the Yorkists gave out that he had 'died of pure displeasure'. Henry's body was exposed at St. Paul's. He was buried at Chertsey, but now lies at Windsor. Reports of miracles prove his reputation for saintliness. Modern examination of Henry's skull suggests violence. There are two fifteenth-century biographies of this good but ineffective man. Both are pious testimonials, though one does venture the criticism that it is a pity that the sea was not better kept free from pirates by his navy.

The life by John Blakman, a Fellow of Eton, was probably written in support of Henry VIII's effort to get Henry VI recognized as a saint. Blakman describes Henry's patience during his long imprisonment in the Tower. See pl. 28 and p. 227.

M. E. Christie, *Henry VI* (Kings and Queens of England), 1922.
T.S.I.H., i, 204 (Henry's virtues). See pedigree, p. 178.

RICHARD NEVIL (1428–71), Earl of Warwick, called 'the Kingmaker' and 'the last of the barons', had twice as much land as any subject had held before. His father had married Alice de Montacute, heiress of the Earl of Salisbury's estates, and he himself married Anne Beauchamp heiress of the Earls of Warwick. Of their ancestors Guy Beauchamp, Earl of

Warwick, had been an enemy of Piers Gaveston, the favourite of Edward II, and William de Montacute, the first Earl of Salisbury (1337), had served Edward III. It is Warwick's own fault that no record of his personal appearance survives. He promised to supply historical materials to the historian Jean de Wavrin (1469), but was too busy at his base of Calais. He received the governorship of Calais as a reward for supporting Richard, Duke of York, his uncle by marriage, at the first Battle of St. Albans (1455). In 1459 his Lancastrian royalist

Ann Nevil and Warwick the Kingmaker (Rous Roll)

enemies sacked Ludlow and 'whenn they hadde dronkyn inowe of wyne that was in tavernys and in othyr placys, they fulle ingoodely smote owte the heddys of the pypys and hoggys hedys of wyne, that men wente weteschode in wyne, and then they robbyd the towne, and bare awaye, beddynge, clothe, and othyr stuffe, and defoulyd many wymmen'. Warwick escaped from Ludlow and reached Calais in time to shut the gates on Somerset, whom Queen Margaret of Anjou had appointed as his successor. Warwick returned to triumph at Northampton (1460), to be defeated by Queen Margaret at the second battle of St. Albans (1460) and to triumph at Towton (1460). It was he who made Edward IV, the heir of the Duke of York, king (1461), and for the first three years of the reign he was the real ruler of England. His naval victories off Calais (1458–9) and the captured Spanish and Genoese ships which he had brought thither had made him a popular hero; and however selfish his purposes may have been, any Londoner who knew any of his servants might take as much meat from his kitchen as could be carried on a dagger. Retainers with his badge of the Bear with the ragged staff were many, and wherever he passed cries of 'Warwick! Warwick!' rang out. He was splendidly dressed and he would greet civilly those who hailed him. He seemed 'the moost corageous and manliest knight lyvyng' and a political song called him 'of Knighthode lodesterre, borne of a stok that evyr schal be trewe'. At Edward's accession Warwick was rewarded with the captaincy of Dover, and the wardenships of the Cinque Ports and of the Scottish Marches. The Nevils were already powerful in the Welsh Marches. Warwick was bitterly hurt to find that Edward IV preferred a Burgundian alliance and a marriage with Elizabeth Woodville to a French marriage alliance of his own designing (1464). Favours received by the new queen's family aroused his indignation. By 1469 London was full of malicious rumours circulated by Warwick and the Woodvilles against each other. That year Warwick actually captured Edward for a time, but had to retire again to Calais when Edward escaped (1470). By a masterstroke of diplomacy Louis XI reconciled Warwick and Queen Margaret, the Yorkist hero and the Lancastrian heroine, though each had brought to death those near and dear to the other. Warwick invaded England on behalf of Margaret and liberated her husband, Henry VI, from the Tower. Edward fled to Burgundy (1470) but returned in 1471 and managed to kill Warwick at Barnet. His body was exposed at St Paul's to prove that he was dead, and he was buried at Bisham Abbey.

C. W. C. Oman, *Warwick the Kingmaker*, reprinted 1926.
T.S.I.H., i, 207 (first battle or St. Albans, 1455) and 212 (rivalry with Woodvilles, 1469).

REGINALD ELY (d. 1471) was an outstanding architect of his century who died aged at least sixty after a working life of thirty-three years. He came from the country north-east of Norwich to Cambridge, worked at Peterhouse (1438) and was the first master mason responsible for building King's College (1444–61) with its superb chapel for Henry VI. Perhaps his last work was the Schools Quadrangle, begun shortly before his death. He left his best belt of green silk bossed with silver to Thaxted Church, Essex, with bequests to churches with which he had been connected as far afield as Boston, Lincs., and Thelsford, Warwickshire.

J. Harvey, *English Mediaeval Architects, a Biographical Dictionary down to 1550*, pp. 94–99.

ALICE CHAUCER, DUCHESS OF SUFFOLK (*c.* 1404–1475), was the grand-daughter of Geoffrey Chaucer. Her father, Thomas, was chief butler to Richard II, Henry IV, Henry V and Henry VI, Member of Parliament for Oxfordshire in most parliaments of 1400–31 and at times was the Speaker. Alice's first husband was Thomas Montague, fourth Earl of Salisbury, who served in France from the beginning of Henry V's invasion (1415) until his death (1428). At the siege of Orleans he was mortally wounded by a stray shot just after the capture of the Tournelles, two strong towers commanding the south end of the bridge. Alice married Montague's brother officer and successor, William de la Pole, fourth Earl of Suffolk. She became duchess when he reached the summit of his power in 1448. Suffolk soon became a scapegoat for disasters in France and was accused of being pro-French. He escaped to sea from the London mob, but was captured in the Channel. Some sailors took him aboard the 'Nicholas of the Tower' and beheaded him, to the delight of England. The Duchess lived on as widow for twenty-five years. In 1437 Henry VI gave the pair licence to found an almshouse and school at Ewelme (Oxon.). Both are still in use in the original buildings. Her funeral effigy at Ewelme (pl. 29) shows her wearing the Garter. This one was quoted to Queen Victoria as a precedent for the way ladies should wear the garter, on the left arm.

GEORGE PLANTAGENET, DUKE OF CLARENCE (1449–1478), was son of Richard, Duke of York. He rebelled against his brother, Edward IV, but changed sides and fought for him at Barnet (1471). He married Isabel, daughter of Warwick 'the Kingmaker', and on her death (1476) annoyed

George, Duke of Clarence (Rous Roll)

Edward IV by seeking to marry Mary of Burgundy. He was executed for high treason in the Tower at the age of twenty-eight, and was said by three contemporaries to have been drowned in a butt of Malmsey wine. He was buried in Tewkesbury Abbey. See pedigree, p. 178.

MARGARET OF ANJOU (1430–82), a handsome daughter of the elegant count René, married Henry VI when she was aged fifteen. It was a triumph for Cardinal Beaufort and Suffolk, who wanted peace. Margaret had a son soon after Henry had gone mad in 1453 and thereafter she became politically important. Her friendship with Suffolk and Somerset made her an enemy of the Duke of York. Throughout the Wars of the Roses she was the relentless champion of her husband and son until their deaths in 1471. Shakespeare makes York call her, what Edward II's queen had been called, 'she-wolf of France'. She spent five years in custody, with her friend the Duchess of Suffolk as her keeper. In 1475 Louis XI ransomed her and she returned to France where she died in poverty.

J. J. Bagley, *Margaret of Anjou Queen of England*, 1948.
T.S.I.H., i, 211 (an adventure with a robber).

EDWARD IV (1442–83) was the son of Richard Duke of York (d. 1460) and Cicely Nevil and until he was eighteen and his father fell at Wakefield his fortunes rose and fell with those of the Yorkist faction of which his father was leader. Edward returned from France with the Yorkist earls, Warwick and Salisbury, and defeated Henry VI at Northampton (1460). In 1461 he was again victorious at Mortimer's Cross and Towton. After Northampton he swore allegiance to Henry VI, after Mortimer's Cross he proclaimed himself king, and after Towton he was crowned. At Northampton he had been Earl of March, at Mortimer's Cross he was Duke of York and at Towton he was king, thanks to the Earl of Warwick. After Towton a Londoner wrote, 'I am unable to declare how well the Commons love and adore him, as if he were their God. The entire kingdom keeps holiday for the event, which seems a boon from above. Thus far he appears to be a just prince, and to mean to amend and organize matters otherwise than has been done hitherto'. It was the turn of Yorkists to get promotion and for Lancastrians to stand their trials, but Edward was determined to control the unruly gentry and to promote new followers so as gradually to become independent of Warwick. Edward was openly said to rule by his virtue. It was Warwick's brother, George Nevil, the Chancellor, who later became Archbishop of York (1464), who first arranged at a meeting at Clerkenwell for Edward to be invited to take the crown; and in Scotland they described Warwick as conductor of the realm. In 1464 Edward married Elizabeth Woodville. This and the consequent promotion of her relations enraged Warwick so much that it achieved the miracle of bringing about an alliance between Warwick, the mainstay of the Yorkists, and Margaret of Anjou, the mainstay of the Lancastrians. Edward's unreliable brother George, Duke of Clarence, was persuaded to join Warwick's plots. Confused fighting began (1469) and a movement called the rising of Robin of Redesdale ended in the defeat of Edward; but in 1470 he was victorious at 'Lose-coat-field' and proclaimed Warwick and Clarence traitors. Soon, however, he had to flee to Holland (26 September, 1470) thanks to the sudden treachery of Warwick's brother, Montague. The story is told by Philip de Comines. The Duke of Burgundy enabled Edward to return (1471), to capture Henry VI, to slay Warwick at Barnet, and to capture Margaret of Anjou at Tewkesbury. He invaded France (1474), but Louis XI astutely persuaded him to desert his ally, the Duke of Burgundy, at the Treaty of Picquigny, as described in intimate detail by de Comines, who was present. Edward was six feet three inches tall and the vivid words of de Comines led nineteenth-century writers to dismiss him as handsome, but merely selfish and luxurious. De Comines was writing to contrast him with the wisdom of his own hero, Louis XI, just as Stubbs in his *Constitutional History* tends to contrast Yorkist tyranny with Lancastrian constitutionalism. In fact Edward was a forerunner of Henry VII as the kind of busy administrator who fulfils the ideal of our own bureaucratic age. As a monk of Croyland writes, 'He appointed inspectors of the customs, men of remarkable shrewdness, but too hard . . . upon the merchants. . . . He also examined the register of rolls of chancery, and exacted many fines from those whom he found to have intruded and taken possession of estates without proving their rights in form required by law. . . . These, and more of a similar nature than can possibly be conceived by a man who is inexperienced in such matters, were his methods of making a purse'. The monk of Croyland portrays Edward as busy with commerce as well as administration: 'Having procured merchant ships, he put on board of them the finest wools, cloths, tin, and other productions of the kingdom, and like a private individual living by trade, exchanged merchandise for merchandise by means of his factors among both Italians and

Greeks'. In a coronation proclamation Edward had deplored 'the oppression of the people, the manslaughter, extortion, perjurie and robberye amonge theym, the . . . verrey decay of merchandise wherein rested the prosperity of the subgetts' and

Edward IV, Edward V and Elizabeth Woodville (Lambeth MS.)

his parliament of 1463 made many statutes to protect trade from cheap foreign prices. An Act of that year even protected for the first time from 'truck' payments cloth workers who had been 'dryven to take grete part of their wages in pynnes, girdles, and other unprofitable merchandise, under such price as stretcheth not to th' extent of their lefull wages, and also delyveren unto them wolles to be wrought by over excessive weight, which hath dryven and dryveth men and women into discorage of such labour'. Another Act ordered English shipping to be used when possible, and Edward owned ships, La Grace de Dieu, Le Henry, Le Antony, Le Great Portingale, Le Spagnard, Le Henry Ashe, The Mary and John (900 tons) and the Mary Redcliffe (500 tons). Laws prohibited the export of currency, and forbade 'inordynate, excessive and outeragious' dress, sub-standard gold and silver articles, and, significantly, a new fulling-mill which could 'fulle and thikke' more caps in a day than could be done 'by hand and fote'. He raised forced money by compulsory loans called 'benevolences', but though his Court was splendid, he died free of debt. The names of his many mistresses, except for Jane Shore, are forgotten. They had no political importance, except that Jane Shore persuaded him not to confiscate the endowments which Henry VI had given to Eton College. Edward loved sport.

'In summer time when leaves grew green
And birds were singing on the tree
King Edward would a-hunting ride
Some pastime for to see.'

Not only fine ladies would accompany him. The citizens of London would come with him hunting at Waltham and feast in a 'pleasant logge of grene bowhis' on 'as well seasoned mete as it had been dressed in a stondyng place' with 'wyne cowched, reed, whyte, and claret whereof they had good plentye'. Jane Shore was said to be daughter of a Cheapside mercer married to a Lombard Street merchant. Edward felt that the great nobility had enjoyed a monopoly of high places for long enough, and his popularity in the City reflects his sympathy with the merchant's outlook. See pedigree, p. 178.

C. L. Scofield, *The Life and Reign of Edward IV*, 2 vols., 1923.
T.S.I.H., i, 221, 227 (De Comines and Thomas More on Edward IV).

EDWARD V (1470–83), son of Edward IV, was born when his mother, Elizabeth Woodville, was in sanctuary at Westminster. His father made him Prince of Wales after the death at Tewkesbury of Henry VI's son, also called Prince Edward. He became King at the age of thirteen (1483), but it was his uncle Richard, Duke of Gloucester, who obtained power and Elizabeth Woodvile returned to sanctuary. Edward's coronation was repeatedly postponed, his parents' marriage was declared invalid, and Richard became King. Edward and his brother were murdered in the Tower (see p. 256). (See plate 31, fig. p. 252 and p. 178.)

RICHARD III (1452–85) will remain one of the worst of stage villains so long as Shakespeare's play lives with its declaration 'I am determined to prove a villain'. For the Tudor rulers and historians, as well as for the great dramatist, Richard III typifies all that is evil, destroyed by their hero, Henry of Richmond (Henry VII), at Bosworth (1485). In *The Union of the Noble and Illustrious Families of Lancaster and York*, 1548, the marriage of Henry VII and Elizabeth of York, a symbolic end of the quarrel of the houses of Lancaster and York and a practical fusing of their family interests, is represented as no less than the union of God and man in Christ. By contrast Richard III is thought of as a devil, and about 1490 John Rous described him as a monster and tyrant born under a hostile star and perishing like Anti-Christ, born with teeth and flowing locks after lagging sullenly for two years in his mother's womb. About 1513 Sir (St.) Thomas More wrote a very readable *History of King Richard III*. This describes him as he seemed to his enemies 'little of stature, ill fetured of limmes, croke backed'.

Lovers of paradox or fair play have tried to show that Richard was not so black, and of course good and bad are seldom concentrated unmixed in one human being.

Even enemies must admit that Richard was brave and generous. He appreciated books and was a patron of architecture and encouraged trade. He founded a college for priests in All Hallows Barking (London), gave a charter to the College of Arms, endowed Queen's College, Cambridge, with 500 marks per year, made gifts to various Yorkshire churches, and refused a bribe from Louis XI (1475).

Richard was the eleventh child of Cecily Nevil and Richard, third Duke of York. After a childhood disturbed by civil war he loyally supported Edward IV, his brother. He accompanied Edward IV in exile (1470) and led the van at the victories of Barnet and Tewkesbury (1471), after which he was said to have murdered Edward, Prince of Wales, and Henry VI. He married Anne Nevil, daughter of his first cousin, Richard Nevil, Earl of Warwick, 'the Kingmaker', and Anne Beauchamp, heiress of the fifth Earl of Warwick. Anne Nevil had been previously betrothed to Edward, Prince of Wales, and her sister married

Queen Anne Nevil and Richard III (Rous Roll)

Richard's brother, George of Clarence, who hoped to keep all 'the Kingmaker's' vast estates. Richard was therefore suspected of having helped to bring about Clarence's death (1478). He hated, as did many other nobles, the growing influence of the large and greedy family of Edward IV's queen, Elizabeth Woodville. Edward IV died on April 9th, 1483, leaving his family and realm in the charge of Richard, for Edward's son, little Edward V, was only thirteen. He quickly and completely overthrew the Woodvilles and then showed himself dissatisfied with his own title of Duke of Gloucester and determined to assert his own right to the throne. On June 22nd, 1483, a sermon at Paul's Cross accordingly explained 'that King Edwarde's children wer not ryghtful enheritous unto the crowne, but that the Duke of Glowcetir's title was bettir than thers'. He had already managed to have Edward V, and a little later, his other nephew, Richard, Edward's younger brother, placed in the Tower; and he had executed his ally, Lord Hastings, because Hastings would have given a lead to those who joined Richard in hating the Woodvilles, but would not join him in usurping the crown. Richard III assumed the crown on June 26th, 1483. Thereafter, says Fabyan in his *New Chronicles of England and France*, 'He fyll in great hatrede of the more partye of the nobles of his realme, insomuche that suche as before louyd and praysed hym, and wolde haue imparted lyfe and good with hym if he had remayned still as protectoure, now murmuryd and grudgyd agayne hym in suche wyse, that fewe or none fauouryd his partye, except it were for drede or for the great gyftes that they receyuyd of hym. By meane whereof he wanne dyuers to folowe his mynde, the whiche after deceyued hym'. People were disturbed by ugly rumours about the Princes in the Tower; 'Some said they were murdered atween two feather beds, Some said they were drowned in malvesey (wine) and some said they were sticked with a venomous potion'. There is no reason to doubt that the bones of two children found in 1933 were those of the princes and that, despite ingenious arguments to the contrary, they were murdered by Richard. A revolt by the Duke of Buckingham ended in the Duke's execution (1483); but Henry, Earl of Richmond, landed and defeated Richard III at Bosworth (1485). See p. 178 and plate 32.

J. Gairdner, *Life and Reign of Richard III*, 1898.
P. M. Kendall, *Richard III*, 1955.
T.S.I.H., i, 229 (Thomas More's description), 230 (Bosworth).

INDEX OF PERSONS

Page references to main entries are in heavy type

INDEX OF PLACES

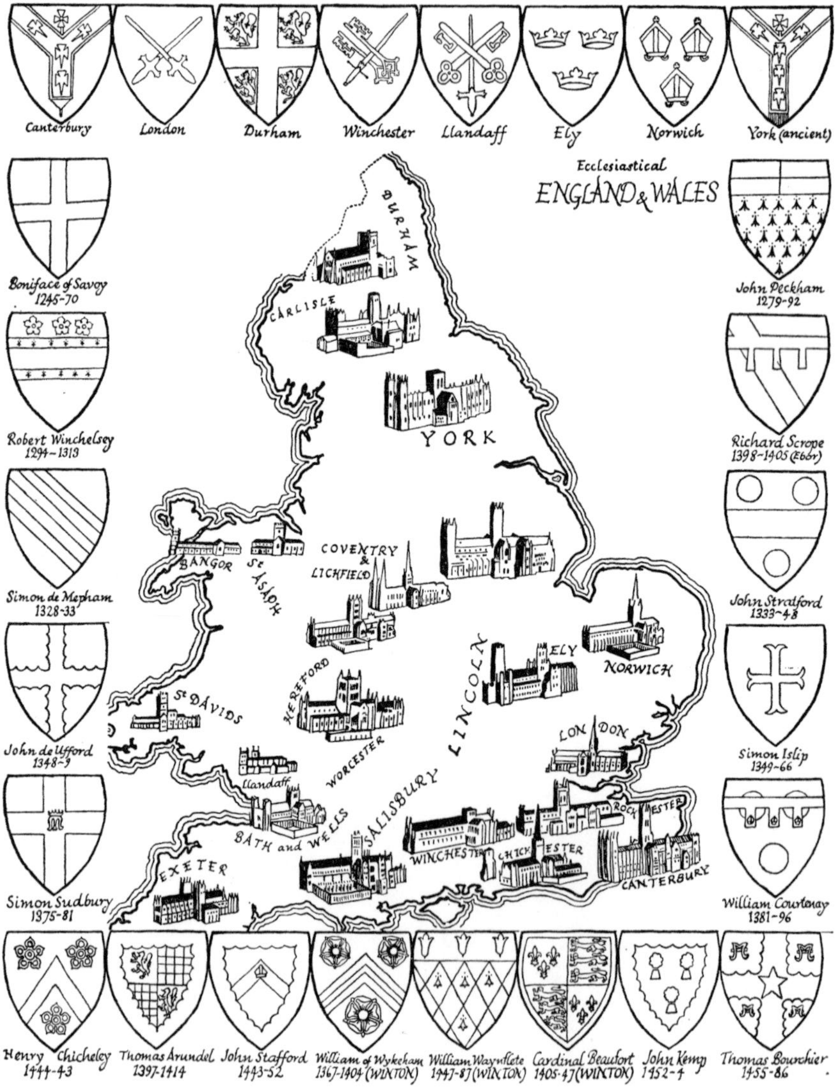
Canterbury
London
Durham
Winchester
Llandaff
Ely
Norwich
York (ancient)
Ecclesiastical
ENGLAND & WALES
Boniface of Savoy
1245-70
John Peckham
1279-92
Robert Winchelsey
1294-1313
Richard Scrope
1398-1405 (Ebor)
Simon de Mepham
1328-33
John Stratford
1333-48
John de Ufford
1348-9
Simon Islip
1349-66
Simon Sudbury
1375-81
William Courtenay
1381-96
Henry Chicheley
1414-43
Thomas Arundel
1397-1414
John Stafford
1443-52
William of Wykeham
1367-1404 (WINTON)
William Waynflete
1447-87 (WINTON)
Cardinal Beaufort
1405-47 (WINTON)
John Kemp
1452-4
Thomas Bourchier
1455-86
DURHAM
CARLISLE
YORK
BANGOR
St ASAPH
COVENTRY & LICHFIELD
LINCOLN
ELY
NORWICH
HEREFORD
WORCESTER
St DAVIDS
Llandaff
LONDON
SALISBURY
BATH and WELLS
ROCHESTER
WINCHESTER
CHICHESTER
CANTERBURY
EXETER